The Unwritten
Enlightenment

The Unwritten Enlightenment

*Literature between Ideology
and the Unconscious*

✦

Nathan Gorelick

NORTHWESTERN UNIVERSITY PRESS
EVANSTON, ILLINOIS

Northwestern University Press
www.nupress.northwestern.edu

Printed in the United States of America

10 9 8 7 6 5 4 3 2 1

Library of Congress Cataloging-in-Publication Data

Names: Gorelick, Nathan, author.
Title: The unwritten Enlightenment : literature between ideology and the
    unconscious / Nathan Gorelick.
Description: Evanston, Illinois : Northwestern University Press, 2024. |
    Includes bibliographical references and index.
Identifiers: LCCN 2023040786 | ISBN 9780810146761 (paperback) |
    ISBN 9780810146778 (cloth) | ISBN 9780810146785 (ebook)
Subjects: LCSH: European fiction—18th century—History and criticism. |
    Enlightenment. | Subconsciousness in literature.
Classification: LCC PN3495 .G67 2024 | DDC 809.3033—dc23/eng/20230830
LC record available at https://lccn.loc.gov/2023040786

For my teachers

CONTENTS

ACKNOWLEDGMENTS

This book would not have been possible without generous assistance from the many colleagues and friends who read and responded to some or all of the manuscript in its earlier, much less developed forms, including Alex Bove, Peter DeGabriele, Michael Drexler, Sara Guyer, Ryan A. Hatch, Brian McGrath, Matthew Rigilano, Michael Stanish, and most especially Richard Garner, Shane Herron, and Lydia Kerr. The book's core theoretical interventions also developed through conversation and sometimes spirited, if always friendly, debate with many of my peers among the Freudian and Lacanian academic crowd, particularly Karyn Ball, Christopher Chamberlin, James Godley, A. Kiarina Kordela, Alexander Miller, Ed Pluth, Frances Restuccia, Russell Sbriglia, Roland Végső, and Cindy Zeiher. Thanks also to Ben Crossan, Todd Goddard, Allen Hill, Forest Lewis, Shannon Mussett, Mark Pingree, and Michael M. Shaw, for their encouragement, loving skepticism, and willingness always to hear me out as I tried, and tried again, to say just what I mean.

I have benefited immeasurably from Todd McGowan's mentorship and Adrian Johnston's support; they helped bring this project to Northwestern, vouched for its promise, encouraged my long efforts at revision, and continue to remind me by their example that serious critical inquiry ought to be undertaken with good humor, camaraderie, and joy.

A (very) early version of chapter 1 was workshopped at the Center for Eighteenth-Century Studies at Indiana University. A partial draft of the epilogue was presented at the invitation of the Graduate Program in Culture and Theory at the University of California, Irvine; special thanks to Roy Cherian, Taija Mars McDougall, and Horacio Legras.

My warmest appreciation goes to the anonymous manuscript reviewers, whose incisive and challenging critiques pushed me substantially to rethink and rewrite my formulations and to assert my ideas with both boldness and due deference to the many thinkers and writers who have come before. They helped me see past the clutter and into the heart of my own argument, with honest humility and even some surprise. The result, I believe, is a different and much better book than what might have been. Of course, any outstanding faults or errors are entirely my own.

It has been a true delight working with Northwestern University Press, especially Faith Wilson Stein, who inherited this project mid-stream but believed in it immediately, advocated for it, and shepherded it into the world.

Her thoughtfulness and professionalism are matched only by her genuine conviviality. Thanks also to Anne Gendler and her excellent editorial team.

Finally, while this book is dedicated to all my teachers, some of you operated a direct and profound influence upon this project from the beginning: Joan Copjec, Tim Dean, Rodolphe Gasché, Graham Hammill, Shaun Irlam, Steven Miller, Kalliopi Nikolopoulou, and Ewa P. Ziarek. I also want to thank my teachers of clinical psychoanalysis at Gifric in Quebec City: Willy Apollon, Danielle Bergeron, and Lucie Cantin.

As it happens, my best friend and the love of my life, Melissa A. Wright, is also my greatest teacher. Nobody better personifies the ethics of inquiry, of criticism and analysis, which I can only attempt to schematize, theorize, and exercise throughout the following pages. Nobody does so with more compassion, patience, and authentic avidity. Like so much else in this book, my gratitude for the great good fortune of having found so remarkable a partner must remain unwritten, though it is everywhere in what follows.

The Unwritten
Enlightenment

Introduction

✦

Literature, the Unconscious, the Enlightenment

Whatever else it may be, the Enlightenment is a myth. This is not to say it is unreal, but to emphasize that it is a way of ordering reality, a narrative scaffolding and interpretation of its origins which wants to imbue the ensuing history with a sense of destiny or inevitability, as if it could not be otherwise. As with any ideological formation, every deployment of the Enlightenment—cynical or recuperative, vaunting or vituperative—imposes an artificial coherence upon a social and historical situation which is fraught, contested, contingent, and contradictory. The myth's terms and conditions developed largely in the eighteenth century, but it overflows any strict periodization because its meaning and value are not in its referents but in its function, which varies according to the interests it is made to serve and the circumstances of its use. Thus can the Enlightenment name the long march from dogma and theocracy to experimental knowledge and deliberative debate, or the rupture after which the free exercise of reason, determined on its own principles and not by any arbitrary authority, became the organizing principle of thought and politics: the "Age of Enlightenment" as the dawn of modern science, universal human rights, liberal democracy, and rational economics. Or it can be defined according to its material foundations and the violence they continue to exact: the efflorescence of bourgeois wealth atop the ground of colonialism and chattel slavery; the investiture of market capitalism with the regulatory prerogatives of the state; the confluence of science and industry in the new machinery of mass society, mass production, and mass destruction. In any case, the Enlightenment is not and never was a neutral term. For better and for worse, it is the master signifier of modernity.

The Unwritten Enlightenment largely concerns what this myth *is not*: that which it wants to silence through the very processes of its articulation, what it attempts to drown in its sea of discourse that yet refuses to slip below the surface. And it is about the ways in which these efforts at erasure rebound upon, subvert, and derange the signifier's pretensions to a masterful totality.

Attending to the other, unwritten side of the signifier, this book does not attempt to resolve the conflicted history of the present, nor to rescue the idea of the Enlightenment from its myriad deficiencies, its cultural chauvinism, or its moral incoherence. It does not rehearse the debate over the Enlightenment's dominant tendencies or radical undercurrents, offer an apology for its unrealized universalism, or excoriate its hypocrisies. It does not diversify its holdings or proffer a more inclusive account of its influences and effects. It does not consolidate its proliferation of possible meanings on the way to a more objective, somehow non- or post-ideological definition. It does not suppose we can be done with the Enlightenment simply by recognizing its mythic status and refusing any longer to believe in it.

When Roland Barthes famously formulated the semiology of modern myth, by which he designated any interpellant speech that elides the contradictions comprising the social construct we call reality, any everyday instance of ideology at work, he discovered myth's ability to assimilate and redeploy its own critique.[1] Nowhere is this recuperative, parasitical trickery more apparent than in the Enlightenment, the very name of which is a declaration of independence from myth. Its greatest seduction is the moral imperative to leverage the agency of thought against an unbearable inheritance, as if thereby to escape it. We cannot think against the Enlightenment without thereby surrendering to this interpellation, reifying the object of ideology critique through precisely its criticism.

This book avails itself of ideology critique and draws liberally from scholarly disputes over the Enlightenment's defining characteristics. But it does so, it historicizes (denaturalizes, politicizes) the Enlightenment, digs through the roots of the myth, only on the way to another way of reading some of its most formative inscriptions: negatively, according to what they want and fail to say, or what they want but fail to hide, or what they cannot acknowledge about their own formal or semiotic constraints without falling into incoherence, or how they revel in this incoherence and either suffer or celebrate it (or both at once) as the condition of their articulation.

Although their shared historical context helps delimit the myth's foundations, what better unites these inscriptions across their many differences, and what justifies or demands their treatment here, is, first, that they are all experimental refusals of their own histories, exercises in imagining what it might mean to be human, alone or with others, after history has been exhausted and without the false assurances, ancestral obligations, or prefabricated destinies it provides. In this quest for radical freedom, these texts position themselves at the outer edge of language itself, at the limits of its capacities, where the truth they are after can only be structured like a fiction. Second, each of these experiments exemplifies rather than exhausts a broader, ongoing effort toward the constitution, elaboration, and cultural sedimentation of a particularly modern conception of the individual and brand of individualism. It is in this way, as early experiments in the modern art of individualistic representation, as novel formations of the subject to whom the Enlightenment's interpellant speech is addressed, and not according to some law of genre to which they are themselves happily indifferent, that these literary-philosophical fictions deserve to be called *novels*. Similarly, my use of "the Enlightenment" designates the contentious process of creative experimentation that constitutes this myth's addressee and enduring ideological bequest: the modern *subject of reason*. In short—since much of what follows will involve this formula's elongation and complication—the Enlightenment is a signifier which represents a subject, nowhere more emphatically or explicitly than through the novelistic discourse that took shape, with great variation, throughout the eighteenth century.

We will return at length to this question of the Enlightenment, its novelistic elaboration, its periodization, and its periodicity. From the start, however, we must note that if it is a signifier which represents a subject, it is not self-transparently so. In this, it is not unique. As Jacques Lacan famously established, the signifier of a subject "cannot represent anything except to another signifier."[2] The negativity which orients, provokes, inspires, but also tortures, teases, and finally confounds the Enlightenment, which is there among but irreducible to the signs of its elaboration, the *other* signifier for the subject of reason—the Enlightenment's own, inassimilable shadow—is what Lacan calls the subject of the unconscious.

Why the unconscious? If it is its shadow, the unconscious is unthinkable without the Enlightenment. Psychoanalysis, the science of the shadow's discovery, develops from and proceeds according to Enlightenment principles of inquiry, even as it fatally undermines reason's desire for internal unity or self-assured coherence. But this does not mean psychoanalysis is merely a consequence and ex post facto accident of a prior and primary movement. It is rather the index and proof of the lack of self-transparency specific to the Enlightenment subject, the study of the *internal* limit to this subject's quest for knowledge and self-assured totality. The unconscious is what sustains reason's irreconcilability with itself, incompletes the Enlightenment from within, guarantees its indeterminacy and contingency, contests it according to its own representational parameters and investigatory procedures. The unconscious is what happens when the Enlightenment reads itself *otherwise*.[3]

Following the action of the unconscious within and against the Enlightenment, then, does not mean to cure the latter of its lack of self-transparency. Instead, it makes clear why such a cure is impossible. *The Unwritten Enlightenment* is about this impossibility and its untreatable effects. Without dismissing their radical discrepancies or imposing some false compatibility— rather, by amplifying their incompatibility—this book reframes the subject of the Enlightenment according to *another logic* that the myth of rational freedom, in constituting itself, represses or otherwise fails to admit: a logic of the unconscious, or what Lacan, emphasizing its proximity and irreducibility to consciousness as well as the desire which motors it, calls the logic of fantasy. Each of the following chapters tracks the confluences and discrepancies between these two irreconcilable logics—of rational will and unconscious desire—in works of literature that both exemplify the momentous philosophical and political transformations of the long eighteenth century and subvert the same ideological formations to which these texts and transformations gave rise. This subversiveness, this internal and potentially radical disturbance, is not self-evident to these texts, their authors, or the ideologically saturated histories of reading that have situated them as emblems of the Enlightenment; it is realized, rather, through a critical practice and ethics of reading that emphasizes their status as *literature*, and that stresses literature's untimeliness with respect to its historical context, its refusal to be exhausted by that context and its potential to trouble it anew and from historically afar. As will be made clear throughout, finding the unconscious in the Enlightenment is in fact a refinding of it.[4]

Although this arrangement can be posed only from our later point of view, it is neither anachronistic nor arbitrary. Literature, the unconscious, and the Enlightenment form the three vertices of a historical and conceptual triangle, such that any two of these points can be seen to radiate from the third. They are distinct yet inseparable, and it is the aim of this introduction to show how their distinctions scaffold their inseparability. While literature forms the core of this study, a shift in perspective, a turn of the triangle, reorients the schema to suggest that, if literature is the site at which the subject of the unconscious and the subject of reason intersect and entwine, so too is the Enlightenment the common ground of literature and the unconscious; one more turn, and the unconscious is the vector from which the other two radiate and in relation to which they are conjoined.

The values of this triangulation are manifold. In the first place, it forces us to consider that the eighteenth-century novel and the novelistic discourse it engendered are more than artifacts or epiphenomena of their wider historical context—that they were formative of that context and still secure its endurance into the present. This was where the Enlightenment's emergent brand of individualism was imagined and how it was popularized. New experiments in narrative fiction innovated strategies for the representation of individual experience that captured the moral and epistemic authority with which the Enlightenment's conception of the subject could unfold and acquire its cultural currency. The following chapters—on instrumental rationality, education, and aesthetics, all in relation to the problematics of subject-formation—will show that this is no exaggeration. The novel is a key technology of the Enlightenment.

As literature, however, and as these studies also make clear, the novel demands to be read. Its complicity with the Enlightenment is not an inevitability or a simple matter of fact. That complicity is rather the effect of a history of reading, one that by no means determines the novel's limits or potentials. Alongside and against this history, the Enlightenment novel demands to be read in ways that resist its own ideological parameters and purposes, without, however, mistaking this for a means to escape them. In short, the novel and its discourse inscribe a resistance to the Enlightenment at its core, and invite that resistance's animation through an alternative, psychoanalytically informed practice of reading.

This introduces the second value of our triangulation: it can correct a stubborn lacuna in the psychoanalytic study of literature and literary theory, namely, the question: *Why psychoanalysis?* If psychoanalysis has always been less a discourse or a theory than a clinical practice oriented around a domain of lived human experience, if its discourse and theory result from and reply to rather than determine the action of the unconscious, then what has it got to do with literature? Why does literature need psychoanalysis or, conversely, why might psychoanalysis need literature? This raises a prior question: *Should* psychoanalysis and literary criticism have anything to do with one another?

Setting aside the sort of disciplinary fundamentalism or territorialism which, as a rule, is more an allergy to theory than a rigorous consideration of the value of the encounter, this question of critical responsibility has run aground on the debate over whether psychoanalysis can or ought to treat literature as anything more than a means of exemplifying its own concepts or generalizing the otherwise singular specificities of clinical experience.[5] Is literature merely a bank of examples from which the analyst may freely withdraw? Even if so, do its clinical uses teach us anything about the work of literature that the work could not teach on its own, without this ill-fitted prosthesis? If literature therefore deserves some distance from its application to psychoanalysis, what, then, of the application of psychoanalysis to literature? What does this mean for the lived experience of the unconscious? What even is "applied" psychoanalysis? Must it be merely a web of concepts divorced from their contexts and reduced to implements in the critic's toolbox? Does psychoanalysis not also deserve some distance from literature, or at least literary criticism? In short, does literature's usefulness for psychoanalytic inquiry or psychoanalysis's usefulness to criticism justify this (mutual or antagonistic) instrumentalization, or is something of the essence of both literature and the unconscious lost through this instrumentalist reduction?

Such questions are already at the heart of the psychoanalytic tradition in literary criticism. Works like Francesco Orlando's classic *Toward a Freudian Theory of Literature*, Marthe Robert's *Origins of the Novel*, Peter Brooks's *Reading for the Plot*, and Leo Bersani's *The Freudian Body* variously consider the semiotic dimension of the unconscious according to its resonances with literature and literary form.[6] The first two of these works absorb literature and its history into the logic of the unconscious; the latter two, inversely, mold the Freudian text into an object of literary criticism and an extension of its literary-historical context. In every instance, one half of the relation is subordinated to its other.

The Unwritten Enlightenment carries on in the semiotic and structuralist tradition these great works helped define, but offers another way through the impasse they mean to treat by systematizing the differences between criticism and psychoanalysis according to what they have in common, and, at the same time, situating these commonalities under the rubric of their differences. We will find that what literary criticism and psychoanalysis share, yet what they both realize in their own ways, is an *ethics* of inquiry at the limits of representation—an ethical concern for what those limits exclude, excise, foreclose, or repress, and for how these remainders of representation continue to haunt the field of the sensible, the knowable, the meaningful, and the valuable, from the margins of sense, knowledge, meaning, and value. They exercise this concern, moreover, from within these same limits, which were core fabrications of the Enlightenment and help define its pervasive effects upon the present.

By considering these ethical modalities with respect to this history of representation and its limits, this book does not introduce a new model of literary criticism so much as it pulls into the foreground a critical sensibility already at work within the concept of literature as well as the Freudian discovery. This shared sensibility at once operates within and is directed against the representational parameters of the subject to which the Enlightenment gives form, therefore also within and against the ideological consequences that unfold from them. Literature and psychoanalysis, separately and together, are two related but distinct instances of the Enlightenment reading itself otherwise.

We can draw this separate-togetherness, this common difference, further into relief by turning our triangle a third time, such that the unconscious is the point at which the other two vertices converge and from which they radiate. Once again, this configuration is not anachronistic. It reflects the fact that psychoanalysis names the (belated) discovery of that against which the Enlightenment was always oriented and which for this reason still clings to it, or better, is its own obscene underside. Obscene, because the Enlightenment banishes it to another scene, to what Lacan, emphasizing its recalcitrance against every endeavor to obliterate or (the same thing) encapsulate it, calls the real. With literature and psychoanalysis, through the ethics of reading that directs and, in fact, constitutes them, we can detect and help amplify the kernel of the real at the center of the fortress of reason, the interior strangeness that orients and perpetually frustrates reason's totalizing ambitions.

In this introduction, I elaborate and theorize this triangulation according to the ethics of reading it informs and invites, beginning with the eighteenth-century novel and its structuring importance to the development of "literature"—not as a vague aesthetic domain but as a discrete concept and an object of theory and criticism, originating with the early German Romantics' conception of the literary absolute. Considering how this concept and its criticism initially unfolded as a means to the Enlightenment's subversive radicalization will permit us to situate psychoanalysis alongside, rather than overlaying it upon or subordinating it to, literature; in this way, we can attend to the differences between psychoanalysis and literature in order to clarify how, across these differences, the discovery of the unconscious was and remains an inherently literary endeavor. Differently put, the unconscious is proximate but irreducible to literature and literary criticism—*analogous* with, therefore not identical to, literature's insurrection from within the Enlightenment.

Through this analogy and its experimental elaboration with a few of the most enduring novelistic contributions to the philosophy, politics, and aesthetics of the subject of reason, the readings in this book demonstrate how psychoanalysis can inform literary criticism, literary history, and the relation or non-relation between them. Along the way and at the same time, we will consider the reverse: literature's capacity to inform psychoanalytic theory and the clinical practice it represents. My readings of the psychosis of reason in Daniel Defoe's *Robinson Crusoe*, the encounter between Jean-Jacques Rousseau and the Marquis de Sade in the unlikely field of education theory, and the ways in which Laurence Sterne explodes the constitutive sexual frustration at the heart of eighteenth-century epistemology and aesthetics, thus do not aim to treat literature with psychoanalysis, as if thereby to diagnose or cure it. Nor do I reduce these works to illustrations of Lacanian and Freudian concepts abstracted from their experiential, clinical foundations. Nor still do I pretend to uncover some treasury of truth buried beneath the surface of these texts. Instead, I follow Lacan's insistence that the unconscious is neither transcendentally above nor the subterranean below of consciousness, but is immanent and occluded within it. These works' strange, surprising resistances to the Enlightenment are drawn right on the surface: in the contradictions and repetitions, the gaps and fissures, the falterings and failures, that index an internal limit to what the language of the Enlightenment can say and, in so doing, direct its untreatable ambition to say more.

Here, we should heed Joan Copjec's admonishment against treating the animating desire at stake in any cultural formation as a depth waiting to be plumbed: "it is dangerous," Copjec writes, "to assume that the surface is the level of the superficial. Whenever we delve below this level, we are sure to come up empty." Rather than pressing some naive empiricism, however, as if the apparent and the real could ever coincide, Copjec instead enjoins us to make legible the discrepancy and interplay between them, because this, and only this, "is the condition of desire."[7] Following Copjec's invitation, and adding to its development among other psychoanalytic critics like Tim Dean, Todd McGowan, and Tracy McNulty, this book operates with the rhythm of this "between," where history, ideology, belief, and the identities they organize become non-coincident with themselves. It does so in ways that make clear why the apparent and the real, consciousness and the unconscious, ideology and fantasy, are co-implicated, radically proximate, but definitively *not* identical phenomena, and why distinguishing between them is a matter equally of conceptual, ethical, and ultimately political responsibility.

This is no mere theoretical conceit. Ideology circulates among what Barthes designated "the decorative display of *what-goes-without-saying*"—among contingent cultural formations that, in their very flagrancy, permit the values and imperatives they represent to appear necessary and inevitable, that is, natural; this is why ideology critique entails a denaturalizing demonstration of these formations' historicity and the "ideological abuse" they enable.[8] While there is no outside of ideology—such a supposition, of course, would be the quintessence of ideology—tracking the logic of fantasy reveals that there is *within* any ideological formation a remainder or residue, a non-sense that it cannot fully assume, a dynamic structure of unconscious desire which does not "go without saying" so much as it traces the limit of the sayable and the receivable, the limit of the social link and its ideological imperatives. Without this uncertain limit, ideology would be total and resistance not so much futile as inexistent.

We will return to this more exhaustively in the book's epilogue, once we have established the necessary conceptual grammar and concrete historical and ethical stakes through a patient reading of our literary texts and contexts. For now, it is enough to assert somewhat axiomatically that fantasy is what orients the subject of the unconscious, which is the irreducible remainder of ideology and the various technologies of interpellation and subjectivation that produce and reproduce it. Without fantasy, ideology would have no need for its various abuses, no need constantly to promote the myth of its inevitability. The minimal distance between fantasy and ideology thus is what ensures that a hegemonic field is always open to contestation, struggle, and resistance—and it is here, I insist, in and as this resistance, between ideology and the unconscious, where the work of literature takes place.

The Subject of Literature

When Shoshana Felman introduced the now-canonical collection *Literature and Psychoanalysis* with the provocation that, "in the same way that psychoanalysis points to the unconscious of literature, *literature, in its turn, is the unconscious of psychoanalysis*" (her emphasis), she crystallized a critical intuition that had guided psychoanalytic literary theory for decades.[9] This foundational volume's effort to stage the intimate—or, to borrow an apposite neologism from Lacan, the *extimate*—relation between them supposes that literature and psychoanalysis are inseparable and unique, unique also in the nature of their inseparability, that each is bound and inassimilable to its ownmost other. But despite Felman's insight, the terms, techniques, and above all the ethics of this extimate relation still demand to be thought. Such a demand imposes a special difficulty: it asks us to attend to the essential differences between literature and the unconscious within the frame of their essential commonality, or the same in reverse.

To name this differential commonality from the outset: literature and the unconscious are two peculiar *structures of address*, peculiar because neither the subject of the address nor the addressee exists prior to their structuration. Literature's addressee is the critic; the unconscious addresses the analyst; and it is through this very address that both halves of each structure, addresser and addressee, are not only conjoined but constituted.

The phenomena which concern psychoanalysis are as old as the human itself, as ancient as the non-relation between the subject and the signifier. Where there is language, there is the unconscious. Yet strictly speaking the unconscious did not exist before Freud discovered it. There is no unconscious without psychoanalysis. To disentangle this apparent contradiction, we should recall Lacan's insistence—already evident in Freud, despite the occasional rhetorical confusion—that the unconscious is not a fulsome intrasubjective depth imbued with some definite mental content, waiting to be mined or excavated by the analyst's prying curiosity. It is not simply what we do or experience beyond the limits of our awareness or intention. The unconscious addresses the analyst, and in so doing calls the analyst into being; at the same time, the position of the analyst constitutes this address as, precisely, of the unconscious.[10] The subject of the address, moreover, is not the subject with an unconscious but what, with Lacan, we already have called the *subject of the unconscious*: a logical position, the barred subject, $, the mark of the lack in the Other that stands for the singular being of the human as an infinitely peculiar creature of desire.

Analogously (from the Greek: *ana-*, "toward," "against," or "upon"; and *logos*, "ratio," "ground," or "reason"), the question of literature is a constitutive address to its critic. The question of literature calls the critic into being, inasmuch as criticism is a special posture toward the literary that recognizes in the work of literature something more than an expression of the author's mysterious creative genius (self-expression), or an opportunity for a reader's affective engagement with a text (individual impression), or a historical occurrence (cultural artifact). This same constituting question thus also brings literature into being, since it is from the position and through the desire of the critic that the work of literature becomes an object and cause of concern. Literary criticism surely does not exist without literature, but nor does literature exist without criticism.[11]

For criticism, then, the analogue of the subject of the unconscious, and the more precisely defined third point in our triangulation with the Enlightenment subject of reason, is the *subject of literature*. The desire of the analyst is the interminable desire to know the truth of the subject of the unconscious, and it is this desire which specifies that to which the unconscious responds in its search for an addressee. In the same way, the desire of the critic is inextricable from the subject of literature whose address calls the critic into being and specifies the critical encounter.

We must take care, however, to qualify this and all other coincidences of the clinical and the critical. Analogy is the overlaying of two subjects, the isolation of a resemblance or similarity between them, not so as to collapse them into a single entity but rather in order to clarify and differentiate them according to what they have in common. The value of our analogy with respect to the extimacy to which Felman sensitizes us is that it illuminates points of relation without eclipsing the distance between the subjects thus analogized. This may correct the unfortunate tendency, as tedious as it is prolific, of applying psychoanalysis to literature as one applies paint to a fence, mapping concepts onto texts without regard for those concepts' clinical specificity, either ornamenting the literary text with the trappings of psychoanalysis or effacing the resistances those texts raise against what thereby becomes a diluted, abstract theory. If we hold to the conviction that psychoanalysis is not a theory but an experience and a practice, and if we then situate it as an analogue rather than a tool of literary criticism, we can retain the structure of address proper to the clinic while also permitting that structure to inform without subsuming the experience and practice of reading at stake in the work of literature. Inversely, we discover the truth of Felman's insight, the literary dimension of psychoanalytic practice, without, however, denying—indeed, while avowing and insisting upon—the essential differences between the subjects of literature and the unconscious.

The Work of Literature and the Poetry of Reference

That both subjects substantially unfold from a shared historical antecedent, the eighteenth-century novel, reveals why our analogy is far from arbitrary. More than any other genre and more clearly than in any other literary epoch, yet also prior to the moment at which "literature" as we know it was initially delimited as a concept and object of critical, ethical concern, the novel invested the order of the signifier with the ability and imperative to articulate the individuality of the individual, to invent the individual through its narration. In this way, the novel functioned historically, and still does so today, as a powerful site of interpellation wherein the reader recognizes and identifies not so much with the individual thus narrated as with the paradigm of individuality to which novelistic character gives form. The reader thereby assumes, and even finds pleasure in, their subjection to the ideological imperatives of individualism and its institutional supports.[12] At the same time, however, the novel makes equally clear that the "self" is not a static entity or a given fact, but a story: a compendium of experience which is rendered intelligible and made meaningful only through its narrative organization. This story will tend to exclude or efface those elements of experience and possibilities of meaning that trouble or undermine or simply do not fit within this intelligible narrative frame. Psychoanalysis or psychoanalytic criticism concern whether and how that frame is haunted by its own exclusions and by the anxiety of its incoherence, how the unsaid and the unthought disarticulate or derange the urge to intelligibility, and how attention to these disturbances opens the subject—of literature or the unconscious—to an unforeseeable potential. We will return to the novel's importance to the formation of the psychoanalytic clinic, remaining for now with the question of criticism.

If it concerns what a given text fails or refuses to articulate, criticism considers the historically specific mechanisms and parameters of intelligibility that structure the language out of which novels and novelistic discourse are fashioned—but only insofar as these considerations are the condition for the possibility of calculating the recalcitrant remainder of this historicity. It is here with the remainder where the work distinguishes itself as literature, and thus where its desire to be read endures beyond its local, historical situation.

The notion that literature names such a recalcitrance and remainder has its own history. It begins, the very *concept* of literature begins, at the end of the eighteenth century, through the early German Romantic notion of the literary absolute. It was here, among the Jena Romantics and in the pages of their influential but short-lived *Athenaeum* magazine, that the question of literature—What is it, how is it distinct from other modalities of experience, and what does it want?—was first articulated and from which it continues, however obscurely, to direct literary theory and criticism today. As Philippe Lacoue-Labarthe and Jean-Luc Nancy have observed:

> This does not simply mean that [Jena] romanticism, strictly thought, is the place where the question appeared, or if you prefer, that romanticism opens the very epoch of literature. Nor does it simply mean that romanticism consequently can be defined only as the perpetual auto-referring of the question: What is romanticism?—or: What is literature? Rather, it means that literature, as its own infinite questioning and as the perpetual positing of its own question, dates from romanticism and as romanticism. . . . This is why romanticism, which is actually a moment (the moment of its question) will always have been more than a mere "epoch," or else will never cease, right up to the present, to incomplete the epoch it inaugurated.[13]

Any practice of reading that either implies or produces a theory of its literary object operates within the question opened by Jena Romanticism, no matter how far the critic seems to wander from this origin.[14] Ours is still this incomplete and incompleting moment of Romanticism. If the Freudian discovery established that the unconscious is inextricable from the address to the analyst that constitutes them both, unconscious and analyst, the *Athenaeum* group similarly established, a century earlier, that the object of literary criticism is inseparable from the act of criticism. Criticism both constitutes its object and is constituted by it. This is why any strict distinction between the creative and the critical, in the work of literature, does not hold.

The New Criticism, with its investment in what Allen Tate called the "specific objectivity" of literature and John Crowe Ransom dubbed "the autonomy of the work itself," is conceptually remote from the early Romantics but is an especially cohesive effect of their insight.[15] Rigorously differentiating literary history from literary criticism, the New Critics subsumed content under the heading of literary form, the latter being the "residuary quality" in which the work's aesthetic freedom inhered and which it was the critic's responsibility to defend against history, biography, morality, or the reader's personal affect and impressions. Translating literature into these other domains of inquiry, or into any register of discourse other than that of the work itself, could not but subordinate it to a "prose logic" through which the work's status as literature was lost.[16]

A core deficiency in this effort to sanitize the relation between literature and its criticism is that the modern novel, especially in its eighteenth-century instantiations, is a quintessentially prosaic literary phenomenon. From the genre's beginnings, the novel announced an unprecedented alignment of literature with history.[17] Thus did Mikhail Bakhtin define the novel as "a genre-in-the-making, one in the vanguard of all modern literary development," or stronger still, "the genre of becoming," which is why the term "novel" perfectly describes this genre whose essential characteristic is its generic inessentiality: its incompatibility with all fixed, preexisting literary forms, its inseparability from the unstable and ever-renewing reality in which it appears.[18] So, while to reduce the novel to its history may mitigate its status as literature, too militant a defense against literary history will betray precisely the specific objectivity and aesthetic autonomy the New Critics, in pulling literature away from history, wished to preserve.[19]

The way out of this dilemma (and past the stale and false dichotomy between historicism and formalism against which the novel so obviously protests) is Roman Jakobson's schematization of the *referential* and *poetic* linguistic functions, which enables us to explore the novel's peculiar mix of the historical and the literary at its most basic level: that of its artistic medium, language.[20] The referential function involves language's use as a technology for the exchange of information or as an instrument with which to describe and order a perceptible reality; it operates within the structure of signification that most interested Ferdinand de Saussure, wherein the differential play of the structure's constituent (signifying) elements produces meaning in accordance with a given, shared context. Reference is the language of observation and analysis, of history and natural science—through and after the eighteenth century, it structures the relation between subjects of thought and objects of knowledge. And it grounds the origins of the modern novel: Samuel Richardson's *Pamela*, for instance, which vaulted the emergent genre to a previously proscribed cultural respectability, could relate events both material and psychological for an audience to whom the eponymous narrator and her life were entirely unknown, and could insist upon the veracity of her

testimony, because the language in which these events were delivered operated according to the apparent objectivity of meaning the referential function
affords.[21] Daniel Defoe's literary brilliance involved a language so ordinary,
so familiar to his audience, so very referential, that the distance between fact
and fiction seemed to disappear, hence Edgar Allan Poe's oft-quoted praise
for the "potent magic of verisimilitude" in Defoe's works.[22]

As literature, however, the novel introduces a profound subterfuge. It uses
the referential function to invent a world that resembles but is not the one its
readers inhabit—another world, constructed wholly out of language, therefore irreducible to the world of empirically determinable objects from which
it borrows its style and terms. In this way, it manifests the classical (Aristotelian) conception of *poiesis*: the creation of some new thing out of existing
materials, creation as recombination. More than this, even with Richardson and Defoe, especially within the formal constraints of verisimilitude, the
novel subordinates reference to its contrary, the poetic linguistic function.
This function, Jakobson explains, entails a "focus on the message for its own
sake," so that the relations among the signifiers within a poetic matrix, as
well as the materiality or shape of the language itself, are the keys to its interpretability. With the poetic function, interpretation can proceed indefinitely
because, undetermined by any external context, "Ambiguity is an intrinsic,
inalienable character of any self-focused message."[23] This is not to say that
poetry puts referentiality out of operation, nor that ambiguity has no place
in referential communication, which indeed is built precisely to contend with
it in order to arrive at semantic exactitude. The point, rather, is that while
the novel indulges reference, while it exploits the communicative powers of
reference, it does so poetically; its "potent magic" is that it situates the poetic
within a referential frame. The novel is the poetry of reference.

This helps clarify why for the Jena Romantics the novel was the highest expression of literature and the literary absolute. Their notion of poetry
obviously is not identical with the New Critics' later, more fundamentalist definition, or with Jakobson's structuralist formulation. The interplay
of poetry and reference nevertheless harmonizes with Friedrich Schlegel's
pronouncement that the novel is "simultaneously poetry and the poetry of
poetry."[24] Writing at the turn of the nineteenth century, Schlegel and his
Athenaeum cohort would have been thinking of the eighteenth-century
novel and its few antecedents (Boccaccio, Cervantes), even if only to orient
Romanticism's inspired departure from this, its own foundation. In the novel,
Schlegel saw both creation and criticism, creation as criticism and criticism
as creation. Operating at the undecidable limit between the creative and the
critical, reflecting upon and refracting its own history, reinventing itself from
itself (all of this is essential for Bakhtin, as well), the novel best represents
the radical potentialities of *the work of literature*, which for the Romantics
was not a noun but a verb, an interminable process—anticipating Bakhtin, a
poetry of becoming.

Schlegel's related assertion that "Poetry can only be criticized by way of poetry" does not mean that criticism must articulate itself through the devices of the artist (it may do so, but not by necessity; and as we have already seen, creativity is never foreign to the task of criticism), nor does it mean that the critic and the artist should be one and the same person. Instead, Schlegel insists that criticism's cause—both the origin and object of its desire, its reason for being, the constitutive core of its responsibility, that from which it springs and for which it stands—is the absolute singularity of the work of literature. This is why criticism is not a secondary additive but an essential property of the work, essential to its always becoming and never arriving. The work of literature has no meaning outside its critical reflection, none which can be reduced to and localized within a prior existing objective reality, however defined. Through the infinite reflective mediation and counter-mediation of artistic creation and literary criticism, the work of literature departs from the world of empirically determinable objects and determining subjects, actualizing itself as an interminable experience. Criticism thus may begin with reference in order to locate the text with respect to its historical and linguistic circumstances, but it undertakes this beginning in order to return the work to itself as "the absolute," as an absolute singularity, absolutely unique to the critical-creative relationship, absolutely unlike any other object or idea.

Systematizing the Romantics' notoriously asystematic conception of criticism, Walter Benjamin isolated this "coincidence of the objective and the subjective side in knowledge" as the site at which "the self-knowledge nascent in the object" is made to shine forth; "or rather it, the observation, *is* the nascent consciousness of the object itself."[25] Criticism, in other words, is the object thinking itself, through its mediation and refraction by its critical other. This route, from objective self-enclosure to subjective engagement and back, frees the work from the sort of historicist reductionism to which the New Critics alert us. But it does so by undermining the distinction between subject and object that orients the referential function—and with it, the whole intellectual edifice of empiricism, of representation's adequacy to truth, upon which the New Critics' concern for literature's "specific objectivity" is built. As Benjamin makes clear, "not only did Schlegel's concept of criticism achieve freedom from heteronymous aesthetic doctrines," such as, for instance, the empiricist aesthetics that predominated throughout the eighteenth century, "but it made this freedom possible in the first place by setting up for artworks a criterion other than the rule—namely, the criterion of an immanent structure specific to the work itself."[26]

The question of criticism, then, is not primarily epistemological or aesthetic or juridical, but *ethical*: How can the critic elucidate the specific structure of the work itself without imposing an extrinsic system of reference or appropriating the work to such a system—without, in other words, betraying the very cause of criticism, the singularity it is supposed to realize and without which neither literature nor the critic would exist? What does it mean to collaborate with the text in a joint enterprise of which neither text nor critic is the authority? Without that authority, what authorizes criticism and what is the responsible extent of its authorship, beyond which it betrays its own conditions?

The ethics of criticism is all the more challenging with respect to its own historical foundation, the eighteenth-century novel, since, as we have just observed, the latter openly courts appropriation—particularly by history and historicism—and cannot be thought without it. But if it is not without its history, this "not without" need not force us to cede the novel to its historical determinations. It is with its history, within it, one of its animating forces; but by inscribing that force through the poetry of reference it opens history to the ambiguity of the poetic function, an ambiguity which demands that the novel *and* its history be read otherwise. The novel formalizes an essential relation between identity and narrativity, lays the imaginary and symbolic ground upon which the modern concept of the individual takes hold, and serves as a tool of interpellation and ideological subjectivation; it is also the aesthetic field through which the empirically indeterminable, interminable experience of the literary absolute, of literature as such, as a work and a process and an experience with all its incalculable possibilities, was first articulated, and from which its reverberations continue to be felt.

The Work of Analysis and the Poetics of Fantasy

In part, and as the following chapters will bear out, the novel was integral to the development of the modern subjectivity, the philosophical and political model of the subject of reason, within and against which Freud articulated (that is, invented) the unconscious. This fact alone would justify the analogy we are developing here. More importantly, psychoanalysis is an especially powerful ally with respect to the structure of address that orients the subject of literature in the early novel because it sensitizes us to those same limits of representation that demarcate the referential from the poetic. The work of analysis is constituted out of a concern for the dilemma between history, form, and the singularity of experience that is also at stake in the work of literature.

This consonance helps clarify that although the singularity of the literary absolute names an excess over empirical knowledge, this excess is not a super-referential abundance; it is not a quasi-spiritual or transcendental beyond, or an inexhaustible "too much" of experience that overruns the referential function's desire for exactitude. It does not presume or induce a metalanguage. Like the unconscious, the work of literature indexes a *lack* in the field of empirical knowledge, a hole in the order of the signifier, an internal limit to the referential function and the logic of exchange which structures it, within which the work takes place and finds its place, interminably.

But analogies are not unidirectional; otherwise, they are useless. So, while psychoanalysis helps us see how literature is like the unconscious, we need to invert this likeness to see why *psychoanalysis is an essentially literary endeavor*. This mutual refraction by which literature and the unconscious are magnified and made strange to themselves reveals that while psychoanalysis is a science of representation, so, too, is the work of literature; conversely, the work of analysis is a poetry of poetry. Viewed in this way, we can respect the differences between the clinical and the critical while harnessing the latter to complicate and enrich our understanding of the truth at stake in psycho-analysis: the truth of the subject of the unconscious, which, as Lacan often reminds us, "has the structure of fiction."[27]

Consistent with Benjamin's characterization of Romantic criticism as an expropriating mediation of "the self-knowledge nascent in the object," psy-choanalysis offers the analysand a way of expressing this truth, the truth of her own desire, which she knows very well even though she may want to know nothing about it, through the mediating action of the analyst. The ana-lyst is no expert, is not the "subject-supposed-to-know," does not hold the knowledge the analysand seeks; strictly stated, the analyst is not even another person but, again, only a position within a structure of address, a position that sustains the hole in discourse, the opening in language, the lack in being, to which the subject of the unconscious corresponds and into which its truth can unfold. Like the work of literature, then, psychoanalysis must be simulta-neously expository and creative: it is attentive to the referential systems and historical or social contexts in which its object, the unconscious, is embed-ded, even as it works toward the elaboration of a truth which can never be exhausted by these systems and contexts: the singular truth of the subject that, as such, resists all structures of equivalence or systems of exchange.

To *interpret* is to work within such a system of exchange. Interpretation is a trade in signifiers that wants to reproduce and render more or differently intelligible the meaning to which they refer. This exemplifies Saussure's basic semiotic fact that in any system of reference signs refer only to other signs, that their reality is entirely psychological. In principle, interpretation can pro-ceed to infinity not because what it interprets is infinitely large, but because its referent is absent from the system of reference within which interpretation takes place.

Around the same time Saussure was developing the new science of semi-ology, Freud encountered this same limitlessness in *The Interpretation of Dreams*, where he discovered that the dream itself is an interpretation. This bears repeating: interpretation is not merely overlaid upon a dream-narrative after the fact, as though the latter were pure truth awaiting its semantic elu-cidation; the dream is already an instance of symbolic exchange, already at a remove from the truth it means to convey, already an interpretation. And what it interprets, here under the heading of "wish-fulfillment," is the trouble at the core of psychoanalytic inquiry: the conflict between an unconscious desire and the repressive force of the social link through its avatar the ego, which censors the desire's realization, avowal, even its articulation. Through the intermingling of condensation and displacement, the dream interprets this conflict, translating it into symbols that evade the censorship of waking life. Each new iteration of the dream's latent significance within the work of analysis thus does not aim to establish a final "meaning." Interpretation is not explanation. Instead, every embellishment of the dream adds another relation of exchange from signifier to signifier, along a chain of associations that carries on until it encounters an unintelligible abyss, what Freud calls the "navel" of the dream: the kernel of non-knowledge that sets the play of displacements and condensations on its course, the black hole from whose orbit these signifiers cannot escape, the dream's unspeakable origin and destination, a truth so specific to the dreamer that it cannot but be lost in translation.[28]

For the purposes of our analogy with the work of literature, the key insight here has less to do with the metapsychological terms in play—repression, the unconscious, and so on—than with the fact that interpretation is built around an internal limit which is also a lack: the constitutive absence of the truth animating the play of signifiers within the signifying chain, the non-presence in language of what it wants to say but can only approximate through an imperfect representation.[29] This is a foundational axiom of the Freudian discovery. As with the literary absolute, the truth exists, but not as an object among others, not as one more term within the ego narrative or the regime of sense with which the ego fabricates the illusion of its sovereign infallibility. Nor is this a transcendental truth, and psychoanalysis is not some kind of secular negative theology. The truth is there where language falters, at the edge of representation, at the margins of sense. Interpretation therefore is just as essential to the work of analysis as it is to the work of literature, in the same precise and restricted sense: its progress refines our apprehension of the limits of representation, the extent of empirical knowledge, and the ways in which a given work occupies, reproduces, or disturbs those limits.

Freud well knew that the limitlessness of interpretation is its own kind of limit. This is why from the beginning he twinned interpretation with another clinical tactic that could define, however provisionally, the evasive truth of the subject of the unconscious: the technique of *construction*. With this, Freud innovated a means to arrest the interminable spiral of interpretations that could unfold from any investigation of the unconscious by presenting, in narrative form, the logic which organizes and orients the interpretive chain.[30] Construction is not opposed to interpretation, but complements it by presenting a story in which the disparate inscriptions of the unconscious, the trajectories of association and interpretation that occupy the work of analysis, are configured relative to one another, much as an archaeologist reconstructs a civilization's way of life by organizing its scattered remnants into an intelligible, coherent cultural system.[31] Unlike archaeology, however, the value of the analytic construction is not measured by its correspondence to empirical events or discoverable historical facts, since what it aims at is not fact but what Freud calls *historical truth*: some archaic impression or event that, of logical necessity, must have taken place, since otherwise the ensuing, factical history could not have happened. Construction is the assertion of a necessary postulate, a counter-myth to the myth of the subject's self-contained coherence, a psychoanalytic fiction that nevertheless speaks the truth—a narrative of the *form* of desire and its effects.

Because a historical truth can be constructed only out of the materials that emerge from the series of interpretations it itself makes possible, it has to be understood as an aftereffect of its own effects—an origin, in other words, which is immanent within and inseparable from what it originates, present only as the absence that its repetition tries and fails repeatedly to re-present. This is why historical truths are primal, not primitive, originary, not original: these counter-myths are origins at which the analysis arrives and not from which it departs. Historical truth is not a sense found but a sense *made*—it is the narrative elaboration of an organizational logic, a "making sense" of the unconscious fantasy operating on the other side of consciousness, guiding the chains of association that foment interpretation. It is not the truth after which interpretation seeks, but the truth of interpretation itself. In more practical terms, historical truth is not some buried past awaiting excavation like the ruins of a forgotten city. It cannot be forgotten because it has not been remembered. It is alive and active here and now. Historical truth is the logic of the present.[32]

Freud's narrative technique makes clear that calculating the logic of fantasy by assembling a historical truth does not mean to impose a static assignation, nor can the work operate from some metalinguistic or metaphysical position; any construction can only ever be provisional and incomplete. Since it is mutually constituted by both analyst and analysand, the construction is the result of a critical/creative mediation, the temporary terminus of an interminable process of critical reflection, a joint calculation of the constitutively incalculable. The analyst is not the master of the unconscious but only ever its collaborator.

Before further delimiting the points of correspondence between the work of analysis and the work of literature, it is worth considering how and why Lacan emphasized this peculiar calculation of the incalculable by substituting Freud's constructions with his notorious mathemes, famously inscribing the formula of the fantasy thus:

$$\$ \lozenge a$$

The formula stresses fantasy's status as a *logic* and the unconscious as a consequence of this logic's elaboration within the analytic scene. Here and with his other formulas, Lacan wanted to correct the pervasive (and persistent, and obstinate) misunderstanding that the unconscious is a container of archaic memories and other definite mental contents. By formalizing the stakes of construction, Lacan could insist upon the universal dimension of psychoanalysis—to be human is to be split by the signifier, riven by lack and driven by desire. At the same time, he could retain the singularity of unconscious fantasy that marks every instance of the human, that binds and distinguishes all such instances from the order of the signifier, also ensuring the subject's intractability in the face of the positivist and behaviorist turn in psychology, the empiricist fundamentalism, to which Lacan's contemporary "Freudians" proved all too susceptible.

The bar over the S on the left side of the formula marks the effect of the signifier that, in constituting the subject of the unconscious, simultaneously excludes it from the symbolic, without remission. "The signifier does not designate what is not there," Lacan explains, "it engenders it. What is not there, at the origin, is the subject itself."[33] This subject is paradoxically an effect of its own negation by the signifier that constitutes it, and therefore exists only as barred.

On the right side of the formula Lacan replaces what Freud called the "lost object" with the little "a," the *objet petit a*, the impossible object-cause of desire the subject of the unconscious seeks in quest of its satisfaction. To somehow attain such an object would be to close the rift cleaved by the imposition of the signifier, putting an end to the movement of desire, the subject's very condition of being. By evacuating it of a definite content, substituting a logical variable in place of Freud's peculiar constructions, Lacan makes clear that this little object is another, simultaneous effect of the subject's constitutive negation. It does not exist any more than the barred subject exists. It can only be experienced as an absence, as the lack in a field of empirical perception, as the hole in reality to which no actual existing object (in Lacan's terms, no *imaginary* object; in Freud's terms no *partial* object; neither of them ever sufficient to the real object of desire) can ever correspond, but which for this very reason directs the interminable desire that would fill it.

Fantasy, therefore, is emphatically not the imaginary.

It is, however, radically proximate to the imaginary because it is what compels the subject to seek the impossible object of its desire, in its own peculiar way, within that register. Every object thus found is at best the placeholder of that impossibility; at best, it can provide a mere substitutive (temporary, inevitably disappointing) satisfaction. Fantasy is what ensures that every possible object of satisfaction is not *the* object. The subject is existentially dissatisfied because the object is impossible.

Since language literally defines—names, describes, indexes—the parameters of possibility and fantasy aims at the impossible, Lacan's formalization of fantasy, his stripping it to its minimal articulation as a logical formula, is an essential supplement to Freud's constructions. The logic helps us see how psychoanalysis, properly and ethically defined, operates always at the limit of the referential function—at the edge of thought where common sense falters and the meaning with which a signifying chain is imbued becomes objectively inscrutable, singular, untranslatable. It is at this limit, along the seam which conjoins and divides consciousness from the unconscious, where the analytic construction is built. As narrative, construction is not primarily representational but *representative*, in the sense that it is a surrogate apparition of that which is not and cannot be included within any representational frame, for otherwise it would need no such representative and the unconscious would not be.

This is where psychoanalysis's essentially literary—stronger still, its *novelistic*—qualities are most evident. Historical truth, the technique of construction through which we arrive at it, and its logical formalization all recall Jakobson's insight that the poetic function demands a "focus on the message for its own sake," where the referential function is not totally decommissioned but subordinated to the internal logic of signification structuring the poetic message's constituent elements in relation to one another, as a closed system. The fabric of associations that unfold from the analysand's speech comprise a closed system oriented by a singular psychic reality, knitted together from terms borrowed from the world of reference but deployed otherwise, thus not according to any possible objectivity of meaning. Fantasy has its reasons. The signifiers of the unconscious are logically ordered. But the logic of this system does not obey the laws of reference that permit and proscribe the use of language as a medium of interpersonal and social exchange, or as the structure of the social link. Constructing the fantasy according to its organizational logic therefore can be considered a clinical variation on Benjamin's "immanent structure specific to the work itself." As with the critical mediation, fantasy is a radical specificity which is created by the analytic mediation, a structure which is the effect of its structuration, and not a precedent fixture awaiting its discovery.

This further recalls Schlegel's definition of the novel: "simultaneously poetry and the poetry of poetry." Psychoanalysis is the poetics of the unconscious, and this poetics is itself articulated poetically, as a creative/critical reflection whose logic is internal to the relations and non-relations among the signifiers which compose it. Through the work of literature, criticism and creation are collapsed into each other and reconstituted as absolute. The work is infinitely variable because no two absolutes are alike, because by definition the absolute is beyond compare. So, too, with the unconscious. The singularity of unconscious fantasy is calculated through the work of analysis, which operates a simultaneously reflective and creative expropriative mediation that cannot be separated from the specificity, contingency, and infinite variability of the experience, the analytic experience, through which the poetry of fantasy, the interplay of interpretation and construction, finds expression.

Again recalling Benjamin, this work can proceed only if the unconscious is permitted a margin of "freedom from heteronymous aesthetic doctrines," and only if the work undertakes an ethical defense of that same freedom. Analysand and analyst together elaborate the logic, make sense, of unconscious fantasy, which from a purely referential point of view cannot but seem like nonsense. They do so through a steadfast commitment to the truth of the subject, however strange it must appear, regardless of the pain such commitment inflicts upon the ego, despite or because of the ways in which the work of analysis can dis-order the ego narrative and its ideological entrapment within the social scene, therefore also disordering that scene itself.

In sum, the novel is foundational to the concept of literature as we know it and, more importantly, to the ethics of reading it invites or demands. It is also foundational to the model of rational, individualistic subjectivity upon which both the work of literature and psychoanalysis intervene. In this regard, criticism and psychoanalysis are two varieties of the same ethical injunction to read otherwise. To situate the work of literature and the work of analysis within this ethical frame makes clear that psychoanalysis is a poetry of poetry, and this means historically and conceptually that it is a novelistic enterprise.[34] Thus situated, it can inform the specific challenges of the literary, it can help calculate the subject of literature at stake in the novel, without colonizing or assimilating literature's structure of address.

Our analogy cannot, however, suppose that psychoanalysis is a continuation and repetition of Romanticism or that the clinic is merely a specialized application of a prior critical insight. Tracking after the truth of one's unconscious fantasy, the person on the couch can dispute, accept, develop, abandon, puzzle over, work through, or simply ignore the analytic construction. The pages of a novel do not. A text does not dispute or concede an interpretation or rearrange itself to defend against a troubling critical insight. A novel does not dream. Psychoanalysis supposes a subject of the drive, while literature can only ever be the drive's trace or sublimation.

This is why, while they make famous and extensive use of literature, Freud and Lacan never adopt the position of the critic with respect to the texts they engage. With Sophocles or Shakespeare, Dostoevsky or Duras, Racine or Rimbaud, they treat literature not in itself but only as a means for illustrating or evoking the clinical experience. This needs emphasizing. Literature is an especially useful tool for the transmission of psychoanalytic knowledge—no doubt because of its privileged position with regard to the poetic function, as well as its relatively greater accessibility as compared to the enclosed reality of the clinical scene—but it is not yet itself such knowledge.[35]

The Other Side of Enlightenment

To state the obvious even more obviously: novels are not actual human beings, and human beings are not novels. Literature and the unconscious concern two related but distinct dimensions of the human experience. But although the ethical resonances between the work of analysis and the work of literature do not permit us to collapse them into one another—we have seen how their consonant ethics refuse any such homology—they do resound from a common historical origin, reverberate within the same walls to which the Enlightenment gave rise, echo from the margins of solicitude it established, and, most importantly, are both constituted through their attention to those margins. The extimate relation between literature and psychoanalysis thus can be traced to their complementary *unworking* of this mutual genealogical antecedent—unworking, because they work upon the Enlightenment subject of reason, but in service to what that idea of the subject excludes or tries to erase.[36]

To bear this out, we have to revisit the question of the Enlightenment's periodization and periodicity to which I earlier promised to return. I have thus far positioned it with respect to the eighteenth-century novel, but you recall that to understand the Enlightenment as a discrete historical period is an insupportable simplification. Nor, given its internal diversity and contentiousness, is it a unified or unifying intellectual movement. And since it is inseparable from its colonial, imperial material conditions, as well as their contemporary ramifications and revisions, it cannot be considered an exclusively or essentially European phenomenon. As Charles W. Mills insists, for instance but crucially, apropos of the "racialized optics of modernity" that literally colors the history of the subject of reason, "the plurality of reference of the concept must be borne firmly in mind: the space, time, and politics of enlightenment are all variable."[37] This variability makes clear that any attempt to imbue the Enlightenment, the myth and master signifier of modernity, with an exhaustive meaning cannot escape the epistemological constraints of its social and historical standpoint. Every deployment of the term "Enlightenment," including its use in the title of this book, is an ideological maneuver. But as we earlier established with Barthes's critique of myth and its recuperative capacities, one does not avoid ideological commitment by presuming to keep one's hands clean, nor, therefore, should one aspire to such false neutrality. My intention in redeploying such a fraught signifier thus is not to ignore its political valence but to amplify it.

Accepting the plurality of reference comprising "the Enlightenment" without, in so doing, consigning the term to semantic vacuity, Clifford Siskin and William Warner helpfully give it some provisional historical boundaries by defining it as "an event in the history of mediation."[38] For them, it names a rupture with previously dominant investigatory procedures and the culturally extensive emergence of a new relation between objects of knowledge and their means of constitution. The most typically repeated characteristics of the Enlightenment include suspicion toward received truth, a positive revaluation of nature and materiality, a (supposed) tendency toward secularization, the unification of moral and aesthetic sensibility, and—though Siskin and Warner do not explicitly account for this—the consolidation of moral and intellectual value around a racial hierarchy that privileges whiteness and debases blackness. These are the material consequences of this event in the history of mediation, this new way of thinking about thinking and about the tools of thought, whose most representative characteristic is an emergent imperative of *systematicity*.[39] In physics or metaphysics, abstraction or concretion or anywhere in between, the Enlightenment was that long and lingering moment at which the validity of any truth claim, the very truthfulness of the truth, became inseparable not simply from its representation but more particularly from the representational system that produced it.[40]

From that corner of the Enlightenment which most concerns us here, the cornerstone that is the formation of the subject of reason, this systematicity moves along two paths whose bifurcation it itself produces: toward the sensible/empirical, and toward the rational/metaphysical. Regarding the order of the signifier with respect to the empirical, John Locke's *Essay Concerning Human Understanding* established the referential function as the domain of rational deliberation, the medium within which the collective work of reason, including any reasoning over personal identity, must take place. After him, any phenomenon that could not be situated in relation to the other phenomena that together comprise the total system of reference, or even challenged the system's smooth functioning, would be denied entry into the order of knowledge, or—to put a finer point on this newfound sovereignty of systematicity in relation to truth—into the kingdom of reason. A century later, Immanuel Kant drew this newfound power of the system to its rational conclusion. Searching for the a priori transcendental conditions of experience—the pure forms of reason—Kant innovated a lexicon with which to represent representation itself, and then invested this lexicon with a universal moral and aesthetic authority. With both Locke's empiricism and the transcendental metaphysics Kant developed in his three *Critiques*, reason became the universal property of human being, thus also the foundation for a new notion of common humanity.[41] To operate according to reason's (eternal, metaphysical) principles was therefore a moral imperative for anyone who would claim a place within the human community thus conceived (the "Kingdom of Ends").[42]

The political end-point of the Enlightenment, its conception of human freedom (defined by both Locke and Kant, despite important differences, as *freedom from desire*), is the product of this philosophical revision of the limits of reason and its dependence upon the referential function. The notion of the human being as a rational, autonomous subject is thus inseparable from the systematic organization of knowledge within a well-ordered, equally autonomous field of representations that alone could guarantee the universal applicability of its methods, the truth of its conclusions, and the communication of its values. All other truths and values thus were denied moral solicitude on these supposedly objective, universal grounds.

This is where the Romantic insurrection begins. From its opening salvo, the anonymous "Oldest Programme for a System of German Idealism," Romanticism accepts the philosophical and moral imperative to realize universal human freedom but shifts freedom's possibility from systematized reason to the domain of the aesthetic, where the system per se becomes an object of aesthetic reflection. Only by constructing a "mythology of reason" that grasps the system in its totality, the "Oldest Programme" declares, "will *equal* development of *all* our powers await us, for the particular person as well as for all individuals."[43] With this founding provocation, Romanticism clearly does not overturn the Enlightenment, but radicalizes it and its claims to universality, valorizing an equally radical particularity that in Jena would find its articulation as the singularity of the literary absolute.

This coupling of reason with the aesthetic is at the heart of Romantic literary and philosophical practice, most apparently in the widespread use of *the fragment*, the passion for which was inspired by Enlightenment systematicity and its dependence, from Locke to Kant, on the core unit of thinking: the idea. For Locke, ideas are the basic units of thought and can always be traced to some sensory, empirical experience. Kant goes further, defining ideas as concepts of pure reason, empirically or "pathologically" irreducible, so that they "can only be approximated," as Rodolphe Gasché explains, "in an infinite process." Situating this with respect to Schlegel's *Philosophical Fragments*, Gasché continues: "fragments, strictly speaking, are then ideas in presentation. They are not leftover pieces of an integral whole, broken parts of a former or anticipated totality; they are that whole itself *in actualitas*. . . . Fragmentation, consequently, rather than implying some loss or lack of presence, represents the *positive* mode in which presentation of the whole occurs." In short, "As fragment, totality occurs."[44] From this perspective, Romanticism follows the Enlightenment's paradigmatic systematicity by positioning itself not beyond but at the limit of representation, as an aesthetic exploration or even celebration of this limit, from which vantage the total system, condensed into the idea in its fragmentary presentation, can be expressed.

The psychoanalytic construction is also a fragment in which totality occurs, but one that re-situates desire at the foundation, rather than beyond the pale, of reason. Construction discloses not only the organizing logic of fantasy orienting the subject of the unconscious with respect to the impossible object of its desire, but also the logic of the ego narrative and its orientation toward the social link. It is a narrative tableau of the unconscious fantasy and an account of the ways in which and the reasons why consciousness is a repetition, or a defensive reaction-formation, or in any case a symptom, of this same fantasy. As with the Romantic fragment, the fantasy is not a leftover piece of an integral whole, severed from an otherwise complete, conscious being. It is the logic of the system of representation comprising the subject's reality. Its construction is the positive presentation of the logic of the whole that, as such, can only appear in a fragmentary, fictionalized form.

Distilling fantasy into a logical formula, Lacan thereby insists that fantasy is another form of reason operating at the limit of consciousness—or better, it *is* this limit. It is discerned in what Lacan calls an "imaginary short circuit," a wavering or wobbling of the ego's reality. It is there where the narrative of a personal identity and the procedures of its constitution prove insufficient to account for some aspect of that reality and its experience.[45] After Lacan, Willy Apollon similarly defines fantasy as "the window of the unconscious to the real world serving to define its meaning, join[ing] the social bond to the unconscious on the imaginary level."[46] A poorly fitted pane of glass will shudder in a window frame when put to the test of a gust of wind, indicating its unfitness as a shelter against the outside. So, too, will reality shudder when put to the test of the fantasy, which, being extimate to consciousness, is an internal outside. Like any frame, it is the point of delimitation, of disjunction and conjunction, between the inside and the outside of the image it structures.

This is why psychoanalytic practice, no less than literary criticism, must be both scientific and aesthetic. Rigorous attention to rational knowledge and its constraints within the order of the signifier is necessary to discover the remainder that escapes it: its own frame, the total system in which each instance of systematic mediation takes place. This totality can only be expressed, if it can be expressed, poetically. Such is equally the case for a particular patient's primal scene or for Freud's civilizational construction describing the murder of the father of the primal horde, or for Lacan's formulaic revisions; all these variations on construction, what I above called the counter-myths of reason, are exercises in what the "Oldest Programme" already called the mythology of reason, articulated from the position of the subject of the unconscious.

Like the work of literature Romanticism inaugurated or induced, the basis of the Freudian discovery—that which the work of analysis works upon, unworks, and finally reworks into the fragment called construction—is the Enlightenment's crowning achievement: the individual. This work does not take place in a vacuum. It requires a sustained attention to history, to Enlightenment systematicity and its legacy, just as Romanticism's insurrection against the limits of the universal worked from within the moral and epistemological systems that founded it in order to insist that a mythology of reason cannot proceed without the reason it mythologizes. The ethics of psychoanalysis and the Romantics' ethics of reading are animated by the same concern for what the Enlightenment both establishes and represses: the residue of singularity that clings to the individual but cannot be located within the field of consciousness and social belonging and which, because of this un- or dislocation, does not cease its search for an addressee.

The Unwritten Enlightenment

Literature and the unconscious resonate with one another not because one repeats the other, but because they are different addresses on behalf of this residuary dimension of the human experience. Their addressees, the critic and the analyst, are constituted through an attunement to the differences that work within and unwork identity, those instances in which a narrative system becomes non-coincident with itself and undoes, in its own way and on its own terms, its self-proclaimed authority and coherence. For it is there, in the residuary dimension of the narrative, that the imaginary and symbolic collide against the unassimilable real, collide and shatter into fragments more unique than any individuality and unrepresentable within any ideology of individualism. The work of analysis and the work of literature, historically situated, are different ways of reading—and through the reading, recomposing, rewriting as fragment—that same indelible mark of the real inscribed by the history of ideas that calls itself the Enlightenment. This means reading within, alongside, around, against, and beyond the parameters of possibility (the ideology) this history establishes and enforces.

One of Lacan's terms for this impossibility, and a key inspiration for the title of this book, is "that which 'doesn't stop not being written.'" The awkward double negative conveys that the unwritten remainder which evades and defies the referential function and undermines any (Enlightenment) conception of the autonomous subject of reason is not utterly alien to the written. To borrow another of Lacan's favorite turns of phrase, what doesn't stop not being written is *not nothing*. Even though it names a lack rather than some positive content or attribute, the lack, the negativity of the written, is generative. It is there with and within what is written, with the "doesn't stop being written'" (the necessary; what could not be otherwise) and the "stops not being written" (the contingent; what becomes necessary through its inscription). What doesn't stop *not* being written enjoins and acts upon the relation between them, dis-orienting and dis-organizing that relation of necessity and contingency, urging the writing on, driving it, not transcendentally beyond but immanent within yet irreducible to every instance of the letter.[47]

Lacan further specifies that what doesn't stop not being written, or what he also calls *the impossible*, is the sexual relation. To say that the sexual relation is the impossible is immediately to recall that sex, after Freud's radical redefinition of it, is inseparable from fantasy. What drives sex is a desire not for reproduction but for the attainment, or creation, of what does not exist outside of the subject's yearning. Every actual existing entity within what is called reality—every imaginary object of desire—is made available to desire only insofar as it substitutes for the impossible object of the fantasy. But nothing within a frame is inclusive of its frame, and so no imaginary substitute for the real object of the fantasy exhausts desire, no matter how well it seems to fit the parameters the fantasy imposes; at best, the substitute may afford a partial, imperfect, therefore dissatisfying satisfaction. Along the path which traces the subject's historical inscription—the history of its dissatisfaction—the sexual relation which would conjoin subject and object, the reason and motive force of the subject's inscription, the logic of the fantasy which quests after the impossible, doesn't stop not being written.

What this means in simple, practical terms is that any supposed intimacy between subjects is inevitably a missed connection. No two fantasies coincide. We are always alone with the fantasy; it is the singular parameter of our existential solitude, the way in which we live our finitude. Every imaginary relation is a missed connection because all such relations are patterned after the non-relation the fantasy structures, between an inexistent subject and an impossible object. The fantasy, precisely because it is fantasy, cannot be dispelled or dissolved by any reasoning or reality. Paradoxical as it may seem, the fantasy is real, it is *the real* of the subject. The sexual relation is real because it is impossible. Every effort to write it, every record, every entry into the ledger of history, misses its mark, re-marks and repeats this impossibility, and does so interminably. As long as there is desire, the subject will be inscribed there in what doesn't stop not being written.

The sexual relation is what incompletes necessity from within, on and with its own terms; it is where Lacan discovers the contingency of necessity. Tracking what I am calling the unwritten Enlightenment means tracing this contingency. It means writing what doesn't stop not being written, constructing the logic of desire that motors the textual history of the subject of reason, in order to disclose the internal impossibility of this subject's realization. It means giving the fantasmatic dimension of the Enlightenment subject over to the work of writing, writing the fantasy at play in the Enlightenment's novelistic discourse, while admitting and embracing that this work is impossible—indeed, it is the work of the impossible, of the real, upon and through and against the possible. Like any construction, such writing is provisional, incomplete, and specific to the scene of its elaboration. But in its provisionality, we nevertheless define the limits of the possible, as Lacan says, "the limits, impasses, and dead ends that show the real acceding to the symbolic," inviting and invoking an attunement to what exceeds them.[48]

To Return: To the Novel, to the Subject

Literature—the unconscious—the Enlightenment. Our conceptual triangle thus drawn, we can see why the novel is not just contemporary with the Enlightenment, it is that aspect of this event in the history of mediation that popularized and rendered generally intelligible the modern problematics of subject-formation and the subject's organization within the order of the signifier. More than a tool or technology of reason, however, the novel is also the literary frame in which the Romantic insurrection sought to radicalize the Enlightenment through the aesthetic refraction of the literary absolute in the work of literature. And the novel is a precedent for the Freudian discovery and for the experience and practice of psychoanalysis, which involve the historically delimited coordinates to which the subject is assigned, the narrative processes by which that assignation is made meaningful, and the construction of counter-narratives by which the subject is invited to signify otherwise, to signify the logic of its difference from itself. In short, literature, the unconscious, and the Enlightenment are fundamentally (which is not to say exhaustively or exclusively) novelistic phenomena.

The novel is many things. It is nothing if not formally indeterminate. But its importance to the Enlightenment, both as its emissary to the popular imagination and as the gap which opens it to being read along vertices that run contrary to and disturb its self-proclaimed hegemony, is a matter less of its unstable generic properties than of the mode of discourse it engendered. Novelistic discourse in the eighteenth century is far from the first place where the philosophical and the literary inseparably intermingle, but it is where subjectivity and narrativity, experience and intelligibility, truth and its representation, interlace to produce the framework of the modern individual.[49] The conjunction of the philosophical and the literary here precedes and precipitates the generic, conceptual, or disciplinary distinctions that began to take shape at the turn of the nineteenth century. The joint the Enlightenment novel and novelistic discourse forged between the poetic and the referential is the hinge upon which the modern relation between philosophy and literature turns, where rationality and Enlightenment systematicity meet the singularity at stake in literature and the unconscious.

The chapters of this book all bear this out by considering experimental eighteenth-century texts that best represent the period's efforts to pose and respond to the question of the subject—to establish its position and limits with respect to a reformed, rationalized version of the social link—while at the same time introducing, without intention or awareness, a limit to the subject's representability that subverts those same systems of subjectivation. Following the analogy between the work of literature and the work of analysis we have established here, each of these texts asks us to calculate the subject of literature in relation to the impossible object of its desire. In the language of psychoanalysis, they ask us to discover the novelistic unconscious and the logic of fantasy which organizes it, giving priority to the shuddering in the window frame, the wobbling in the imaginary, the symbolic slippages, frustrations, or internal contradictions, that indicate these texts' ill-fittedness, their irreducibility and resistance, to their surrounding reality, to the ideologically circumscribed parameters of the possible structuring that reality, and finally to themselves.

The first such effort, on Defoe's *Robinson Crusoe* by way of Daniel Paul Schreber's *Memoirs of My Nervous Illness*, initiates this attunement to the disconnect between fantasy and ideology by locating Defoe's prototype of the Modern Man at the vanguard of the eighteenth century's emergent imperatives of instrumental rationality and sovereign subjectivity. From Locke to Kant and beyond, and with great variation, such imperatives hold that a properly formed subject is one who systematically forges a mimetic relation between the phenomenal world and the mind, such that they, ideally, mirror one another. Nowhere is this model of subject/world formation more clearly presented than in *Crusoe*. We will find by reading it alongside Schreber's testimony that this sort of mimetic ordering, this overlaying of the rational upon the material, cannot but assimilate all difference into the sameness of its own mental order, fabricating a totality without remainder which is as impervious to self-doubt as it is convinced of its own irresistibility. Defoe's didactic vision of instrumental rationality, with all its imperialist world-ordering pretensions, is structured according to the logic of a psychotic delusion. Far from being the other of reason, we find on Crusoe's lonely island that psychosis is the truth of reason. This comparison finds or introduces a wobbling in the Enlightenment imaginary that therefore recasts its rationalist imperatives and their material consequences as a psychotic project.

The purpose of this designation and comparison is not to harness the history of stigma attached to a putative psychopathology which psychoanalysis radically and steadfastly problematizes, as if we somehow are immune to this psychosis at the foundation of the modern age. We do not stand outside of the history or language Defoe's novel occupies, elaborates, and bequests. Nor is this yet an instance of the sort of standpoint epistemology Charles Mills calls for in his emphasis on enlightenment as a plurality of reference. Our aim rather is to reorient the critique of the European Enlightenment, including criticism of its colonial zeal, its constitutive antiblackness and white supremacy, its hypocrisies and contradictions, in ways that confront the logic of fantasy at its core, from within, at the center of, its colonial mentality.

The critical and political horizon of this investigation is that one does not unsettle the psychosis of reason by reasoning with it. Crystallizing the psychotic Enlightenment through the work of literature, joining a psychoanalytic ethical sensibility with a literary phenomenology of the delusion, instead subverts its imperial ambitions and legacy of violence by offering the Enlightenment and its inheritance an addressee other than the rapacious, all-consuming Other of its own desire.

If *Robinson Crusoe* presents the problematics of the subject and its formation through a didactic literary experiment with the parameters of instrumental rationality, chapter 2 amplifies this relation between didacticism and subjectivation by way of the revolutionary pedagogy Jean-Jacques Rousseau imagined with *Émile: or, On Education*. In this novelistic treatise, Rousseau insists the subject's quest for existential freedom is inseparable from the social order in which that subject is unfortunately inscribed and against which his freedom is in perpetual conflict. After Rousseau, the rational, libertarian educator is compelled to prioritize this freedom against its social and historical inscription in order to reform or reinvent the social link. This was an essential propaedeutic, if not to the development of radical pedagogy and its emphasis on critical consciousness, then at least to modern child-centered education. But the friction between Rousseau's message and the structure of the text by which it is conveyed betrays his pedagogy's

profound conservatism. In a psychoanalytic idiom, Rousseau and the pedagogical liberalism to which he gave voice remain enchained to the pleasure
principle, and this is the quintessence of ideology in action.

The way beyond this entrapment is through an ethical fidelity to the
subject's dissatisfaction not only with its world but with itself, which dissatisfaction is traced by the peregrinations of the death drive. It is such a fidelity
that the Marquis de Sade actualizes in his (ir)reverent rewriting of *Émile*, his
dialogic *Philosophy in the Bedroom*. Locating the truth of the subject-in-
revolt in Sade's revolting subjects—and beyond them, in his graphomaniacal
efforts to articulate this inarticulable, revolting, unceasing resistance to the
order of the signifier, this truth that doesn't stop not being written—turns
the Enlightenment's pedagogical legacy upside-down and exposes its obscene
underside. Following Sade into the boudoir and back into the street, the
consequence of this Sadean subversion is a speculative, impossible political
community, or a community of the impossible, whose basis is *the right to jouissance* according to which a genuinely radical pedagogy might take shape.

This second chapter certainly concerns sex, sexuality, and the logic and
politics of sexual difference, but we will find in the following chapter that,
as far as concerns the unwritten Enlightenment, these problems are best
addressed by way of Laurence Sterne's *Tristram Shandy*. More than any
other eighteenth-century work, as much as any novel before or since, Sterne's
monument to the wildly incalculable potentials of novelistic discourse folds
the Enlightenment into its fictional frame—literally reproducing whole passages of Locke's *Essay* and other eighteenth-century theoretical treatises
on aesthetics and epistemology, re-situating them in the work of literature,
opening them to the experience and ethics of reading such work enjoins. In
formalizing *Tristram Shandy*'s impossible narrative structure, in developing
a formalization of the impossible, the final chapter is the culmination of the
theory of the unwritten within the written—and of what it means for the
work and subject of literature in general—this book hopes to advance.

In *Tristram Shandy*, the eponymous narrator's unceasing effort to constrain
reality to within his narrative's representational frame exposes, operates, and
renders ridiculous the hinge upon which the referential function turns: literally and figuratively, the signification of the phallus. At the same time, an
unpredictable meandering of the signifier defies, subverts, provokes, yet does
not pretend to escape, the phallic function. Together, these two modalities of
the signifier dis-join to form a text which, contrary to most readings, is not
random or unmotivated but *differently motivated*—motivated by sexual difference and driven by the desire of the other. Organizing the narrative around
the two mutually constitutive, irreconcilable modalities of signification Lacan
calls the masculine and the feminine, Sterne effects an aesthetic sublimation
of the drive that at once amplifies and delights in the Enlightenment's futil-
ity. By tracing the devices of this sublimation, we will find that the novel
stages the impossibility of the sexual relation, the existential incompatibility

of the urge to make sense and the urge to signify, the fantasmatic non-relation that "doesn't stop not being written." To draw this out, I venture my own construction of the fantasy, tracing and then narrating the contours and coordinates of the sexual non-relation, the impossibility, the primal scene, from which *Tristram Shandy* springs. Such a construction is not confined to the fantasy structure of Sterne's text; it specifies, singularizes, the effects of the impossible, but in so doing insists that the subject of literature, no less than the subject of the unconscious, is a sexed subject.

Following the constraints and possibilities of our analogy between these two subjects, literature and the unconscious, these chapters draw extensively from psychoanalysis for three interwoven reasons. First, psychoanalysis stands to learn more about itself, its own clinical operations, its primary dependence upon the poetic function, its radical subversive potential, as well as its limitations in this regard, from the work of literature. Second, the Freudian conception of historical truth, as well as its Lacanian revision and formalization, can help break the stale and stubborn impasse between the historical and the historically irreducible that has beguiled the novel and its criticism, and the work of literature as such, at least since the New Criticism and up to the present. The third reason is the stake of the book's epilogue on the inevitable relation and essential difference between fantasy and ideology. As a discourse, a practice, and above all an ethics, psychoanalysis is founded upon the infinitesimal but infinitely consequential difference between the subject and the processes of subjectivation that encircle it and wish totally to exhaust the subject's potential to desire. This difference is more than the special province of psychoanalysis; it structures the early novel—and with it, the Enlightenment, and therefore the whole of the modernity to which we, no less than the works in question or the Freudian discovery itself, remain subjected.

I do not deploy the language of psychoanalysis in order to sort and categorize, to diagnose characters or authors or readers, or to pretend to a detached, clinical neutrality.[50] Such would be to maintain or impose an untenable distance from these texts and the work they invoke. My aim rather is to follow the analogy between the critical and the clinical elaborated here in order to draw into relief the infinitesimal distance between, on one hand, a text's social and historical location, explicit moral investments, and political or didactic intentions, and on the other hand, those aspects of the text that undermine, refuse, or otherwise resist all such assignations as the subject of literature pursues its quest for something other or more than what these histories, moralities, and intentions might demand. Because infinitesimal distances are nevertheless infinite, I make no claim to critical exhaustiveness, nor does my emphasis on the eighteenth century and the Enlightenment suppose that other epochs, signifiers, myths, or aesthetic forms are less amenable to the critical, ethical sensibility that a psychoanalytic attunement enjoins. Nor, finally, can we imagine that what doesn't stop not being written in the

Enlightenment will cease its incessant unwrittenness merely because of the writing that follows, that always only follows.

I hope instead that *The Unwritten Enlightenment* will operate like a Freudian construction but from another angle and in a different but essentially, extimately related domain of human endeavor and experience. Arresting, however approximately and imperfectly, the work of literature's movement through language and history, this book offers a few provisional calculations of the subject of literature: traces of the effect of the subject whose persistent murmuring beneath the din of history is the invitation to read otherwise, to read against, again, or anew, interminably. "That is what happens," Lacan says, "when you scribble something."[51]

Chapter 1

✦

The New World Delusion

Robinson Crusoe and the Psychosis of Enlightenment

Prologue: The End

Young Robinson will not act the part. Instead, he acts out. Abandoning his home, taking to sea despite his total inexpertise and without considering the consequences for either his parents' peace of mind or his shipmates' safety, undertaking an adventure with no determined destination, he endeavors to carve a channel for his uncertain, itinerant desire, come what may. The result, at the edge of the earth, is the end of the world.

It could not be otherwise. Crusoe never had a chance. The catastrophe begins well prior to the abortive slaving expedition that will maroon him upon his island of solitude, in the novel's first lines and at the earliest possible scene of this private history—the family scene, site of ancestral origin and inheritance:

> I was born in the Year 1632, in the City of *York*, of a good Family, tho' not of that Country, my Father being a Foreigner of *Bremen*, who settled first at *Hull*: He got a good Estate by Merchandise, and leaving off his Trade, lived afterward at *York*, from whence he had married my Mother, whose Relations were named *Robinson*, a very good Family in that Country, and from whom I was called *Robinson Kreutznaer*; but by the usual Corruption of Words in *England*, we are now called, nay we call ourselves, and write our Name *Crusoe*, and so my Companions always call'd me.[1]

From the beginning, "Crusoe" is not his father's name and he is not his father's son. Unlike the man who raised him, the boy is rebellious, impulsive, and restless; foolhardy and fickle; self-interested, obstinate, and ambitious— entirely unfit for "the middle State," the life of tranquil mediocrity, to which the old man would consign him (5). Above all, he refuses to read in his father's exhortations the script that Providence has prepared for him in the book of eternity. Thus severed from his inheritance, he is set upon a wayward journey into the savage wilderness where his world will end and where, alone with the scraps and remnants of that wasted reality, he will have to begin again.

The catastrophe is already the sign under which the whole text proceeds; the writing of the disaster is there in the name, *Robinson Crusoe*. Its inscription at the top of the text, before the narrative's beginning, will have marked the loss, more profoundly the foreclosure, of a special signifier: the name of the father. Special, because the signifier's inability to gain any purchase on the son's life is far from insignificant; in the symbolic economy of the novel, the discrepancy between "Kreutznaer" and "Crusoe," the gap or gulf in the name, is the sign of the failure of the father's law, and of the divine Law for which it stands, to imprint itself upon young Crusoe and restrain his impetuous, unruly, imperial desire and channel it toward more modestly domestic enterprises. Thus is the name also a "No," a paternal prohibition that would have assigned the son's middling place in a preordained universe, subduing those "rambling thoughts" (4) surging from an irresistible "I know not what" (12): an unnamed, impetuous, ruthless agency driving him across the planet in search of ever more money and blood to fortify his plantation soils. The foreclosure of this "No" and this name is the very cause of the narrative's being; this is what dislodges the child from his father's house, breaks him away from the middle state and destines him instead for a state of exception in which he will discover both destitution and deliverance—for himself and for us all.

Foreclosed, it is not that this signifier on which the hero's fate hangs has been refused or displaced; it is as if it never existed. Its rejection and return therefore operate according to a logic other than that of the repressed and the symptom, a logic that aims to make sense, to build a new world of meaning, out of the catastrophe of its loss. If there is a symptom here, it is extensive with the hero's whole being; it is the end of the old world and the creation of the new.

Nor is the signifier's foreclosure a simple absence. It is doubly marked by the mother: first, by her ancestral name, Robinson; and again by the mother tongue, which usurps the place where "Kreutznaer" should stand. His father is from elsewhere, a German, a stranger to the mother country and the mother tongue. "Crusoe" is what results when the foreign is overwritten by the familiar. Through this consumption and reproduction, this genealogical cannibalism, the name of the father is appropriated and transformed, and the usurpation is inscribed upon the son, who himself is nothing but an inscription—a name and a narrative, a work of fiction whose every mark re-marks, repeats, the insatiable conquest of Mother England. As Robinson Crusoe spreads from the rim of the metropole outward toward the infinite horizon, he overwrites and absorbs, conquers, secures, and domesticates; he brings the catastrophe with him.

He is the end of the world.

Reading the Psychosis of Reason

Can we avoid the Freudian overtones in this dynamic, according to which the subject of the adventure, on the way to self-discovery and self-determination, occupies one corner of a triangle of desire whose other two vertices are the (symbolic) father and mother? Whose symbolic position is calculated from the start according to this triangulation? Whose very being begins with the trouble of this dual, dueling inheritance?

This resonance with Freud's Oedipus is not anachronistic. On the contrary, *Robinson Crusoe* is one of the very conditions of the Freudian discovery. More exactly, the novel is that condition's supreme articulation. It is the arrangement—in the conceptual and clinical language of the last chapter, the *construction*, the narrative structuration of a logic—of the quintessentially modern myth of the Self-Made Man. The eponymous hero and narrator is the emblem of the struggle, in a world deprived of its ancient assurances, to fashion a meaningful life out of the ruins of a decaying past and the raw materials of a chaotic and indifferent universe. This is a universal, ancient struggle that nevertheless takes on new flesh through and after the eighteenth century: that of the sovereign, therefore solitary, individual, whose sovereignty is both the origin and consequence of the story he tells, both its constituting and constituted power. In this regard, Crusoe is older than Oedipus. It was Crusoe who first separated himself from his proto-bourgeois origins in the family romance.[2] It was his author Daniel Defoe, not Sophocles, who constructed (which is not to say invented) this model of the subject through, upon, and against which the invention of psychoanalysis later took place. *Crusoe* does not modernize the Oedipal drama of the subject's dilemma regarding desire, inheritance, and allegiance or obligation to the two irreconcilable halves of the parental dyad; it precedes it.

Defoe's novel is the source material for the myth of the Modern Man, thus also the historical basis of its psychoanalytic mythology, in part because nobody better imagined, personified, and made generally legible the ordeal entailed by the Enlightenment myth as such: Enlightenment as cultural adolescence, an ambivalent rupture with an unbearable inheritance, a contradictory embrace and repudiation of its ancestry in search of some new, superior vantage from which to determine another destiny. Neither strictly beholden to older theological structures of knowledge and power nor a fully realized champion of Enlightenment rationalism or liberalism, Defoe's hero, like his Protestant author, occupies and exemplifies an interval during which the doctrine of an all-powerful God operating an eternal cosmic order struggled to reconcile itself with an emergent scientific and philosophical materialism and a new faith in an all-powerful Nature. With one foot in the past and another striding toward the future, Defoe consolidated and compressed numerous political-philosophical controversies surrounding the question of human nature.[3] He also helped smear the veneer of nature and natural determination upon emergent racial hierarchies, ideologies of conquest, and the profound inhumanity they still enable.[4] His fictions displaced the earlier literary model of spiritual biography, repackaging the latter's proselytism in the more insidious didacticism of a novel narrative design.[5] His most successful novel more than schematized, it demonstrated and popularized, the difference between reason and desire at the basis of the eighteenth century's epistemological shift and presaged several of its later touchstones, including Edmund Burke's aesthetics of the sublime and Kant's metaphysics of morals. *Robinson Crusoe*—character, author, text, reception, and legacy—is an emblem of the Enlightenment.

Thus does our troubled and troubling hero, with hardly a thought for the familiar shore of the old world receding behind him, cast away and cast himself, and with himself the whole of the modern age, into the abyss of freedom. Eventually, he will repent of his foolhardy intransigence and crawl back to the Law of the Father, since his adventure is the story of a religious conversion, an entertaining lure toward the author's peculiar blend of Nonconformist Protestantism and early capitalist entrepreneurship. One man alone on an island, armed with no special skills against his unfamiliar environment, led by no priest and no king, abandoned to this terra incognita with nothing but a few spare Bibles to guide his spiritual awakening, discovers through Reason and the voice of Conscience the key to spiritual—and, by extension, worldly—contentment: a joyful obedience to the Father's inexorable commands.

But this resolution to the classically Freudian neurotic dilemma, this happy Oedipal reconciliation, is a ruse.

One man alone, utterly so, left in the lurch at the end of the world, suffering from auditory and at times visual hallucinations, debilitating paranoia, and chronic anxiety, discovers or divines through Reason and the voice of Conscience that he is a modern prophet divinely elected to bear a singular testimony of world salvation. And saving the world entails nothing less than creating the world anew, in his own image. In the end, at the dawn of this new beginning, he does not accede to or reconcile with the Father's law, but triumphs over it. For while it is a conversion narrative masked as an adventure story, *Crusoe* is also and more exactly an adventure story masked as a conversion narrative.[6] The hero's journey from destitution to deliverance and on to deliverer surreptitiously transubstantiates the spiritual into an extension and effect of the worldly. Posing Crusoe as a humble object and servant of God's grand design, Defoe thus makes Reason, Conscience, and Providence servants to his (and his Enlightenment's) limitlessly self-aggrandizing, representationally and materially imperialist purposes.

In short, the outcome of the end of the world, the response to the catastrophe, the sense of it all, is the novel construction of a New World delusion.

"Delusion" is neither a pejorative term nor a sign of unreason. It is an entirely reasonable, not uncommon response to the end of the world. Worlds end all the time. Delusion is one strategy by which the subject at the center of such an apocalypse—what psychoanalysis calls the psychotic—seeks a way out of the disaster, seeks some other to whom the historical truth of the catastrophe can be addressed, an other who thereby can afford some relief from the crushing solitude of that truth, some distance from it, by helping the subject articulate it in the direction of a broader collective. Delusion is the structure of address proper to the truth to which the psychotic testifies. As we have already begun to discern, it is also the structure of address through which the subject of literature here, at the foundation of the myth of modernity—within and against the fiction of the Self-Made Man, modernity's most outsize, most celebrated mythic hero—calls its critic.

This chapter therefore contends that *Robinson Crusoe*—not merely the character, but the emblem the whole text has become, the subject it signifies—is a key variant of the delusions of modern reason that together constellate the Enlightenment. Venturing this hypothesis with the work of literature, and with this work in particular, reveals why the autonomous, morally culpable, conscience-driven subject—the hero of the modern age; the basic unit of universal moral account; the ideological wellspring of bourgeois revolution and republican democratization; the beating heart at the center of the myth of the Enlightenment even today—has the structure of a delusion. To take up this structure means not so much to excavate as to construct it, and in so doing to calculate the position of the subject of literature which the emblem elides and refuses. To occupy the position of the other of this subject's address, to constitute and be constituted by this peculiar structure of address, will require that we reconceive the Enlightenment's purchase on reason as a psychotic one. Its conception of the autonomous individual is a variation of psychosis. Its world-ordering ambition, realized in the long history of representational and real violence against the ancestries, lifeworlds, and bodies of its many others, is a psychotic project.

As with the clinical treatment of psychosis, or with any worthwhile case history, such a reading presents particular difficulties. In the first place, we must set aside the false assurance that we occupy a zone of inquiry "beyond" the delusion; nor, relatedly, can we assume psychosis is a pathology or sickness that ought to be cured, if to cure means to dissipate the psychotic's reality and replace it with another, more supposedly objective one. As Freud notes, delusion is its own sort of construction; faced with the catastrophe of a collapsed and ended world, the delusion *is* the cure.[7] If we remain under the shadow of the Enlightenment, even if it is a myth, even if it is only the master signifier of an illusion we would rather see deposed or dissolved, our world is the delusion. The Enlightenment is the psychosis we are still living, some of us undoubtedly more habitually or comfortably or desperately than others. As Defoe's novel is formative of the delusion, we remain *Crusoe*'s benefactors or its victims, or in any case its readers, but there is no transcendental outside of the history over which this name is inscribed. To the extent that we participate in this history, belong to it or act upon and within it, we are like Defoe: more than readers, we are authors of the delusion, which does not stop being written merely because we cease or refuse to accept it.

Our aim, therefore, is not to pathologize the Enlightenment or to cure it, but rather to read Defoe's construction and the logic it exemplifies in order to formulate the question prior to any possible treatment of the Enlightenment and its legacy. We have to ask after the historical truth that orients the Enlightenment in order to gather how that truth replicates and perpetuates itself, as well as how, unless they contend with this compulsion to repeat, even the most well-meaning and rigorous critiques of Enlightenment cannot but reproduce and reify this collective psychosis's terms, values, and conditions of possibility. Proceeding in this way, holding hands with this emblematic, mythical figure and venturing to the heart of the New World delusion, we may find another path from which to subvert the ideological complex and the lived and living violence for which the novel still stands, according to its own parameters and within the limits it established and still sustains.

Such a subversion is an example of what the psychoanalytic "cure" can mean for psychosis. This cure is not the successful application of a ready-made diagnostic taxonomy, of some abstract, disembodied truth, from a hypothetically metalinguistic, "sane" position of authority. That position, like Crusoe's God, is precisely the crux of the delusion we mean to treat. We must instead exercise our analogy between the ethics of psychoanalysis and the ethics of reading by giving the psychotic subject of literature a proper hearing, really listening to what that subject has to tell us about the historical truth—not the facts but the unconscious, fantasmatic structure to which the facts belong and in which they take place—of our present. Our critical task is to occupy the position of the other to whom the delusion may be addressed, and through whose critical, creative mediation the delusion's truth returns to the subject in another, differently illuminated form. To do this, we have to trace the work of the psychosis in the body of the text, according to the logic of its operations, and attend to the ways in which it makes sense of the shattering of the old world upon its collision with the new. Thus can we trace the truth of the catastrophe called modernity.

We therefore follow Lacan's insight that psychosis, first and foremost, designates a certain relation to language, a relation which the psychotic lives at the level and in the materiality of the body. Nowhere is this more observable than in the writing of the delusion. Writing gives the truth of the psychotic's experience over to recognition, inviting its addressee into a joint investigation of the causes and extent of the catastrophe to which the delusion responds. This is why Lacan's seminar on *The Psychoses*, where he introduced the linguistic turn into the Freudian field, primarily concerns another famous text and monument to the Enlightenment, Daniel Paul Schreber's *Memoirs of My Nervous Illness*. The linguistic dimension of the delusion is already apparent in Freud's analysis of Schreber's *Memoirs*, as it is the only one of his case histories whose central figure Freud never met and who was present, so to speak, only as the text.[8] For Lacan, Freud's textual encounter with the psychotic evinces a semiotic dimension of psychoanalysis and its concern for the subject of the unconscious that Freud did not yet have the conceptual grammar to articulate. This semiotics therefore needed to be drawn out of Freud through Schreber, through the limitations and failures that confounded Freud's efforts to see in the psychotic anything other than an especially acute neurosis. The Freudian text needed to be dis-appropriated from itself in order to reveal from this intimate distance what Freud had discovered but was not able to name.

In this regard, Lacan's maneuver is not unlike the concept of criticism Walter Benjamin extrapolated from the Jena Romantics. Like the literary critic operating through the work of literature, Lacan returns the work (on Schreber; of analysis) to itself according to its immanent but as yet unarticulated structure. In this chapter I want to repeat Lacan's operation, this time through Schreber's effect upon *Robinson Crusoe*, in order to discover what the novel says without knowing, and what its emblematic status effaces, about the Enlightenment articulation of the subject. To do so, I will consider the form and structure of the novel, how it works and why, alongside what we may term the *functional structure* of Schreber's delusion.

This connection with the work of literature is not arbitrary. For Lacan, the abiding value of Schreber's text is the window it opens onto the "problem of literary creation in psychosis."[9] At stake, then, in the semiotics of the psychoses is a psychoanalytic literary criticism or a literary-critical psychoanalysis that contends with the delusion's aesthetic dimension, its creative energies and their frustrations, but does not aim to resolve—indeed, explores and enriches—the text's enigmas, ambiguities, and contradictions. It is not that the delusion is literature, nor is the psychotic subject at stake in the *Memoirs* a work of fiction on the same order as a fictional character. There is little romance in the psychotic's experience. But the delusion nevertheless is not without literature, since the subject articulated there, like any subject, has the structure of a fiction. The literary dimension of the delusion cannot be thought without literary criticism, since, as we established early in the introduction, criticism is the site at which the work of literature takes place, or else it does not exist. With the psychoses, psychoanalysis needs literary criticism, if by the latter we mean not a ready-made collection of interpretive techniques but an ethical sensitivity to the text's irreducibility and its inseparability from the practices of reading that animate it.

As Lacan insists, "since we don't know Schreber the subject, we have to study him via the phenomenology of his language . . . , around the more or less hallucinated, parasitic, foreign, intuitive, and persecutory phenomena of language at issue in the case."[10] In what follows, I will show why the same should be said of Defoe's novel. Elsewhere in his seminar on *The Psychoses* Lacan called *Robinson Crusoe* "one of the themes of modern thought," and its response to the question, "what happens when the human subject lives all alone?" an analogue of the psychotic's experience.[11] Pursuing this analogy, taking up Lacan's cryptic provocation, means reading psychosis not as literature but on the way to literature, as the singular testimony of a real experience—a making sense, a construction, thus a necessarily poetic elaboration and mediation, of the experience's otherwise insupportable immediacy; and it means the same in reverse: reading literature on the way to psychosis, constructing with the text a literary phenomenology of *Robinson Crusoe* that discloses the logic of the response to the disaster, the logic of the delusion, which calls itself the Enlightenment.

The only way to generate such a phenomenology is to follow the entanglements among the novel's constituent elements. As we are tracking after and constructing the subject of literature at the margin of an emblem, we must understand the novel as a signifier which is overdetermined—stacked with various, distinct, sometimes complementary and often contradictory symbolic values. If along the trail of disentanglement we seem at times to wander in the direction of character study, this is only because Crusoe is one aspect of that overdetermination. The formation of the character is inseparable from the form of the narrative, therefore also from the formulation of the Enlightenment subject. Crusoe is only a fiction, but it is precisely as a fiction that he is the representative of the Enlightenment's real, enduring, material effects.

We will return to this question of material consequences, as well as what reconceiving the Enlightenment as a general psychosis means for the future of thought, politics, and their moral frameworks, at the chapter's conclusion. First, however, we must continue to elaborate, on its own terms, the text's coincidence with and treatment of the end of the world.

An Undeniable Compliance of Chance

The existential solitude around which Lacan's gnomic association of *Robinson Crusoe* with the structure of the delusion pivots is by no means exclusive to the psychotic. It is a fact of being human that at some point each of us is compelled to ask a fundamental question, a question of foundations: "What am I there?" What is my being according to its symbolic inscription in the domain of the Other? What is my place there in the social link, in the language which structures it? What does the Other want of me? Logically, such a compound question is inarticulable without the subject's, every subject's, radical, constitutive alienation from the symbolic. One does not ask existential questions for which one already has the answer.

Now, it often happens that what Lacan calls the Name-of-the-Father (sometimes also the "paternal metaphor") affords such an answer. This name is not a referent but a function. It is what assigns the subject's ill-fitted, inherently unsatisfactory symbolic position, the "there" to which the question of the subject's being is addressed.[12] The subject can then depart from that assignment on the way to self-discovery or self-realization, or may venture forth only to return and live with the convenient dissatisfaction the original position provides. If this primordial signifier is foreclosed, however, this opens another course. It leaves the psychotic, as Schreber says, "in the lurch"; his "What am I there?" is answered not by an impotence but by an emptiness, a gap in the symbolic where the Name-of-the-Father would be; the site of his being is a missing link in the chain of signifiers comprising his world, the discovery of which can cause the whole rigging to collapse.[13] Without the symbolic position that constrains the subject to negotiate its desire according to the shared parameters of the social order—thus also without a position with respect to which that order, too, must negotiate its desire for the subject—the subject is abandoned to an unbearable oppositional relation to the whole of the imaginary. A holy onslaught.

Assigning the subject its (non-)place in the symbolic performs an additional function: it negates the subject's status as the *object* of an otherwise boundless maternal *jouissance*.[14] As Danielle Bergeron explains, the father is "the entity," not the man (or woman, for that matter) "that makes symbolic castration the kernel of coexistence and guarantees that the child will never be enslaved as the exclusive object of the jouissance of an other [the mother] to whom the child must be devoted."[15] This prohibitive aspect of the name is why it is also a "No," an originary interdiction.

Similarly, "mother" does not designate the gestational origin of the subject any more than Robinson Crusoe or his mother are real human beings—a fact some critics of psychoanalysis too easily forget, but which should be obvious considering that the subject's origin is not in the womb but in its vanishing beneath the signifier. Organicity ends where the subject begins, and the latter is what concerns psychoanalysis. It is thus only retroactively, after the origin that divides the subject from its organic determinations, and not according to any biological relation, that the position of the mother is constituted as a coordinate of desire. In other words, it is the position of the desire of the mother within the unconscious fantasy of the subject, and not the human being who calls herself or is called "mother," that gives the signifier "mother" its significance. The maternal *jouissance* which the paternal prohibition interrupts, or which entraps the subject for whom this primordial signifier is foreclosed, thus is not the *jouissance* of the woman who holds the infant in her arms. Rather, it is that bitter flavor of enjoyment the subject savors through its own fantasy of being the object of this originary Other's rapacious desire, the missing piece, the key to that total plenitude, that oneness without separation, which lures the subject from the other side of symbolic castration toward an impossible, annihilatory, satisfaction.[16]

Mother, father, and child are symbolic assignations for the constituent elements of a fantasmatic configuration that, as such, can be too easily conflated with this or that individual in the imaginary. This is a misunderstanding that has plagued psychoanalysis since Freud's foundational construction of the Oedipus complex. What is neither symbolic nor imaginary but *real* are maternal *jouissance*, the Name/No-of-the-Father, and what they mean for the reality of the subject.

Here we can begin to calculate the coincidence of the psychotic's delusion with the subject of literature in Defoe's text. The catastrophe from which both unfold and which both want to contain is the primordial foreclosure of the paternal metaphor and the subject's abandonment to the indomitable Other for whom there is no other (for Crusoe, as we have seen, this Other is Mother England and her mother tongue), who always wants but never gives, before whom the subject is but the object of a ruthless and bottomless, apocalyptic enjoyment.

Schreber presents this crisis as a torrent of auditory hallucinations, especially voices, which he experiences as outside impositions. These constant castigations and senseless imperatives constitute an "unholy turmoil" issuing from the divine rays that bind him directly to God.[17] He can only alleviate this anguished confusion once he has built a new, makeshift symbolic order within which to sort and contain his experiences. He is a *bricoleur* borrowing signifiers from the language, history, and systems of knowledge he has already known, but imbuing them with other meanings gleaned from the chatter of the divine rays and their "basic language." Against the traumatic onslaught of perceptive phenomena, Schreber reasons, "I had to solve one of the most intricate problems ever set for man and I had to fight a sacred battle for the greatest good of mankind." From this, he discovers that he has been singled out for a sacrificial mission to restore the Order of the World. "When I think of my sacrifices," he laments at the end of his record, "the picture emerges of a martyrdom which all in all I can only compare with the crucifixion of Jesus Christ."[18] So the delusion brings deliverance—not from the violence of a voracious omnipotence, which to the end does not stop its persecutions, but from the *senselessness* of that violence. The sense he makes of it, the meaning of the violence, is that only he can deliver the world from a deranged God whose apocalyptic desire has created an ontological rift at the center of which Schreber stands, as if his ravaged body hangs over an abyss, arms outstretched, Christlike, holding the universe together lest it and we collapse into inexistence.

What Schreber is living at the level of an embodied and real experience is the defect in the symbolic, the fact that the world was not built with him in mind, was not designed to afford him a place there; there is constitutively no symbolic location for the subject bearing his name. The same is true for all of us—indeed, this lack is the universal basis of psychoanalysis. What distinguishes the psychotic's difficulty, then, is not that he is outside of language (his entrapment by it is all too apparent) but that he lives this lack as a singular persecution, and must undertake to correct the defect in the symbolic all on his own, as if—you already will have gathered—as if stranded on some uncharted island at the end of the world.

Consider now Crusoe's variation on the existential question, "What am I there?" voiced from a place of radical solitude in a moment of immense consequence for the narrative, at the turning point after which Crusoe will discover his direct attachment to God, the solution to his unbearable isolation. According to the journal he sometimes keeps, it is June 28, and Crusoe is recovering from a terrible fever dream. Reflecting upon his sorry state, he is for the first time in his life entertaining thoughts of genuine repentance, not the *faux* contrition of the sailor amid the storm praying from terror and the urge to self-preservation. Sitting and staring out at the endless ocean, he initiates a conversation with—who else?—himself, by way of an ontological question. "What," Crusoe asks, "is this Earth and Sea of which I have seen so much, whence is it produc'd, and what am I, and all the other Creatures, wild and tame, humane and brutal, whence are we?" Immediately, he imposes a theological conclusion—"It is God that has made it all"—and from this apparently self-evident reply he deduces the limitlessness of Providential influence, and therefore that Providence is the cause of his own, peculiar misfortune. This is the realization that provokes his appeal to the Other, phrased here in the language of exceptional persecution: "*Why has God done this to me? What have I done to be thus us'd?*"

In response, the Other does not hesitate: "My Conscience presently check'd me in that Enquiry, as if I had blasphem'd, and methought it spoke to me like a Voice; W R E T C H ! *dost thou ask what thou hast done!* Look back upon a dreadful mis-spent Life, and ask thy self *what thou hast not done?*" (68). The text is unequivocal. In this transformational moment of reflection upon his place in the universe's grand design, when Crusoe asks why he has been left in the lurch, so despicably used and abandoned, he begins hearing voices.

The acousmatic rebuke responds to Crusoe's blasphemous self-pity, his Job-like "Why me?" or Christ-like "*Eli, Eli, lama sabachthani?*" by disclosing the divine Reason of his predicament. This is no mere internal conversing of thoughts. The term *wretch* returns from without.[19] Yes, it is in Crusoe's head, but like the chatter from Schreber's divine rays it is external to his deliberative consciousness, accusatory, uncontrolled and uncontrollable. Nor is Conscience's epithet arbitrary or random: it closes a metonymic circuit joining God, Reason, Providence, and the Name/No of the Father. The first node in the circuit is old Kreutznaer's arrogation of God's will to himself in his early protest against his son's seafaring intentions. "If I did take this foolish Step," his father tells him, "God would not bless me" (6). On the eve of Crusoe's break away from home, his father laments (these are his last words): "That Boy might be happy if he would stay at home, but if he goes abroad he will be the miserablest Wretch that was ever born" (7). When, nine years later, at the farthest end of his disobedience, the voice of Conscience here answers Crusoe's ontological appeal, its explosion marks the moment at which the wayward son assumes the charge of his wretchedness, when the curse Kreutznaer had uttered in God's name erupts with such rage that even the typesetting struggles to convey its fury.

It is impossible not to hear in Crusoe's lament a resonance with the leit-motif running through Schreber's *Memoirs*, the persecutory *liegen lassen*, the dread of being forsaken. Against this dread, Conscience's "*W R E T C H*" is not merely an accusatory reminder of the father's dissatisfaction, cloaked in morality, in which we are tempted to recognize the Freudian superego. More than this, it is an imperfect repetition of the foreclosed primordial signifier, the lost name and "No" of the Father, which reasserts the originally ineffec-tual paternal prohibition through its return here as a holy rebuke.

Coincidentally, "wretch" is the same word with which Schreber's English translators render a special term of abuse leveled against him by God: the German *Luder*, which Schreber tells us is a common expression in the basic language, designating "a human being destined to be destroyed by God and to feel God's power and wrath."[20] *Luder* also could be translated as "whore"; relatedly, Lacan preferred "lure," since Schreber's awful intimacy with God results from the latter's attraction to Schreber and his solitary, helpless body.

As with this moment in Schreber's delusion, the world in which Crusoe finds himself after the voice's effraction into his lonely island is not the world from which he has been exiled. Because it is an outside that imposes itself from within, subjecting him to its ferocity without distance or defense, it thereby demands a total reconfiguration of the parameters of the self, a sub-ordination of the self to the Other, an acquiescence to the status of *object* with respect to the voice in his head—and finally a complete reinvention of the character's worldview and the terms for its expression according to what Conscience, the tip of God's spear, demands of him.

This is the pivotal moment at which Crusoe abdicates his claim to rational autonomy and undertakes to (re)construct the Order of the World according to the dictates of divine Providence. His narrative now shifts from a private history of ambition, adventure, destitution, and despair to a testimony of gratitude and spiritual devotion through prayerful self-examination.

What must be emphasized is that this liberation from an existential anxiety hinges upon its author's reduction to an instrument of the fantasmatic Other's dreadful desire. Only as such an instrument can Crusoe (or the author behind him, Defoe, who through his character positions himself as the instrument of his divine Author) construct a new social link, and therefore a new language, a novel symbolic order, out of the tattered remnants of the old order. And so he does, since it is through this objectification and consequent obedience to an irresistible and ruthless intruding agency that he can recast the whole pre-ceding narrative as a necessary trial on the way to deliverance—for himself and, because the testimony is addressed to a sea of anonymous readers, for the wide and wayward world. Through this "cascade of reworkings of the signifier," as Lacan terms it, his text is a textile with which he quilts the rags of his prior reality into another reality that can better represent—contain, explain, and offer some relief from—the otherwise insupportable real of his experience.[21]

Such coincidences between *Crusoe* and the *Memoirs* abound. That both Schreber's trouble and Defoe's novel are animated by the foreclosure of the same sort of signifier, and that this signifier returns in a similar place, even under a similar epithet, is happenstance. But when working with psychosis, these strange, surprising adventures of the signifier are never "mere" coincidence. Every such coincidence, every instance of what in another context Freud approvingly called the "undeniable 'compliance of chance,' " however random, is a potential point of contact with some otherness beyond the insatiable, persecuting Other of the delusion.[22] It is an indispensable ally for any encounter that does not replicate and reinforce the psychotic's radical isolation. Coincidences offer a way, not out of the delusion for the psychotic, but *into* it for those of us wishing to grasp something of its logic and its truth, offering the possibility that our distinct but equally legitimate realities might be negotiated, emphasizing those points of uncanny contact that can be reasoned with but not reasoned away.

From Coincidence to Construction:
The Functional Structure of the Delusion

Although this compliance of chance is not yet sufficient evidence of a literary psychosis, it is an invitation to further inquiry that, after Lacan, requires a phenomenology of the language at work in and between these texts. What literary criticism can offer here is attention to the shared elements of form with which such a phenomenology may be structured.

The question of form, as Lacan shows us in his formalization of the Freudian construction, is the question of the universality which bounds a field of singularities. So, while every delusion is unique, we learn from Schreber and the semiotic structure of his experience that the form of the delusion can be distilled into five organizing characteristics, defined, like the Name-of-the-Father, not by their content but according to the functions they perform:

1. Delusion is a *testimony*, the personal narrative of an exemplary truth which is inseparable from the position of the one who bears it.
2. It is a *rationalization* of the experience to which the psychotic attests. Whence its internal logic, its making sense of an otherwise unbearably senseless situation through a rigid scaffolding of signifiers that is not an unreasonable response to the catastrophe that invokes it. On the contrary, such a response is intensely, desperately rational, even or especially in the face of experiences that threaten its consistency and coherence.

3. Following from this, the delusion often will evince some par-
   anoid, persecutory, *prophetic knowledge*, as the subject sees
   beyond the ruins of what Schreber calls The Order of the World
   to the corruption at its foundation, and there discovers the means
   to repair this fatal defect, saving the world or restoring it to its
   proper destiny.

4 and 5. Because this special knowledge and philanthropic purpose befall
   the subject as if from outside, from an internal outside, they
   bring a sense of *exceptional election* to a *salvational mission* he
   is powerless to refuse.

Testimony, rationalization, prophecy, exceptional election, and philanthropic
enterprise together form a lonely island of understanding, a radical solitude
that cannot be perforated through any appeal to a supposedly objective reality outside of this frame, and which forms and secures an absolute certainty
in the truth of the delusion.

Situating these five functions of the delusion within the work of literature
and upon the ground the psychotic has prepared permits us to critically comprehend the structure of the New World delusion of which *Robinson Crusoe*
is formative and exemplary. Through this work, we will find ourselves standing alongside the mythic Modern Man, contemplating what remains after the
end of the world, and where or how or if to begin again. We will consider
these structuring functions in turn, sequentially in each of this chapter's following five sections, in order finally to consider not how to free ourselves
from this history of delusion, but how more ethically to inhabit it on the way
to another future.

Testimony: From Catastrophe to Knowledge

However else we may try to understand it, Schreber's *Memoirs* is a testimony, and testimony is a particular genre of truth-telling.[23] Because it is by
definition unique to the witness who bears it, it is unverifiable; it can be true
only insofar as it might be false.[24] The truth of any testimony—or really, any
autobiography or, in eighteenth-century parlance, any "private history"—is
never a matter of fact, but only of the good faith the witness evokes from his
audience. We, Schreber's audience, therefore must either assume (preposterously) that Schreber fabricated his delusion with the knowledge that it was
false or take Schreber at his word.

From the beginning, even before the beginning, *Robinson Crusoe* imposes
this same choice upon its readers. Writing under the guise of its editor, Defoe
announces in the book's preface that what follows is a private history written
by the man himself, Robinson Crusoe, and "neither is there any Appearance
of Fiction in it" (3). Such claims to veracity were typical of eighteenth-century

novels, but what makes this unusual hero's "Strange Surprising Adventures" so strange and surprising is the absence of any ancillary witness, any secondary spectator, to guarantee or dispute the truth of his report. Unlike the principal characters in other fictional private histories, Crusoe's solitude *is* the story. The prefatory disavowal of the narrative's status as a fiction therefore hangs upon the reader's good faith. As with Schreber's *Memoirs*, we must take the text at its word. Whether the reader is convinced of its credibility (Defoe's public's fascination with reports of actual castaways, reports from which Defoe himself profited, prepared such credit) is irrelevant. What matters is that this formal maneuver seals the text's truth within the hermetic non-falsifiability of the singular witness.

And yet this singularity is internally divided, organized and driven and finally made available to reading by its difference from itself. From the beginning, there are two Crusoes: the character and the narrator.

The first Crusoe, whose tale unfolds rectilinearly and terminates somewhere in the year 1704, we may call the *subject of experience*, to and through whom the story happens.

The second Crusoe is the one to whom the story has happened, who therefore knows what has happened and, more importantly, what it is supposed to mean. This is the *subject of knowledge* who intervenes between the subject and the experience in order to make their relation possible, retroactively constructing the subject of experience from a superior vantage point. Operating from the metanarrative position of an ordering omniscience, the subject of knowledge apprehends the entire narrative timeline at once, giving the facts their proper place, situating them within a temporal order that invests their linkages with a revelatory moral significance.[25]

Through this division, the divine knowledge of Providence and the authorial, authoritative subject of knowledge are made to mirror one another. The result is a total, totalizing cosmology that can account for the origin and end of being itself as well as the logic of its organization, the logos to which the subject of experience is subjected, according to which that subject is inscribed, in whose language the subject is written. Through this inscription the subject traverses his experience, contains it, circumscribes it within the order of the signifier, and thereby becomes the subject of knowledge.

Prior to its inscription, the experience takes place within what Jean-Max Gaudillière and Françoise Davoine, in their seminar *Madness and the Social Link*, have called a "zone of catastrophe," which is distinguished by the absence there of time itself. Having fallen out of the signifying chain, the subject of experience—in Lacanian terms, the one who faces the onslaught of the imaginary without symbolic mediation, the psychotic at the swirling heart of the catastrophe—cannot arrange that experience through concepts such as "past" and "future." The very diachrony of language is collapsed into the synchrony of an all-encompassing *now*. The writing of the delusion affords a way out of this "absolute loneliness" of "anti-time" by mapping the disaster diachronically—narrating it, subordinating it to the linear operation of the signifying chain, so that this map to the delusion's historical truth may be addressed elsewhere.[26]

We therefore are not surprised to discover that the first act of writing Crusoe brings to his lonely island, his first attempt literally to compose himself once he has exhausted himself with the panicked histrionics of a desolate survivor on the other side of the apocalypse, is a calendar, made in the shape of a cross, on which every day he cuts another mark of his passing isolation. Beginning from day zero, this minimal writing does not resume but rather initiates the diachronic movement of time. Time is an effect of the sign. Each new mark is a repetition of the last, a groove in the wood that at once retains and extends each previous mark's significance and in so doing extends the reality of the subject for which the calendar/cross stands. Without the re-marking of the mark, the subject would remain entrapped within the anti-time of the original disaster.

That this marking time takes place upon a cross is crucial to the messianic value of the subject's experience. We will return to this. For now, we should punctuate that the instance of the letter is the narrative's condition of address. It is what divides the narrative's two constituent subjects, neither of which exists except as a consequence of this same division. There can be no knowledge without experience, but experience is a senseless torment without the knowledge that organizes it and makes it signify. It is the subject's division that delivers it from a zone of catastrophe to a regime of sense within which it can testify to the catastrophe, that is, express its singular truth. The subject's singularity is an expression of its division.

Rationalization: World, Text, Order and Disorder of the Signifier

This division is not a discrete event in the narrative but the whole process of narrative, narrative as process. Like the marks on the calendar/cross that congeal into the record of a history that thereby guarantees the subject's adventure through time, the process is iterative; the subject is made and remade with every remark upon the journey from experience to knowledge. In the end the journey will have been ordered not arbitrarily but purposively, teleologically, by the cosmic logos. The narrative's ratio and ground, the form it frames, is a divine desire without limit, an eternal Providence that is also Reason Itself, the Reason for all things, irresistible because it is right, right because it is irresistible, perfect because its desire is synonymous with its perfect Reason, because it is the very definition of perfection, the terminus atop the great chain of being.

The narrative begins with the opposition of reason to desire in order to resolve it. Traveling from the myopia of self-interested ambition to the peak of Reason, blazing the trail of a *becoming-reason*, the omniscient subject of knowledge makes clear that it is as a self-interested creature of desire that young Crusoe has set out on his ill-fated adventure, headstrong and stupid, on the way to the end of the world. The shift to what we may call Other-interestedness, through which Crusoe's desire joins in holy union with a perfect, complete Providence, takes place on the other side of that apocalypse. It is once again through writing, the inscription of the self-contained narrative, that this telos will be realized.

The narrative's organizing principle is a rehearsal of the basic tenets of eighteenth-century empiricism: a mimetic relationship between Crusoe's mental composure, the order of his material reality, the mechanics of reason, and the record of his experience. His lonely island is a laboratory where reason can unfold without contamination by secondary influences—tradition, social expectation, political or religious authority, historical contingency: Reason Unbound. In this "meer State of Nature" (86), Crusoe is Natural Man personified.[27] His slow mastery of the island thus naturalizes the dialectic through which an ordering reason subdues and domesticates a disordered external world, transforming the external materiality into an extension and servant of internal mentality. That this mastery accompanies his self-mastery, that in composing his surroundings he also literally composes himself, writes himself into being, makes clear that self-ordering and world-ordering are one and the same.

This mind–world–reason–text relation announces itself in the first instance of writing on the island after the calendar/cross, Crusoe's list of the evil and good qualities of his solitude. The list converts Crusoe's roiling confusion into discrete textual objects that act like weights on a scale: he is destitute and alone—evil—but unlike the rest of his crew he is alive—good—and so on, in essentially Lockean fashion (49–50).[28] With this, Crusoe arrests his racing and repetitive thoughts and carves the path of escape from his torturous self-pity. Writing is a technology of reason, a rational ordering prosthesis. Here on a smaller scale, it mimics the total order of the text, dividing experience from knowledge and, in so doing, constituting both.

The next extension of the writing-prosthesis, Crusoe's journal, is both a plot point and a narrative device, and therefore can take its place only after the narrator's description of the shipwreck and first few weeks of survival. He could not have started his journal any earlier, he claims, because of that same overwhelming "Discomposure of Mind" (51) he had just treated with his list of good and evil. His domestic scene was "a confus'd Heap of Goods, which as they lay in no Order, so they took up all my Place," so that "I had no room to turn my self" (50), no room to write. This last phrase, "I had no room to turn my self," implies an excess of both mental and physical clutter, too much confusion to turn inward and perform the rational self-reflection writing entails. To write his journal, it first will be necessary to "separate every thing at large in their Places" (51). And through its composition, Defoe does the same to the preceding narrative, revising and reordering it, disentangling and sometimes contradicting its prior confusions.[29] Once again, rationalization is an effect of signification.

As is the case with any system, this mimesis among Crusoe's mental state, his material circumstances, and Defoe's reorganization of the testimonial record is nowhere more apparent than in those moments when it all comes unhinged—when the narrator must suspend the rectilinear trajectory of his presentation in order to reinstall the (obviously unstable, unreliable) primacy of reason, like a mechanic servicing a broken writing machine. Thus does the subject of knowledge interrupt the journal's neat chronology, disordering the flow of the story in order to correct the journal's mistaken, because too immediate, record regarding the seemingly miraculous appearance of a few stalks of corn beyond Crusoe's hedge wall (58); and again, when a typhoon and earthquake leave him "like one dead or stupify'd" (59), scattering the journal's chronology in its confusion. Narrator and narrative recover from these astonishments by expanding the bounds of knowledge, describing and defining the island, domesticating it materially, with hedge walls and fences and surveillance points, and with a widening web of signs—maps, territories, an elaborate image-repertoire—civilizing and tranquilizing the wilderness with progressively complex patterns of representation.[30]

No such complexity can fully envelop Crusoe's world, however, so long as it issues from his own, finite perspective. So, after fourteen years of solitude, after Crusoe has fortified his island walls, fenced his livestock, hedged his corn, after all these exhaustive security measures, his tranquility will collapse when he stumbles upon a stranger's single footprint on the shore (112). With the shattering of his mental composure and resulting hallucinatory paranoia, the text itself forgets its chronology, sliding forward and backward by days and months, and the subject of knowledge fails to account for at least two years. In their place, there instead emerges a disordering anxiety.

The novel's most frequently used terms for this anxiety are "astonishment" and "terror," which some decades later are at the center of Edmund Burke's theorization of the sublime. According to Burke's aesthetic extension of Lockean epistemology, the sublime astonishes and terrifies because it exceeds and in so doing exposes the limits of the Understanding.[31] Anticipating this, Defoe suggests that a miraculous crop of corn, an earthquake, or a mysterious footprint are not intrinsically terrifying; they become so, and disturb the narrative's chronology, because they cannot be located within the existing set of references that would allow Crusoe to organize and situate them—write them—among the other objects of his self-wrought rational order. What the sublime reveals with the limits of the understanding is the rational creature's own finitude, the preposterously diminutive compass of its knowledge.

For Crusoe, and for Defoe, and also for the Enlightenment conception of the subject to which his fiction gives form, there is but one effective treatment for this anxiety disorder, one means of security against a world which is not so much hostile as it is uncertain—or hostile because it is uncertain, because it can spontaneously evade the limits of reason, exceed and therefore attack the order of the signifier. The subject of experience may build walls upon walls, fortify his stock of supplies, execute all manner of reconnaissance, but none of this is sufficient unless he aligns his experience with a higher Reason. Within the boundless bound of this divine agency, within the order of this master signifier, anxiety is impossible because understanding is limitless, infinite, and absolute.

And yet, the writing machine is imperfect. To the end, it malfunctions or breaks down. Experience and its knowledge are never quite consistent. It is in the gaps separating experience from knowledge where the narrative falters, and where we detect another non-relation, this time between what the text can say and what it desires to say, between what is possible and what is impossible.

This urge toward the impossible—this desire for an infinite and absolutely perfect Reason—is what the text's anxiety signifies and what the whole written narrative aims to correct. The instances of narrative disorder therefore are not senselessly random; they are organized by a logic which is unbeholden to the narrating subject of knowledge, another logic that gives the lie to the primacy of reason. The self-affirming teleology of the cosmic logos would entomb desire within the divine Reason. With this other logic, the situation is reversed: Reason is subordinated to desire, subverted by it, made into its object, until, as we will see, desire usurps Reason's place and masks itself in Reason's name.

The overt narrative articulates this subterfuge in an inverted form, presenting the subject of desire as the divine Reason's elect instrument through which the fine vibrations of Providence are transmitted at a higher frequency and for all to hear, like the prophet Ezekiel broadcasting his divine interferences from the bank of the Chebar Canal.

A Prophetic Phenomenology

The first evidence of this divine election is the contentment the hero finds on the other side of the spiritual conversion sparked by the voice of Conscience. According to that acousmatic voice, the internal outside that also recalls the chatter of Schreber's divine rays, Crusoe's solitude is a blessing. The mental repose that results once he accepts this blessing (even though, bestowed from the hand of Providence, it could not be otherwise) shows that he is no ordinary wretch, no common recipient of God's amazing grace. He is bound directly and uniquely to God; his testimony, his whole being, Defoe's novel and the myth of the Modern Man it promulgates, is the channel of the cosmic logos, come to deliver the fallen world from its perdition. It is the center of a divinely mandated, salvational enterprise. In imbuing this record with such singular importance, and placing it through various biblical allusions alongside Moses, Elijah, and Ezekiel, Defoe assumes for his hero—and for himself—a *prophetic* authority.[32]

This is why, just as Crusoe's religious conversion converts his predicament from a curse into a blessing, his prison is transformed into a shelter. What had been a solitary confinement becomes a secret intimacy with God which protects him from worldly pleasure and promises a greater, eternal, happiness. He turns his back on "the World," considering it now "as a Thing remote, which I had nothing to do with, no Expectation from, and indeed no Desires about," and sees it "as we may perhaps look upon it hereafter, *viz.* as a Place I had liv'd in, but was come out of it; and well might I say, as Father *Abraham* to *Dives, Between me and thee is a great Gulph fix'd*" (93–94). This reference to the Gospel of Luke not only associates Crusoe with the patriarch of patriarchs, it constructs an analogy according to which the world is Hell and his island is Heaven.[33]

Within this new-made Paradise, on the other side of the "great Gulph" between himself and the world, the whole universe of Crusoe's experience is infused with a secret significance, the signs of which are legible only to him. Each of his experiences is received or reconceived as a mark of the benevolent conspiracy. Everything, every aspect of the narrative, is thereby transmuted into a scrutable sign of God's eternal order. The world, such as it is, is overlaid with a prophetic phenomenology.

The resemblances between the nerve-language with which God communicates directly to Schreber's nervous system and the channels of transmission linking Crusoe with Providence, detailed in the following remarkable and somewhat dizzying passage, are striking:

> How wonderfully we are deliver'd, when we know nothing of it. How when we are in (a *Quandary*, as we call it) a Doubt or Hesitation, whether to go this Way, or that Way, a secret Hint shall direct us this Way, when we intended to go that Way; nay, when Sense, our own Inclination, and perhaps Business has call'd to go the other Way, yet a strange Impression upon the Mind, from we know not what Springs, and by we know not what Power, shall over-rule us to go this Way; and it shall afterwards appear, that had we gone that Way which we should have gone, and even to our Imagination ought to have gone, we should have been ruin'd and lost: Upon these, and many like Reflections, I afterwards made it a certain Rule with me, That whenever I found those secret Hints, or pressings of my Mind, to doing, or not doing any Thing that presented; or to going this Way, or that Way, I never fail'd to obey the secret Dictate; though I knew no other Reason for it, than that such a Pressure, or such a Hint hung upon my Mind. . . . Such secret Intimations of Providence, let them come from what invisible Intelligence they will . . . are a Proof of the Converse of Spirits, and the secret Communication between those embody'd, and those unembody'd; and such a Proof as can never be withstood . . . (127)

Like Schreber, Crusoe is an embodied spirit with whom unembodied spirits converse through a medium more intimate and immediate than any spoken language. It is a nerve-language. He feels the signs of Providence in his body. Schreber, of course, experiences this as an insufferable onslaught. In Crusoe's Protestant, imperial romance, these invisible spiritual emanations guarantee his well-being provided he acts in perfect obedience to their secret springs, hints, pressings, intimations . . .

This special sensitivity drives home the plot and its happy ending. Following his secret intimations, Crusoe triumphs over cannibals, mutineers, and even ravenous wolves by divining, *feeling*, the future. Submitting to Providence and its injunction to prophecy, his testimony will comprise "a Chain of Wonders" strung together by "a secret Hand of Providence governing the World" (197). Crusoe's faith in the protective and guiding influence of his own sort of divine rays is like the good faith his testimony solicits from its readers: it is a matter of conviction. For him, this is a conviction of which he is absolutely, incurably certain.

Such certainty does not result from the eventual correspondence between this or that "secret Dictate" and the reality to which it will correspond, as if Crusoe's conviction were a matter of reality-testing. The "Proof of the Converse of Spirits" is undeniable, it "can never be withstood," because it does not follow from but rather forms the structure of intelligibility, the frame of reference, within which the subject of knowledge *will have situated* empirical reality. Practically, this means his secret transactions with Providence determine the meaning of his experience in advance of its textual emplotment. Within such a future-anterior structure, everything is preceded and predetermined by the prophet's certainty. As with Schreber, any disconnect between the nerve-language and reality is literally unthinkable because reality is secondary to the primary truth at stake in the delusion. Reality only ever follows that truth. Thus do the facts of experience shed their contingency to convey a greater truth, the truth of the logos that unites them according to a secret necessity, a final meaning to which they all do not refer so much as bear witness.

Crusoe, like Defoe, and like us all to the extent that we are interpellated by the myth of the Modern Man, is alone—always alone, save for the desire of the Other and its echo in the voice of Conscience. It is this desire that has singled him out for a greater purpose, and through this special designation it has guaranteed precisely the hero's solitude, and therefore the untouchable certainty with which he asserts his truth.

This is how Crusoe—and behind him Defoe, who is himself only another instrument of Providential transmission, only the author through whose pen flows the true Author's divine Reason, who shapes that Reason into a narrative that accounts for the origin and end of all things, solving the ontological riddle and healing the defect in the Order of the World that is the source of the subject's misery and destitution—this is how the subject of knowledge heals the anxiety at stake in the discrepancy between (finite) knowledge and experience. The emblem of the Enlightenment arrogates an Absolute Knowledge and a knowledge of the Absolute that no reason can shake because *this is itself the dream of reason*, its impossible object of desire, the point of its completion. What makes this fantasy real is the manner in which the prophet of reason reifies it, acts upon it as if obeying the dictate of a divine logos, rearranging the world by rewriting it, clarifying and rectifying it, reconstructing it in the image of its own desire, not out of mere malice but in the spirit of philanthropy, in order to secure the world's redemption.

A New (World) Missionary Position:
From the Desire of Reason to the Reason of Desire

Prophecy thus is not an end in itself but the means to this fantasy's realization. Once he has been saved from the perdition of ingratitude and the terror of his election, the prophet becomes the savior who not only delivers the divine message but delivers the world. So Defoe delivers the Modern Age.

We have just seen that as the narrative proceeds, the division between materiality and spirituality dissolves until the former is merely an expression of immaterial forces and the "Converse of Spirits" with which Crusoe alone is acquainted. As the adventure bends toward its conclusion, the original structuring dichotomy between desire and reason—the adventure's very cause and condition of possibility, the core of Defoe's didacticism—seems to dissolve until self-interested desire is utterly subdued by its opposite. In fact, however, the contrary is the case: the hierarchy of Reason is inverted, so that Reason is transfigured into a conduit for the operations of desire, and is made the key armature against the otherwise limitless, rapacious *jouissance* resounding from the hole in the symbolic where the name and the No of the father have been foreclosed.

It therefore is unsurprising—or is this another undeniable compliance of chance?—that this transposition of desire and Reason takes place, as we will see, at the site of the failure of the paternal metaphor, the default in the symbolic for which Crusoe's delusion is the perfect solution. Having thereby been saved from the anti-time of the zone of catastrophe, and following the logic of the delusion, Crusoe is transposed from saved to savior, that is, from wretched son to holy father.

The shift is driven by "an Impetuosity of Desire" that contravenes the contentment to which Crusoe had been providentially obligated, a desire imposing itself "with such force . . . that it was not to be resisted." Like the fever dream that preceded his religious awakening by the voice of Conscience, this idée fixe also provokes a bodily disturbance: "it set my very Blood into a Ferment, and my Pulse beat as high as if I had been in a Feaver" (143); this fever, too, precipitates a dream upon which his shift in outlook will turn. Unlike the earlier dream, however, this is not a persecutory night-mare. It is a prophetic vision in which he rescues a savage fleeing from his cannibal enemies, reversing the logic of the nightmare in which he was the passive recipient of a heavenly vengeance, re-situating him in the active posi-tion of savior and liberator. Of course his dream will come true. Within the prophetic phenomenology, it could not be otherwise. On the edge of its realization, moments before he saves a poor savage from two other hungry cannibals, Crusoe testifies that "I was call'd plainly by Providence to save this poor Creature's Life" (146), thereby folding Reason into his impetuous desire, cloaking a private motive to end his solitude in the mantle of a heav-enly mandate.

Once the rescue has been accomplished, Crusoe bestows, or imposes rather, the name "Friday" on the accidental refugee, as a father would christen a son. In the same moment, he rechristens himself "Master." Of course, Friday does not have the English to comprehend this as anything other than a name; for the Master narrative, it is not a referent but a function, one which makes clear where in his newfound symbolic universe Friday stands, or kneels. Master then assumes responsibility for his child's cultural, mechanical, and especially spiritual development. He states their relationship in precisely such paternalistic terms: "never Man had a more faithful, loving, sincere Servant, than *Friday* was to me; without Passions, Sullenness or Designs, perfectly oblig'd and engag'd; his very Affections were ty'd to me, like those of a Child to a Father" (151). With Friday, then, Crusoe has succeeded where his own father had failed. "Master" can leave no doubt as to the name of the father who has broken Friday away from the state of Nature to which he had hith-erto been abandoned by God (123–24).

This break is effected by a searing articulation of the culturally chauvin-istic "white savior" archetype, the perfection of antiblackness, according to which the enslaved demands his own enslavement as a condition of rescue or emancipation from his otherwise world-less savagery: Friday places his head under Crusoe's foot, which the latter receives as a "token of swearing to be my Slave for ever" (147).[34] So he is. And even before giving Friday his new name, once again extending the empire of the mother tongue, Crusoe refers to him only as "the poor wretch" (146), repeating the signifier that had formed the closed circuit of his own salvation, here displacing the acous-matic voice of Conscience with the omniscient narrating voice of the subject of knowledge.[35] From saved to saving, son to father, named to naming, and finally from Wretch to Master, Crusoe claims a son who is also his property and his perfectly loyal subject, thereby accomplishing a complete ascendance to the sovereignty of Reason.

Crusoe is now secure in his position as God's specially elected emissary on his island. Consistent with his prophetic phenomenology, the appearance in the plot of any foreign agent or object is no longer a threat or a source of anxiety, but another occasion for the exercise of providential sovereignty. The strange is absorbed into the familiar without remainder, situated according to his domestic arrangements which are themselves the material extension of his mental state, incorporated into the heavenly society in which he alone has been enraptured for so many years.

Once he takes up Friday's religious instruction, Crusoe reflects that perhaps his whole purpose for having been brought to the island, providentially destined for his isolation, was to save the life and soul "of a poor Savage, and bring him to the true Knowledge of Religion" (159). This is not the limit of his messianism. When saving a wayward Spaniard and Friday's father from more cannibals (170), planning to liberate the Spaniard's cohort from captivity among the savages (179), and rescuing an English captain from mutineers (182, 188, 196), the narrator characterizes himself as "deliverer" and his actions as "deliverance," always reaffirming his status as the instrument of Providence.[36] Upon first revealing himself to the English captain and two fellow prisoners, Crusoe presents himself as the manifestation of a heavenly design, a human whose lifetime has been sacrificed in service to the realization of an obscure redemptive enterprise, and whose sacrifice confers salvation upon his fellow Englishmen as an act of divine grace.

It is no accident that the savior's name is an anglicized perversion of Kreutznaer, which contains the German *Kreuz*—cross.[37] Nor, as we suggested earlier, is it insignificant that Crusoe's first act of industry on the island, his first step toward building the world anew, is both a structure and a text: "I cut with my knife upon a large post, in capital letters—and making it into a great cross, I set it up on the shore where I first landed—'I came on shore here on the 30th September 1659' " (48). The calendar/cross is the record of his temporal sacrifice that repeats the prototypical crucifixion to which it so obviously refers; but also, it is the symbol of the missing cross, *Kreutznaer*, the name of the father whose will the son would not heed until he is abandoned at the end of the world. In the end, his island penance, and therefore his whole testimony, is revealed to have been just what Schreber's trial was for him: a sacrificial solution to the defect in the Order of the World, exactly comparable to the sacrifice of God-as-man in Jesus Christ.

By the text's conclusion, the secret whisperings of Providence, the voice of Conscience, the memory of his father, and every other agency he encounters along his pilgrim's progress all become conduits for the hero's escape from his confinement, but not before he has transformed the New World into a perfect reflection of his own desire—for control, order, certainty; for the dominion of whiteness, Englishness, entrepreneurial Protestantism; for a reality that has been totally circumscribed by the parameters of the self. He escapes his confinement only by confining everyone and everything within the narrative web of the subject of knowledge, including the Old World, which does not remain unchanged by his adventure. The subject of knowledge, secure in his position above the text, omniscient and omnipotent, organizing and explaining the secret web of relations joining all the seemingly disparate events comprising his story, finally reveals himself to be the apotheosis of a salvational teleology. The end was inscribed from the beginning. It could not be otherwise.

This is more than a story of one man's redemption. It is an indictment of a fallen, disordered, wayward world and the instrument of a holy mission of universal salvation. It aims to report on and rationalize the catastrophe of the world's end, but also to build it again, to make it new, out of the detritus that remains. The New World Testament—prophetic pronouncement, emblem of modernity, irresistible commandment, myth of the Modern Man, and inscription of the disaster under the sign of Enlightenment.

Certainty and Subversion: Treating the Psychosis of Reason

"Reason" is at the heart of the delusion that allows Crusoe to capture his singular experience within a framework of meaning, to claim absolute mastery of that framework, to secure his vision of the world behind a wall of complete certainty, to disavow (though he cannot disown) the conquering and impetuous desire without which his testimony would not exist, and to invest that desire with a philanthropic moral imperative. In the end, "Reason" is a reflection of desire that, through its textual construction, is made into a reality of his and his author Defoe's own design.

If, recalling Siskin and Warner, the Enlightenment was "an event in the history of mediation," then surely *Robinson Crusoe*, straddling the divide between seventeenth-century religious dogma and the eighteenth century's discourses of freedom, spanning the Atlantic triangle, occupying both sides of the "*great Gulph*" even between Heaven and Earth, finitude and the infinite, experience and knowledge, belongs to this event.[38] In the remainder of this chapter I want to further explore how and why this instance of textual psychosis is a fictive distillation of the Enlightenment as such, and how it opens the subject of the Enlightenment, the subject of reason, to an ethics of reading that demands our attunement to what is unwritten there in the text, to what structures and sustains it: the logic of its organization, the logic governing the network of relations among its constituent signs, without which neither the novel nor the history of ideas it emblematizes hang together.

Crusoe is the mythic symbol of the solitary individual whose faith in an all-powerful God is not contravened but affirmed by his capacity for rational reflection upon a material, empirically determined reality. Both this intellectual capacity and the Order of the World in which it discovers its own image are, in the novel, proof of Providence, the divine Reason. So, too, was this the case in the eighteenth century and its so-called Age of Reason. Even the most humanistic of Enlightenment sensibilities held that human reason could explain itself—could account for its very existence as well as its purpose—only through recourse to an essentially monotheistic cosmology according to which God (or, with Deism, the Supreme Being) *is* perfection: the final resolution of all apparent contradictions within a coherent, complete whole. The secularizing tendencies of eighteenth-century politics and culture were not entirely a reaction against God or an attempt to supplant God with Nature and natural history; rather, they realized a growing disaffection with the rigid authority of religious institutions that privileged obedience over skepticism and fear over serious reflection. Defoe's hero, then, by finding God without recourse to any established religion, is not only a paragon of the author's Nonconformist beliefs, but the personification of this critical spirit, which frees the subject from arbitrary, therefore unpredictable and capricious, external authority without thereby capitulating to the inherent unruliness of desire. Instead, the subject *internalizes* the voice of authority. Whence the voice of Conscience, which is always a bad conscience or else it has nothing to say. At the same time, however, this internalization must be papered over by the ideology of self-determination and eventually the metaphysics of the moral law, exemplified by the Kantian categorical imperative according to which true freedom is freedom from desire through obedience to the conditions of pure (practical) reason.

In the following chapter we will continue to problematize this apparent antagonism between reason and desire. Here, we only need emphasize how *Robinson Crusoe* and the Enlightenment situate reason at the center of their proliferating systems of knowledge concerning both the material and the metaphysical. Through this centering, reason is like the God it displaces: it is exempted from the play of language and thought that comprises and animates these systems. With Schreber's help, we can see that this revision of the order of the world according to an absolute certainty in the totalizing power of reason is a psychotic endeavor.[39] After Defoe's novel, the new God of Reason, like Schreber's God, is an old signifier invested with a new meaning. Empiricism and materialism, with their radical valuation of perception and consciousness—that is, of the concrete and experiential foundations of all thought, including theology—forced a collective encounter with the hole in being where God was supposed to be. This fatal defect in the symbolic precipitated a crisis or catastrophe that deserves to be called apocalyptic.

Against this particular end of the world, the myth of the Enlightenment had to borrow the language of the crumbling symbolic order in order to invent the world anew, which it did on the shores of other continents by attempting to obliterate and replace the other worlds it discovered there, constructing a New World in its own image. Whereas it once was God who created man in His image, Crusoe's transvaluation of desire reveals that, now, it is in his own image that man creates God, who is thus reduced to an instrument of human desire. What remains of God, or what is now called Reason, is the name for an absolute certainty in that desire's rightness and therefore its irresistibility. Such a certainty manifested itself first in the imperial adventure and then in that adventure's recoil upon the metropoles in the form of bourgeois revolution.

The Enlightenment's construction of this new reality required a total revision of the universe in supposedly impartial, objective, universal terms. But this was only a reflection of its own idea of consciousness. Its paradigmatic systematicity claimed to capture the real, but was only the manifestation and rationalization of a fantasy of liberation from the desire at its core, a desire for freedom from desire. Thus enclosed within an impossible circuit, imbued with psychotic certainty, a new Age of Reason shrinks the distance between human knowledge and absolute Truth, until Truth finally is made to serve the very knowledge that desired it. Reality would be made to conform to what reason already knows and to the structure of its knowing. Though it could never admit as much, the ground of the Enlightenment is a prophetic phenomenology.

What does it mean for the future of the Enlightenment and its (literary) criticism to reconceive the vector of its transmission, the mythical hero of modernity, in these terms? Freud's essay on "Creative Writers and Day-Dreaming" affords the beginning of an answer. By "creative writers," Freud means those authors who enjoy "the widest and most eager circle of readers of both sexes," a species to which Defoe certainly belongs, and which his (simplistic and unfair) reputation as a hack writer supports rather than undermines. In fact, Freud's remarks concerning the appeal of popular fiction are a barely disguised allusion to *Robinson Crusoe*: "One feature above all cannot fail to strike us about the creations of these story-writers: each of them has a hero who is the centre of interest, for whom the writer tries to win our sympathy by every possible means and whom he seems to place under the protection of a special Providence." We can already recognize Defoe's Crusoe in this, but Freud goes further: "If . . . the first volume closes with the ship he is in going down in a storm at sea, I am certain, at the opening of the second volume, to read of his miraculous rescue—a rescue without which the story could not proceed." The story's progress, though, is less important than the heroic, even magical invulnerability we readers are thereby invited to enjoy. "It seems to me," Freud concludes, "that through this revealing characteristic of invulnerability we can immediately recognize His Majesty the Ego, the hero alike of every day-dream and every story."[40] The majestic, sovereign ego, in creative writing as in everyday life, is not only a fiction with which the reader sympathetically identifies; by alluding to the "special Providence" in which we place our trust for the security of the heroic ego, Freud points us toward his abiding critique of monotheism according to which faith in an all-powerful God is the common manifestation of an infantile, thus unconscious, fantasy of paternal benevolence and protection.[41] The power of creative writers like Defoe therefore results from their capacity to translate the singularity of their unconscious fantasies into a narrative through which the anonymous reader can enjoy his own fantasies vicariously, obliquely, and without having to say precisely why he so easily, thoughtlessly, happily identifies with his literary heroes.

While it is addressed to the question of literature, Freud's treatment of creative writers is oriented and informed by his clinical investigations, and results from the work of analysis. Shifting the question of unconscious fantasy from the clinic to the work of literature, *Robinson Crusoe* (and Freud's own allusion in the above passage) affords a fictional analogue of the concept of the modern individual both before and after the discovery of the unconscious. In our reading, the narrative of an autonomous individual presumes complete control over his experience, but cannot withstand the unspeakable desire that works its way into the narrative from its own margins, as an unwritten remainder that is yet there in the written, waiting and demanding to be read, instantiating a structure of address other than that of the ego or its literary correlate. Freud positioned *Robinson Crusoe* in "Creative Writers" as a paragon of the ego narrative; its seductive capacities, the source of its popularity, are the same as those of the mirror image with which the ego identifies and, through identifying, invents itself. Our hypothesis of textual psychosis radicalizes Freud's insight. The modern ego narrative of the self-sufficient, self-determined individual is not only a fiction, it is a delusion. It is not more reasonable than the psychotic's version of reality. It is the psychosis of modernity, a psychosis which has slipped the bounds of the solitary subject and become an organizing principle of collective thought and action from the eighteenth century to the present.

Together with the prophetic phenomenology, this minimal difference between these two narratives, called ego and delusion, draws the political implications of *Robinson Crusoe*'s psychosis into relief. If politics and political community are oriented by the psychosis of reason, if the political subject is defined by its subjective autonomy and egoic self-determination, and if all this is guaranteed by the supposed moral rightness of an incontrovertible, necessary order of things, then politics becomes the conduit through which a community attempts to realize its delusion by remaking the world in its own unfalsifiable image, with the inevitable representational and material violence that any such world-ordering entails against all manner of difference. In this frame, as Claude Lévi-Strauss once noted of the European colonial project and its contemporary aftermath, difference is only an opportunity for the extension of sameness.[42]

Consider again the moment at which Crusoe rejoins society—the patently ethnocentric display of superiority in which he assumes complete mastery, even in name, over Friday, his perfect son. This is a literary figuration and crystallization of the Civilizing Mission that imbued European imperialism and the plantation economy with a divine mandate and a perversely humanistic sensibility. If we situate Crusoe's emblematic paternalism within the context and structure of psychotic delusion, then the supposedly moral obligation that motivated the violence of empire cannot be dismissed as an alibi or mere window-dressing for the avarice at its core. English imperialism and, by extension, Continental imperialism, the genocidal colonization of Africa and the Americas, its inheritance in the doctrine of Manifest Destiny, chattel slavery—all those modern militarized endeavors whose stated purpose was (or is) to spread the light of reason and impose its twin institutional representatives, capitalism and democracy—are symptoms of a collective psychosis.

The difference between *Robinson Crusoe*'s psychosis and Schreber's testimony therefore is not formal or generic, but rather a matter of reception: Crusoe found an audience for his delusion, one that craved the outlandish representations of bloodthirsty cannibals creeping at the margins of empire that confirmed their imagined sense of moral, cultural, and civilizational superiority, an audience who wished to be like its literary hero: certain of its divine exceptionalism and attendant obligation to save the world by subjecting all difference to its own hermetic and indisputable vision of pure, nominally God-granted reason. The empire of reason, like Schreber, believes with *absolutely certainty* in the justice of its cause and the truth of its calling. Imperialism was not an accident of the Enlightenment, but its object and cause.

This leaves us, finally, with the problem of morality. It is tempting to reduce the characters in the historical drama of imperialism to villains who cynically misused the language of reason as an excuse for their autocratic ambitions; and it is easy to vilify or scapegoat specific historical figures such as, for instance, Defoe himself, whose most famous hero is a sugar plantation owner, slave trader, and inept sailor who nevertheless is saved from death, perdition, and solitude, develops an intimate acquaintance with God, and assumes the testimonial status of a prophet, because of his good fortune in having been born an Englishman. But to surrender to this temptation to vilify would indulge a desire to rescue the Enlightenment from itself, as though our modern, post-colonial sensibilities could continue to lean upon its standards and systems of reason without being complicit in its terrible excesses. The urge to blame can too easily shift the question of responsibility from the present to the past, as if we could refuse our inheritance simply because we despise it. The trouble, our trouble, is that the psychosis of Enlightenment is not a localized condition. It is the groundwork of the present. We cannot exempt ourselves from its operations except by repeating the very logic of exceptionalism, the same pretensions to metahistorical truth, at the center of our critique. Our challenge therefore is not to scapegoat but to subvert this reality, from within its walls and its own terms.

This does not mean to absolve Defoe or his novel of responsibility for their contribution to the European imagination and its violent legacy. As we have seen, Defoe needs no help with redemption. It means instead to stand with the ethics of psychoanalysis and refuse to either moralize or pathologize psychosis as though it is an evil to be exorcised or a sickness to be cured. After all, pathologizing, too, is a lasting effect of the Enlightenment, an especially powerful strategy around which the eighteenth and nineteenth centuries spun the web of epistemological, political, and moral systems at the historical basis of our contemporary technologies of normalization. To view reason as normal and psychosis as abnormal is an Enlightenment perspective, thus also a psychotic one. We cannot opt out of modernity's founding psychosis without surrendering to the delusion's temptations.

Instead, we should consider that a social order whose security is measured only by the extent to which the world conforms to its own image and its own desires, and whose self-assurance is predicated upon a belief in its own metaphysical or moral purity—any Kingdom of Reason—may resort to all manner of aggression against every difference, interminably, because the primary (primal, originary, fundamental) difference against which reason opposes itself is not the savage cannibal on the shore of another world. That difference is not beyond the Enlightenment, and thus not susceptible to its strategies of domestication or eradication. It *is* the Enlightenment. The Other of Enlightenment reason is its own desire, the desire for absolute reason, which knows no limit because it does not want to know anything about its own limits, because to confront such a limit is the crux of its anxiety, the sublime against which it recoils, stupefied and terrorized. Testifying to reason's powerlessness to recognize its own limit, inscribed under the sign of a constitutively divided subject that wants nothing more than to encircle its whole self within the purview of its knowledge, *Robinson Crusoe* shows us that this is not a theoretical conjecture but a matter of historical truth.

We therefore are not immune to the psychosis of our history. As Freud's notion of historical truth insists, history is the structure of the present. We cannot step outside this structure without falling into Schreber's insufferable position, into the zone of catastrophe. Instead, we can concede the psychosis of reason and, through the interminable work of literature, pry open a minimal distance across which that psychosis can break with its self-enclosed self-certainty in order to find an addressee other than the rapacious, world-ending Other of its own desire.

What opens and sustains that distance is only an effect of thought and a critical-creative practice of reading. It is not the desire for a new reality but an ethical responsibility to negotiate our inherited reality alongside others. We then might begin to imagine new forms of relation to other systems of thought, new ways of inhabiting the history of reason, other outlets for what it has variously foreclosed or repressed. This would be a future without telos or plan. An uncertain future, to be sure, but such is any future worthy of the name. This is why the prophecy of its becoming can best be read, if it can be read, at the margins of history, in the anxiety of the discrepancy between the subject of experience and the subject of knowledge, in the quiet insistence of the subject of literature.

Chapter 2

✦

Pedagogy of the Repressed

Rousseau, Sade, and the End of Education

Psychoanalysis, education, and government are alike in at least one sense: they are all "'impossible' professions," Freud writes, "in which one can be sure beforehand of achieving unsatisfying results."[1] This famous and sardonic comparison appears in his late essay "Analysis Terminable and Interminable," which considers how we can know when an analysis has run its course. When is analysis at its end? Surely not when every repression has been resolved, because new instances of repression, new symptoms, inevitably develop throughout any person's life; at no point will the analysand have reached a state of "absolute psychical normality" since "a normal ego of this sort is, like normality in general, an ideal fiction"; the conflict between the drive and the ego cannot be resolved "definitively and for all time" because they are constitutively opposed; and interpretation and construction can, in principle, proceed interminably because both techniques can only approximate the ineffable truth of the unconscious.[2] The end dissatisfies.

As always, Freud defers such theoretical concerns to the facts of analytic experience, framing the end of analysis as "a practical matter" best illustrated by the analyst in training. That is, it is not a question of expertise, but a matter of education. So, Freud continues, "where and how is the poor wretch" (the would-be analyst) "to acquire the ideal qualifications which he will need in his profession? The answer is, in an analysis of himself, with which his preparation for his future activity begins." This experiential foundation and process of self-discovery need not conclude with the poor wretch joining the psychoanalytic profession. It has achieved its purpose "if it gives the learner a firm conviction of the existence of the unconscious, if it enables him, when repressed material emerges, to perceive in himself things which would otherwise be incredible to him, and if it shows him a first sample of the technique which has proved to be the only effective one in analytic work." Conviction, sensibility, and the rudiments of a technique—and this is still not enough; this end in fact is only the beginning, since "we reckon on the stimuli that he has received in his own analysis not ceasing when it ends and on the processes

65

of remodeling the ego continuing spontaneously in the analysed subject and making use of all subsequent experiences in this newly-acquired sense."[3] An analysis thus terminates, frustrating as it may seem, when the analysand assumes its interminability.

To take responsibility for the unconscious and its effects, to pursue the truth of the fantasy according to the clinical strategies one discovers while on the couch, and thus to extend the lessons of the clinic into an endless education of which nobody—neither the initial analyst nor the ego nor any theory or theoretician—is master: this is the end of analysis, in a double sense of "end," both practical conclusion and ethical objective. Clinical success is marked by the acceptance of its failure. This acceptance is not resignation but commitment and accession to the position of the analyst because a trained analyst is an analyst always in training, a perpetual student whose only true teacher is the unconscious. This is the crux of the ethics of psychoanalysis.

It is because of this ethical commitment that Freud's case histories, those most practical demonstrations of his conviction, sensibility, and technique, are all failures. As he notes elsewhere, at the beginning of the Wolf Man's case, "Analyses which lead to a favourable conclusion in a short time"— which this case certainly did not—"remain for the most part insignificant as regards the advancement of scientific knowledge. . . . Something new can only be gained from analyses that present special difficulties."[4] Psychoanalytic knowledge is never a matter of theoretical certitude or technical application. It is a reflective, uncertain, and dynamic index of the disconnects between theory and experience. Such knowledge therefore advances only through an encounter with its own limits.

Constantly emphasizing his limits, Freud's writing makes clear that neither he nor anyone else can claim a mastery of psychoanalysis. This was the basis of Lacan's ceaseless excoriation of the psychoanalytic establishment after Freud, which reduced his discovery to a set of technical procedures over which its practitioners claimed exclusive authority, lending Freud's name but not his ethics to one more -ism in the catalogue of dogmas that calls itself "the human sciences." Like Freud's case histories, Lacan's notoriously esoteric teaching style—which was always directed toward training analysts and is best comprehended with this in mind—was a performance of Freud's exhortations against theoretical certainty. "The end of my teaching," Lacan explains, "is, well, to train psychoanalysts who are capable of fulfilling the function known as the subject, because it so happens that it is only from this point of view that we can really see what is at stake in psychoanalysis."[5] And the subject for Lacan, of course, is never the sovereign subject. It is the subject of the unconscious, whose being inheres in its vanishing beneath the signifier and which Lacan therefore designates a function—a logical operator within a structure of address. To fulfill this function, the analyst is one who subjects oneself to the question of the unconscious, interminably. As with Freud's writing, then, Lacan's teaching evacuates the pedagogue of his pretensions to sovereignty, to mastery, and in so doing leads his students to the same.

The transference in the clinic, or at least its ethics if not the phenomenon itself, thus is mirrored in the teaching of psychoanalysis. It begins with the students' faith in the teacher's expertise just as the patient arrives at the analyst's office expecting to find a "subject-supposed-to-know"; but, because that expertise is a matter of experience for which no theory can substitute, the training, like the analysis, works toward that initial faith's dissolution and its replacement with an ethics of inquiry. If Freud supposed psychoanalysis to be impossible, Lacan insists this is because it works only by unworking its own conditions of possibility.

We need not confine this insight to psychoanalytic training. For is this not the ethical aim of any education? The teaching of literature or philosophy, for example, surely requires a rigorous attention to texts, their histories, their relations to one another, the network of citations in which they are embedded, the strategies of reading that have animated them, and so forth. But any teacher worth the title will avow that the real aim of such work is not to amass and impose information but to demonstrate the value and skill of questioning, to foster in one's students what Edward Said, after Erich Auerbach and Paulo Freire, called "critical consciousness": a critical orientation toward consciousness; an awareness of the fluctuating history and conditions of one's social location; a refusal to be satisfied by the apparent and the given; above all, an attention to the limits of consciousness and an urge to exceed and thereby transform them.[6]

Critical consciousness knows that education is where the transformative potential of the human in relation to its ideological situation stands or falls because education is the process by which a person becomes, or is made, a social subject.[7] Neutrality is not an option. This is why educational institutions and practices today face accelerating encroachments by a corporatizing ideological agenda that wishes to reinvent liberal education within the later paradigm of neoliberalism, that is, according to individualistic imperatives that displace the collectivist governance strategies of the democratic state with the supposedly less coercive interests of the open marketplace.[8] It is also why contemporary champions of progressive education policy like Henry Giroux, who is exemplary in this regard, insist that education "is always directive in its attempt to enable students to understand the larger world and their role in it. Moreover, it is inevitably a deliberate attempt to influence how and what knowledge, values, desires, and identities are produced within particular sets of class and social relations."[9] Education is the site of hegemonic struggle at which social ideals are supposed to be realized, reproduced, or rethought, where subjects are created in ways that either sustain or contest the socially prescribed limits of the possible.

If education is the battleground of collective aspiration at the gap between what a society is and what it wants or imagines itself to be, the contest of education therefore is the essence of the political. Small wonder, then, as Freud reminds us, that with education, as with psychoanalysis and government, we "can be sure beforehand of achieving unsatisfying results."

The roots of the present conflict between liberal and neoliberal education can be traced to one of the core concerns of Enlightenment thought: the tension between public good and private interest. This was the hinge upon which the eighteenth century's economic, political, and eventually educational reforms turned. In North America or Europe, with the Constitutional Convention or the French Revolutionary Assembly, it was at the heart of the heated debate over what made a modern, enlightened republic. The question was how to reconcile the autonomous individual's self-interest with the demands and constraints of social life, or inversely, how to limit the reach of the public sphere in order to ensure the individual's autonomy. In statecraft and economics, the answer was liberalism. In education, the spokespeople of the Enlightenment hoped that individuals' mental, emotional, and physical development could be choreographed in ways that fostered their own potential and also contributed to the wider society's progress toward its highest ideals. This is why education in the eighteenth century was not merely one object of inquiry among others; it was the screen upon which was projected a vision for the reinvention of the social order according to shared principles of right and reason, or the stage upon which this new society stood or fell.[10]

No one was more instrumental to the invention of modern education, no one more definitively situated it at the base of the whole idea of the Enlightenment or better exemplifies the topic's incurable contentiousness, than Jean-Jacques Rousseau. No other Enlightenment figure more steadfastly engaged the paradox at the core of modern liberal education—namely, that the individual is both a solitary being and a social agent, both existentially free and necessarily bound by the limits of coexistence. Whence the infamous opening lines of his *Social Contract*: "Man is born free, and everywhere he is in chains."[11] The question for Rousseau thus was how to preserve the individual's freedom without renouncing his social responsibility, and inversely, how to define that responsibility in ways that support rather than trample the individual's natural liberty. Rousseau's philosophy was a revolutionary conservatism, then, that demanded a return to Nature (his idea of Nature, anyway) in order to reinvent the social order according to natural principles, even if or precisely because Nature and society are constitutively opposed. Progression as radical regression. Revolution as restoration.[12]

Unsurprisingly, Rousseau's legacy is as controversial as the subject of education. When his novelistic treatise on the subject, *Émile: or, On Education*, was published in 1762, it was burned in the streets of Paris and its author buried beneath what Freud's friend Romain Rolland called "an avalanche of hate."[13] Rousseau was not rescued from the avalanche until decades later, well after his death, when at the apex of the French Revolution "Rousseauism" (another unfortunate -ism) came to signify competing interpretations of what constituted a truly republican national education program, as conflicting voices in the Revolutionary Assembly all claimed that they, and not their political adversaries, were the true heirs to Rousseau's thought.[14] Across the Atlantic and more than a century later, John Dewey credited him as "the most ardent of the early advocates of equality," even as he suspected that Rousseau's ideas on education tended toward absolutism.[15] Today, Rousseau is considered both a "pioneering thinker whose revolutionary ideas about permissive child rearing generated the movement for child-centered progressive education" and "an inconsistent, wildly utopian romantic who introduced anti-intellectualism into modern education."[16]

This fraught legacy suggests Rousseau is both the most influential and the most radical or scandalous Enlightenment theorist of education. The former may be true, but that second dubious honor belongs elsewhere, with the Marquis de Sade.

Rousseau's pedagogical legacy continues to burn bright in the contest over education, while Sade's barely casts a glow. Given his particularly brutal brand of pornographic libertinage, his contemporaries may be forgiven for overlooking his pedagogical insights. More curious, however, is that during his critical resuscitation in the twentieth century even his sympathetic readers, if they considered his thoughts on the topic at all, situated education at most as one unexceptional object within Sade's larger cabinet of horrors—as though his vision of a libertine education belongs on the same level as his endless apologies for incest and pederasty, his sickening and exhaustive descriptions of extreme sexual violence, or his invective against God and religion. What could education be in such a context if not another perversion? But Sade himself resisted such a conclusion. Consistent with his contemporaries' revaluation of education as the ground of social transformation and even with Rousseau's child-centered approach, Sade insisted that the moral, philosophical, and even aesthetic value of his works was in their pedagogical utility.[17] By his own account, Sade was a teacher.

Among the principal players in Sade's French revival, only Lacan seems seriously to have considered this. His essay "Kant with Sade" begins with the observation that "the Sadian bedroom is equal to those places from which the schools of ancient philosophy took their name: Academy, Lyceum, Stoa. Here as there, the way for science is prepared by rectifying the position of ethics."[18] Though prevalent in all his major works, especially *Juliette* and *The 120 Days of Sodom*, the best representative of Sade's ethical corrective to education—and of the practical reforms and political community that would result if his libertine pedagogy somehow were adopted on a grand scale—is his novel written as a series of Socratic dialogues on the very subject, *Philosophy in the Bedroom*.

If, as Lacan insists, Sade belongs alongside Plato, Aristotle, or Zeno of Citium, since like them he reconceived the practice of education through a prior revision of its ethics, then *Philosophy in the Bedroom* certainly deserves comparison with Rousseau's *Émile*, which endeavored to do the same. Like Rousseau, Sade saw his works banned, burned, and condemned, but for blushingly obvious reasons he has never enjoyed his predecessor's redemption among liberal education theorists. Also like Rousseau, he insisted that society stifles and corrupts rather than fosters a person's natural inclinations, and that Nature therefore ought to be the origin and end of a truly free, truly human education. Both writers imagined the reconstitution of the social link at its subjective origin, in the mentally and physically malleable child. By holding that Nature is the only legitimate teacher, both exemplify the Enlightenment's ambition for the universal.

This filiation is neither frivolous nor accidental. Sade's philosophical system was informed by the scientific materialism of Buffon's encyclopedic *L'Histoire naturelle*, d'Holbach's *Le System de la nature* and *Le Bon-Sens*, and La Mettrie's *L'Homme machine*;[19] his literary style, such as it is, was inspired by Voltaire's graceful vituperation and the humanistic sensibilities of the great English novelists, particularly Richardson and Fielding.[20] But he reserved special praise for Rousseau, in whom he found a rare unity of philosophy and passionate sensibility. Of Rousseau's *Julie, ou la nouvelle Héloïse*, to which his *La Nouvelle Justine* is an overt reply, Sade asserted that "this sublime book will never be bettered" because the author's "fiery soul" and "philosophical mind" are "two traits Nature does not bring together in a single person more than once a century."[21] When Sade's wife refused to provide him with a copy of Rousseau's *Confessions* during his incarceration at Vincennes, Sade replied as if defending a good friend: "while Rousseau may represent a threat for dull-witted bigots like yourselves, he is a salutary author for me. Jean-Jacques is to me what *The Imitation of Christ* is for you."[22]

It might seem absurd that Sade placed himself in Rousseau's shadow. This chapter will show to the contrary that Sade is more true to *Émile*'s pedagogical system that even Rousseau himself: he walks in Rousseau's footsteps but goes further to reveal the truth of Enlightenment education, exposing and avowing the radical political potential of the logic of fantasy at work in this historical foundation of modern liberalism.

Émile is the prototypical construction, in the Freudian sense, of critical consciousness as an organizing pedagogical principle; it is the narrative presentation of the fantasy that frames and orients this consciousness within and against its world. With Rousseau, the object of this fantasy is the end of education: it is completed, terminates, *succeeds* in the fully constituted subject of Enlightenment, where we will find that its agitated relation to the social link is quieted to the point of an idealized harmony that is in fact a total stasis. The troubling implication is that liberalism after Rousseau is motivated by the same fantasy of subjective closure, of consciousness at peace with its world, against which critical consciousness is opposed. To neutralize the subject is the dream of ideology.

Consistent with Freud and Lacan's position on the end of analysis, which we now see was always an educational concern, Sade reveals on the contrary that true education succeeds just where it fails, where the subject remains incomplete or unfulfilled, insofar as this failure is situated within an ethical frame that enjoins its interminability. The fantasy at stake in Rousseau resists this more radical end of education, trapping the subject of education within the parameters of the pleasure principle. Sade, meanwhile, pushes Rousseau's conception of education beyond the pleasure principle, refusing the idyllic fantasy of a subject who is fully constituted—complete, contented, and calm. Instead, he sustains the desire at stake for the subject of the unconscious, a desire which is perpetuated by the inevitability of its failure because of the impossibility of its object.

The symptom of this desire, the sign of Sade's failure, is not the content of his text but the writing of it. The subject of literature is there in his graphomania, his obsessive questing after the impossible object where he aims and fails to inscribe it. Sade falls short and begins again, and again, because the subject is constitutively alienated from its object, because their union doesn't stop not being written.

Through the work of literature, *avec* Rousseau, Sade's failure will show us why critical consciousness must account for the logic of unconscious fantasy which frames it. For it is here, at the level of the fantasy, where the subject's existential dissatisfaction pushes it beyond the ideologically prescribed limits of the possible, beyond what is written and writeable, and toward an impossibility that no ideology, no social order, no language, and indeed no consciousness can contain. After Sade, a truly radical, revolutionary pedagogy demands such a reorientation, and can be neither thought nor realized without it.

This chapter concludes by schematizing this radical pedagogy of the unwritten remainder according to a truly revolutionary ethics of education whose roots lay buried in the Enlightenment but do not nurture the flowers of liberalism. To arrive at this impossibility, we will have to follow the circuitous path carved by Rousseau and then retread this path with his greatest and worst acolyte. We begin with a textual anatomy of *Émile*, the relation between literature and philosophy it instantiates on its way to truth, and its place within the broader frame of Rousseau's thought and the Enlightenment more generally. We will then repeat this movement with Sade in order to show how *Philosophy in the Bedroom* takes *Émile* beyond itself and radicalizes its conclusions.

This reconceiving of the Enlightenment's subject of education—on its own terms, with its own texts—will end in failure. The subject of education, like the subject of literature or of the unconscious, will remain unwritten. For it is only in its simultaneous compulsion and evasion of the order of the signifier, only at the limit of the possible, at the edge of language, that such a subject announces the impossibility from which it springs and at which it hopes to arrive.

The Subject of Education: An Inscrutable Inscription

Part fiction, part exposition, and part manifesto, *Émile* joins dissertation
to demonstration by personifying and narrativizing Rousseau's prescriptions for a "natural" education. His eponymous pupil's story, which is also
his whole being, is told in the present tense as it unfolds alongside Rousseau's philosophy. Rousseau is the first-person narrator, so that the student's
story is also his own. The principles and practices of education move hand
in hand from the beginning of the hypothetical child's life to the triumphant end of his tutelage, when he ascends to the place of his author/father/
teacher—Rousseau himself. From the start, however, it is Nature that dictates this adventure. Rousseau is not Émile's true teacher, but only Nature's
surrogate and the instrument of its authorship. His imagined pupil is the
intelligible, chronologically ordered inscription of Nature, the true Author,
the master signifier. What Defoe had called God and Providence, Rousseau
calls Nature.

Unlike the other treatises from which Rousseau took his inspiration
(Locke's *Some Thoughts Concerning Education*, Montesquieu's *The Spirit of
the Laws*), Rousseau's philosophical fiction and literary philosophy is both
artistic and analytic. It is a novelistic discourse (from the Latin *discursus*:
wandering or moving in various directions; dispersal; discharge).[23] This novel
form is an essential quality of Rousseau's thought, which here and elsewhere
concerns a truth irreducible to fact: the truth of the human and its nature.
For Rousseau, this truth is not one fact among others; it is the ground upon
which all observable facts take place. Anticipating the early Romantic ambition to present reason in its aesthetic totality, Rousseau supposes that to fully
represent the human therefore requires a literary philosophical imagination.

For the question of education, Rousseau develops this conjunction of philosophy and fiction in order to model the construction of an ideal subject,
the novel foundation of a better world.[24] This exemplary subject's fictiveness
is inseparable from his exemplarity. "I gave myself a common Emile," he
explains, "to be useful and to make myself understood; for, with respect to
the true one, a child so different from others would not serve as an example
for anything."[25] The "true" Émile thus is more hypothetical, less real, than
the fictional one. If he existed outside the fiction, he would be outside the
order of the signifier altogether—illegible, utterly inscrutable, meaningless.
Organizing his imagined pupil into a narrative is an instrument of Rousseau's
desire for meaning, his desire to make himself understood, to make the unintelligible intelligible, even though he knows the truth cannot but be obscured
by this exemplification. As the basis of a new reality, Émile first must be
invented according to the terms of the present reality he would replace.

We have established with Jakobson and Schlegel that this is also the
province of the eighteenth-century novel. It resembles, reflects, but is finally
irreducible to the surrounding reality from which it borrows its language and

attendant systems of intelligibility; it constructs a new reality, another world, out of ready-to-hand semiotic and cultural materials. This poetry of reference is how we should understand Rousseau's paradoxical claim that his book, and thus his pupil, is an example of what defies exemplarity, and why this truth can only be structured like a fiction.

His novelistic strategy for representing the unrepresentable is also meant to provide a margin of freedom from the heteronymous doctrine and emergent paradigm with which Siskin and Warner distinguish the Enlightenment as event: the paradigm of systematicity, to which Rousseau's name, at least, was eventually assimilated. Here, however, Rousseau declares a contrary freedom of the paradox. "Common readers," he pleads, "pardon me my paradoxes. When one reflects, they are necessary and, whatever you may say, I prefer to be a paradoxical man than a prejudiced one" (93). Reason's characteristic intolerance for contradiction is here positioned as a barrier to thought. Any consistent conceptual apparatus, any system of thinking, wins its consistency only by simplifying and distorting the complexity of its objects, reinforcing its own illusory certainty, confirming its own prejudices.

The novelistic, the fictional, the literary thus are not the ornaments but the engines of Rousseau's writing; here, literature is where true philosophy occurs. Fiction is not an additive but the essence of the work. His vision of the subject of education—and after his revolutionary redemption, the subject of the Enlightenment per se—therefore invites and demands the work of literature, which means an ethical attunement to the subject of literature, the unwritten remainder that haunts, motivates, and unworks the text's elaboration and its legacy. And because *Émile* concerns an exemplary subject (of education; of literature) whose inscription is also its effacement, a subject whose writing yet leaves it unwritten, the structure of the subject's becoming and the framework of its desire for being are an equally exemplary fantasy, with all the paradox this implies.

Telos and the Paradox of Freedom

Along the trail of the subject in this text, we discover a higher order of paradox: *the text's anti-systematicity itself results in a system.* Unlike *Robinson Crusoe*, this system does not so much falter against its various contradictions as it is moved by them, and is as self-contained and self-sustaining as any of the systems against which Rousseau was opposed. Attending to the philosophy's plot, as its novelistic presentation asks us to do, we discover that every stage of Émile's development negates but does not nullify its preceding one, so that every successive movement of his subjectivation retains and complicates its precedents. The study of his physical limitations becomes moral judgment; self-preservation becomes romantic love; and the process concludes with its own beginning.[26]

We can avoid taking the long march through this whole proto-Hegelian narrative by attending to just its key moves, which help situate it with respect to the (psychosis of) Enlightenment we charted in the previous chapter and will prepare us for its Sadean revision.

First, the narrative begins even earlier than does Robinson Crusoe's private history, prior to Émile's birth, when the child is enclosed within himself like a seed awaiting germination. Rousseau's first address thus is not to the pupil but to his mother: "Form an enclosure around your child's soul," he implores. "Someone else can draw its circumference, but you alone must build the fence" (38). This fence is like Crusoe's island: it means not to imprison but to protect the child from the corrupting influence of "all the social institutions in which we find ourselves submerged," which "would stifle nature in him and put nothing in its place" before he could stand a chance of being otherwise (37–38).

This is the extent of the mother's role in Rousseau's drama. The necessary passage from the natural to the social is the separation from the mother, who is thereby left alone in her little fence, not to be seen again. The mother is only the child's organic condition of possibility, a vessel of reproduction, and a womb of the soul. On the other side of this separation stands a guide who can lead the child through the pitfalls of socialization, a protector, an authority—a father. This is the role Rousseau assigns himself.

The foundation of Émile's socialization is self-love (*amour-propre*) as self-preservation, a care of the self that develops in tandem with a knowledge of the limits of his desire with respect to the objects and people populating his world. At this stage in his development, the age of utility, he is allowed his first and only book, at least until adulthood: a model of self-sufficiency and the moderation of desire, a best-selling English novel about a solitary man who masters his environment and his imagination by transforming both into a reflection of his own rational desire; Émile's manual, of course, is *Robinson Crusoe*.[27]

Having traversed this period by learning industriousness and self-sufficiency, Émile will now enter the stage of his development marked by the advent of the passions. "We are, so to speak, born twice," Rousseau opines, "once to exist and once to live; once for our species and once for our sex" (211). This second natality, this being born from mere existence into real life, draws Émile into dangerous territory, from the security of *amour-propre* into the perilousness and vulnerability of love for and by others. His tutor's task at this stage is to engineer a series of lessons within the social sphere that can maintain the student's moral and emotional independence even as he explores the treacherous contours of the wider world.

It would seem that Émile's every step to this point was to provide him with the requisite tools to navigate the social order at arm's length, to engage with it while maintaining his natural right to self-determination. In fact, however, the preceding adventure has actually prepared the ground for his total subjection to Rousseau's tutorial will and, by an infinitesimal extension, the inner voice of reason to which his tutor has awakened him. Now that he is "sufficiently prepared to be docile" (332), his true education can begin.

Here the text interrupts itself and circles back to its own beginning in order to retrace the same movement for Rousseau's ideal Woman, Sophie—an abbreviated repetition which within the geography of the text is secondary to the education of Man, but perhaps no less important insofar as Émile's course will remain incomplete without the complement of his natural feminine other. And if Sophie is, by natural right, inferior in strength and reason, this is offset by Émile's weakness before and dependence upon her as the object of his affection.[28] As with his first lessons concerning the limits of his desire with respect to physical reality, his freedom, and Sophie's, are conditioned by the natural, thus indisputable, imperative of romantic companionship and sexual reproduction.

The most revealing and important element of this schema is *Émile*'s final paragraph, which, contrary to everything Rousseau has led us to expect, does not mark the realization of the educated subject whose upbringing we have followed through hundreds of pages from his earliest germination. Such a realization remains for Émile on a vanishing horizon. "'My master,'" he exhorts,

> "congratulate your child. He hopes soon to have the honor of being a father. Oh, what efforts are going to be imposed on our zeal, and how we are going to need you! . . . Advise us and govern us. We shall be docile. I need you more than ever now that my functions as a man begin. You have fulfilled yours. Guide me so that I can imitate you. And take your rest [*reposez-vous*]. It is time." (480)

So the book ends, Rousseau having given his fiction, his subject, the last word. *Teach me again so that I may become you, and take your rest.* These last words thus close a loop whose two ends are not the seedling and the man into whom it grows, not the teachable and the taught, but the teacher and . . . himself. What seemed to be the story of Émile's development was in fact the story of his author, tutor, and surrogate father. It is he and not his pupil through whom Nature finds its full articulation. The true subject of education, Rousseau himself, is realized—*made real* by assuming his full subjectivation to the will of this Master—when he finally evaporates and is supplanted by his fiction, his student and son, who repeats the movement again with his own children, who must themselves again repeat it with their children, and so on, interminably.

This would be a true repetition, a repetition without a difference, since the end of Émile's becoming-subject is no end at all, but instead his arrival at the beginning of a new adventure, that of the becoming-teacher, the path of which has already been inscribed, determined, as the text which he also is.

Through his teaching and his text, Rousseau has traversed this second becoming to arrive at a happy stasis (*reposez-vous*). Rousseau's terminal paradox, then, is that the subject of education is not the student but the master, who comes to be only at the moment of his disappearance. Only then is he free.

What sort of freedom is this?! For a subject formed in the crucible of Natural necessity, autonomy is impossible. The child is absolutely subjected to his master's will, and is literally never more than a step away from Rousseau at all times. Just as Crusoe had done with the admonishing voice of Conscience and the return of his father's cursed appellation ("*Wretch!*"), the young adult has internalized this will so completely that he cannot, he is engineered not to want to, distinguish between Rousseau's desire and his own. As father, Émile is consigned to repeat the same upbringing with respect to his own child, which he and Sophie will produce according to the dictates of Nature. Finally, the author of the whole process, Rousseau, the real subject of education, is merely the instrument of this higher author-ity; he is only the implement, the perfectly functioning writing machine, by which this master signifier is inscribed.

This is decidedly *not* the kind of freedom imagined by the moral authorities of modern liberal education. It is not self-determination, but what we may call Other-determination; as with Crusoe's psychotic Other-interestedness, Rousseau's exemplary subject is determined according to its instrumentalization by a signifier, Nature, an Other as incontrovertible and indifferent as any god. It is according to, on behalf of, and in service to the desire of this Other, this Master, that the subject of education signifies.

If there is a freedom at stake in any of this, it can only be the freedom to obey, the freedom of the properly educated individual to conform his desire—his meaning, what he wants to say and, so saying, to be—absolutely to the master signifier, thereby also refusing that secondary subordination to the other of Nature, the social link. And since Nature is by definition a tautology, because it is what it is and cannot be otherwise, because this is the basis of its supremacy and incontrovertibility, the subject's alignment with this supreme Master is in truth a concession to absolute necessity.

Nature is a master that cannot be other than what it is, Rousseau is only this master's puppet, and Émile is merely the puppet's puppet until he, too, will take hold of the strings.

The Good Old Days: A Fate Worse Than Death

We cannot grasp what this marionettage means for the constitution of the subject, its position at the foundation of a new social link, or its importance to the myth and legacy of the Enlightenment without situating it within Rousseau's larger intellectual project, which always concerns the same originary division between Nature and society Émile is designed to close. The slash in the Nature/Society dyad that both conjoins and divides its two halves is the hinge upon which all of Rousseau's thought turns. It marks a constitutive antagonism, a strife at the heart of human being, a cut which is the mark of the human as such. The impossible child therefore is assigned a mission fitting for his impossibility: to reconcile the irreconcilable by traversing this existential opposition.

Already in his (in)famous First and Second Discourses, and again in his *Social Contract*, Rousseau formulated this antagonism in his attack against the history of progressive moral improvement through which his age imagined itself to be moving. On the question "Whether the restoration of the Sciences and Arts has contributed to the purification of morals," his First Discourse launched Rousseau to iconoclastic stardom with an emphatic, almost Nietzschean *No!*[29] The text which most concerns the origin of the originary division between the natural and the social, however—the object and cause of Émile's mission—is the "Essay on the Origin of Languages." Here, Rousseau asserts that "speech is the first social institution," which is to say, society begins with language; language founds the social link and is its prototypical form:

> As soon as one man was recognized by another as a sentient, thinking Being, similar to himself, the desire or the need to communicate to him his sentiments and thoughts made him seek the means to do so. These means can only be drawn from the senses, the only instruments by which one man can act upon another. Hence the institution of sensible signs to express thought. The inventors of language did not make this argument, but instinct suggested its conclusions to them.[30]

In the move from the state of Nature to the social order, speech is born of the instinctive need to communicate one's pre-linguistic sentiments and thoughts to another in whom one recognizes—in whom is reflected—something of oneself. Coupling thought with sentiment, Rousseau emphasizes that language is not originally referential, but figurative and poetic:

> Not hunger nor thirst, but love, hatred, pity, anger wrung their first voices from them. Fruit does not shrink from our grasp, one can eat it without speaking, one stalks the prey one means to devour in silence; but in order to move a young heart, to repulse an unjust aggressor, nature dictates accents, cries, plaints: here [then] are the oldest invented words, and here is why languages were songlike and passionate before they were plain and methodical.[31]

Language thus indexes the experience of a feeling or idea that has no representative among the immediate objects of sense-perception yet must be made accessible to some external other. It originally does not facilitate the

organization of a group of self-interested individuals into a community oriented around the distribution of resources. Physical need—pure, unmediated
self-interest—repulses one individual from another, and cannot explain the
origin of the social link. The only sufficient explanation for the human desire
to overcome this primordial separation is thus the compulsion to share "the
moral needs, the passions," and it is from this passionate impulse that speech
arises.[32]

If language originally springs from this natural urge to community, this
poses yet another paradox—the paradox of paradoxes. In order to maintain
that language erupted through the force of Nature, of what he here calls
instinct, Rousseau places this origin at Nature's command and in opposition
to society and its corruptions. And yet, it is only through language that the
pure state of Nature will have been interrupted. With language, Nature introduces a difference into itself, and in so doing gives itself to the perversions of
reference and the perversity of reason.

Early anthropologists misunderstood Rousseau's account of the origins of
the social link as a matter of historical fact and accordingly, a little ridicu-
lously, sought to confirm it empirically through the discovery of actual "wild
men," nameless Crusoes who somehow had survived from birth beyond
the reach of language.[33] In fact, his origin story is a necessary philosophical fiction—once again, a *construction*—that articulates not a historical fact
but a historical truth. Just as with Freud's construction of the murder of
the primal father, this is not an empirically delimited origin but a narrative
organization of the logic of the present. According to this logic, the divide
between Nature and society, the cut which severs them, is fundamental, originary, and constitutive of them both. We will not find any anthropological
confirmation of Rousseau's human nature because the agent of division—the
sign whose irruption into and interruption of the state of Nature is itself
compelled by Nature—creates that which it divides; Nature and society can
only be posited, constructed, situated in and by language, once the division
has taken place.[34]

If the founding of the social link forever cleaves the human from Nature,
initiating humanity's (d)evolution to its current, contemptible state, it is
therefore this same difference against which Rousseau writes; it is because
language disappropriates man of his "inner voice" and installs him within the
social link, alienates him from Nature, that any education must take place.
Education therefore is a re-education, a forward-directed return to what primordially has been lost. Yet, the relation between Émile and his father/tutor
does not exist except in language, as language, as a hypothetical movement
through language to a point beyond and, what amounts to the same thing,
before it. Nature is both the origin and end of education, and yet this end can
be achieved and Nature's integrity restored only through the traversal of its
own antipode. The text's aim and purpose is thus to close the gap that Nature
opened in itself with the introduction of language and the social link, to write

against this gap without which the text, any text, could not exist. Formalizing *Émile* in this context, we can see that Rousseau therefore writes against his own writing and against the whole of language. The text's object and cause, the desire it arrogates to itself on behalf and in the name of Nature, is to cancel itself out by canceling the very condition of its being.

This revolutionary restoration of the undivided origin would realize the uninterrupted plenitude of a primordially lost harmony, unity, and unconditioned enjoyment. "Assume perpetual spring on earth," Rousseau writes, "assume water, cattle, pastures everywhere; assume men issuing from the hands of nature and dispersed throughout all this"; this is a state of "primitive freedom," an "isolated and pastoral existence" perfectly suited to men's "natural indolence," utterly remote from "the slavery, the labors, and the miseries that are inseparable from the social state."[35] This antediluvian paradise can only be assumed, never observed, constructed rather than discovered, since it has been drowned by the tide of civilization which has cast us upon a distant shore. From our exile, we observe or hallucinate the whole of history. "I see Palaces and Cities raised," Rousseau continues, "I see the birth of the arts, laws, commerce; I see peoples forming, expanding, dissolving, succeeding one another like the waves of the sea: I see men clustered in a few points of their habitation in order there to devour one another, turning the remainder of the world into a dreadful desert."[36] The desire of the text, then, is to (re)unite with the "perpetual spring" that lies beyond the monumental desert of history.

This would be a restoration of what Freud in *Beyond the Pleasure Principle* calls "an *old* state of things," the state preceding the scission that alienates the human from its nature and relegates it to the field of desire: "an initial state from which the living entity has at one time or other departed and to which it is striving to return by the circuitous paths along which its development leads."[37] For Rousseau and the Enlightenment education he exemplifies, thus also for the subject such an education would reify, the true logic of its becoming, with all its circuitousness and paradox, is the death drive.

But Rousseau could not avow the annihilatory logic of his pedagogical program. Instead, the author will betray the death drive and forestall his self-cancellation. His becoming is repeated and repeated again, endlessly reproduced according to the supposedly incontrovertible dictates of natural necessity—including, with the late introduction of Sophie, the necessity for sexual reproduction as self-preservation. This compulsion to repeat is not true to the death drive that motors it. It is instead the drive's attenuated representative: the self-perpetuating tension and release of the pleasure principle.

Unlike the death drive in its fullest sense, the pleasure principle baits the subject with the lure of fulfillment, offering a reprieve, however slight or fleeting or false, from the constitutive tension between the subject and the impossible object of desire, muffling the fantasy's protest against an always insufficient reality. This is why the pleasure principle is the operative principle of ideology, which wants only to reproduce, without tension or remainder, the conditions of possibility, the very terms, of the reality it prescribes. In the end, the horizon of Rousseau's critical consciousness, the true object of his desire particularly with regard to the question of education, the end of Enlightenment education, is the total coincidence of consciousness with its reality. Such a coincidence is no freedom: it is the essence and aim of ideology.

Despite Rousseau's panegyric on the good old days before language opened a rift in being and divided it from itself, before the text which would write this division away or close it through a return to the happy repose from which it was forced to depart, a life determined by the pleasure principle would be a fate worse than death. It would mean the seamless repetition of the same, a life without difference, a history without movement. It would mean a reality without fantasy. Perhaps Rousseau, that brightest firebrand of eighteenth-century thought, for all his vituperation against the prejudices intrinsic to systematic coherence, could not assume the truth of his desire because it is the truth of the system he nevertheless constructed. Or perhaps this was always the horizon of this thought—to resolve all his proliferating paradoxes, to write the image of his own perfect subject and thereby to write himself out of existence, into the illusory plenitude of a being beyond desire.

But the text remains, monument to this movement's failure, testament to the impossibility of its ambition, agent of its own disillusionment. Writing, the mode of the fantasy's transmission and the means to its actualization, is also the medium of its perpetuation, the trace of the fantasy's refusal to bend to the language and the reality it frames. The trajectory of Rousseau's thought thereby takes us beyond him, beyond the pleasure principle, and into the vicious and deathly terrain of the Marquis de Sade. For it is here, among Sade's grotesquerie and fury and the revolting joy (*jouissance*) of his writing, where the truth of Rousseau's critique is drawn or wrenched into the cold light of a more radically revolutionary Enlightenment.

Yes Future: Education as Expenditure

To begin again, we should recall that the end of psychoanalysis, too, is the cancellation of its own conditions. At least in this vital sense, psychoanalysis belongs to the pedagogical tradition Rousseau exemplifies. As with an analyst in training, Rousseau shows that the student does not ascend to the status of an autonomous subject by adopting the position of the teacher; the work of education is complete, so to speak, only at the moment of the teacher's withdrawal, when the student assumes the responsibility for his own desire upon the model provided by the one who has come before.

The difference is that for psychoanalysis this model is not an instance of mastery or a method for realizing the desire of the Other. The end of analysis is not a terminal point but an interminable quest. In the clinic, this turns upon the transference, the function of which is to push the analysand beyond the imaginary support of the subject-supposed-to-know, into an attitude of perpetual learning with respect to the unconscious, which is neither master nor mastered.[38] Rousseau retains and embellishes precisely this illusion of a master beyond the order of the signifier. His authority over his student, up to and beyond Émile's passage to the position of the teacher, is perfect and unimpeachable. Émile's desire is only Rousseau's desire, which is itself only Nature's desire for self-cancellation, and so it is into Nature's arms that the perfect, fully formed subject will be contentedly enfolded, like a puppet placed back in its case.

After Rousseau, Sade also situates himself as an author and pedagogue in service to Nature, and for the same reasons. Like *Émile*, Sade's *Philosophy in the Bedroom* figures the incompatibility of Nature and the social through the fictional education of a child. Sade's pupil is a young woman, Eugénie, whose education proceeds in tandem with the novel's plot. Her teacher, Sade's philosophical mouthpiece, is the libertine Dolmancé, who like Rousseau begins his lessons from the conviction that society disfigures the natural subject. And like Émile, Dolmancé's ingenue is delivered at the end of her tutelage from the irrational prejudice, superstition, and false virtue, all the stupidity and derangement, of her social milieu.

The essential difference between them is that Nature for Sade is not a zone of pastoral plenitude. Its embrace is not warm. Nature is violent. It is not cruel but morally indifferent, and only appears cruel from the removed perspective of arbitrary moral prejudice. Thus does Sade repudiate any Rousseauistic sentimentalism or nostalgia. To align one's desire with the dictates of this amoral force, to craft oneself as the instrument of this ferocious Other's desire, requires a new notion of the subject which recognizes and, indeed, celebrates the annihilation of its own conditions. To reinvent the social link according to a concept of social justice erected upon this molten ground is to abandon the dream of a future in which all discords are resolved into a "perpetual spring on earth." For Sade, *the subject is discord*.

As with Rousseau, the best way to discern the logic of fantasy organizing Sade's text—the (non-)relation between what it says and what it desires but fails to say—is to situate the end with respect to its beginning. Here we find that while the end of *Émile* closes a circuit which guarantees its own interminable repetition, *Philosophy in the Bedroom* concludes with the pupil's full assumption of her desire, which, according to its natural dictates, pushes her toward the annihilation of her own origin, without recuperation or repose.

The novel opens with Eugénie's arrival at Dolmancé's notorious academy, having been delivered to his capable hands by her father who wishes that she receive a proper education. Through the ensuing seven dialogues, she is molded into the perfect libertine—for Sade, the ideal enlightened subject. As Dolmancé and company's philosophical dissertations become more extravagant, so too do their exercises in sexual extremism. As usual, Sade's imagination is unmatched in the peculiarity—and, after a while, the mundanity—of its erotic assemblages. Bodies pile upon bodies as every orifice of every character is variously penetrated, every limb used for penetrating, every exposed bit of skin whipped and flogged, fluids multiply swapped, incest and pederasty indulged . . . all framed by a simultaneously unfolding paean to Nature and a crescendo of invective against God and law.

During the third dialogue, in response to Dolmancé's claim that Nature prefers destruction over conservation, his accomplice the Madame de Saint-Ange interjects, "Do you know, Dolmancé, that by means of this system you are going to be led to prove that totally to extinguish the human race would be nothing but to render Nature a service?" to which he happily responds, "Who doubts of it, Madame?"[39] Later, in a rare interlude from the lubricious proceedings and speaking under the influence of Buffon's study of the history of species extinction, Dolmancé asks, "Why! what difference would it make to [Nature] were the race of men entirely to be extinguished upon earth, annihilated!" He quickly answers his own question. "The entire species might be wiped out and the air would not be the less pure for it, nor the Star less brilliant, nor the universe's march less exact. What idiocy it is to think that our kind is so useful to the world that he who might not labor to propagate it or he who might disturb this propagation would necessarily become a criminal!" (276). Such is the core lesson of the Sadean system, grounded as it is in a contemporaneous scientific materialism. Sexuality, and thus the education it forms and informs, is true to Nature only if it operates by a principle of expenditure, within what Georges Bataille would call a general economy, according to which energy is discharged without any expectation of return.[40] Sade's sexuality has no exchange-value. Its aim is not, as with Émile and Sophie, reproduction or regeneration, because it produces nothing—except perhaps the libertine's discourse, which repeats and repeats again, and again, that sex is the expenditure of a bottomless desire.

For her part, Eugénie plays the apt pupil. In the final dialogue, she surpasses even her tutor's imperative of expenditure—which remains at the level of a wasteful extravagance throughout—with a symbolic act against her own possibility of being. Her mother, a paragon of the virtue Eugénie has by now learned to despise, arrives to retrieve her from the notorious libertines. Immediately she is variously raped, beaten, and tortured, including by her daughter, who proudly proclaims in medias res, "Here I am: at one stroke incestuous, adulteress, sodomite, and all that in a girl who lost her maidenhead today! . . . What progress, my friends!" (359).

Unlike Émile, Eugénie is not content merely to repeat her lessons under her teacher's approving gaze. As the text moves toward its climax, Dolmancé instructs his syphilitic valet to rape the mother—a detail which conjures Voltaire (one of Sade's favorite predecessors), who often cited syphilis as proof against any religious conviction in a benevolent, omnipotent God since such a Being would not authorize Nature to interfere with His imperative to procreation except by a preposterous contradiction.[41] Once the rape is accomplished and her mother inseminated with the disease, Eugénie stitches her mother's vagina shut with a needle and thick wax thread, "so that you'll give me no more little brothers and sisters" (363). The libertines arrange themselves into a final erotic assemblage, fucking and watching with rising excitement as Dolmancé and Eugénie share the needle with which they pierce and sew her mother's flesh. The student now assumes the position of the teacher, separating from the festivities to direct the drama herself, commanding Dolmancé's movements, directing the flow of his semen. In the end, the group dissipates; "all's been said" (364–66). At the apotheosis of Eugénie's education, the mother, sobbing and bleeding, is forced to kneel and beg her daughter's forgiveness.

Well. In general, reading Sade is not a pleasurable experience.[42] But this is due less to the extent of his violence, which can go much, much further even than it does here, than to the obscene enjoyment with which his writing is imbued and to which it attempts, and finally fails, to testify, or to which it testifies in this very failure. As has been rather exhaustively noted by prior readings of Sade after Lacan, he forces a literary encounter with *jouissance*, that awful enjoyment which pushes characters, readers, and author alike beyond the pleasure principle. This is why sexuality for Sade is not useful— neither for the cultivation of romantic intimacy, nor for the perpetuation of aristocratic lineages and the social order over which they preside, nor for the procreation of the species. It refuses all these diversions from its true aim: *to cancel itself out*. In such a configuration, life, which is always a sex life, names only the singular pursuit of this deathly satisfaction.

In this regard we should note the conspicuous absence, here and throughout Sade's vast catalogue of horrors, of either suicide or necrophilia, as well as the absurdly implausible excesses to which he subjects his fictional victims' bodies before they are finally permitted to expire. Why, after all, does Eugénie not put her teacher's lessons into practice simply by killing herself? Why is her mother allowed to live? How is the poor woman's survival possible given the extent of the brutality to which she has been subjected? Death is absented from the libidinal equation for the same reason Sade requested, in his "Last Will and Testament," that upon his death he be buried in an unmarked grave so that all trace of his physical being "may disappear from the face of the earth."[43] The absence of life is also the absence of the *jouissance* which compels it, and therefore is of no interest to the Sadean system. It is not death Sade is after, but more life. His writing is the inscription, the trace, of the death we are always already living.

To live is to desire, to desire is to be subject to the fantasy of an impossible fulfillment, and *jouissance* is the terrible enjoyment this subjection exacts. *Jouissance* is what compels the perpetuation of the fantasy, thus of the desire it organizes, thus of the life it sustains. To organize an ethics around this enjoyment, to take responsibility for it in a way that is true to the self-canceling movement of Nature, it is necessary to go on living—with Sade, to go on writing.

Introducing *jouissance* to distinguish the enjoyment at stake in the fantasy from the pleasure that lures the ego, and situating it through Sade with respect to an ethics of desire, Lacan punctuates Freud's discovery that death is not the opposite of life. Death is the truth of life, the truth of the desire which compels it.[44] This is another way of saying that the death drive does not negate life but affirms it, affirms each singular instance of life through the circuitous and always unique movement of its self-cancellation. As Steven Miller explains, the death drive "is not true to its own name: rather than designate the living being's inner urge to die, it evokes the much more complex process whereby it seeks to nullify the fact of its own birth."[45] Eugénie's violence upon her mother's body is as clear a symbol of such a quest as can be found in the history of literature. That both she and her mother live on makes clear that the text's aim is neither orgasmic pleasure nor organic death. Its aim and its engine is *jouissance*.

Rousseau saw that language divides Nature from itself, and that this makes possible a writing which wants impossibly to write away this very division, to nullify its own origin. But by parachuting into sentimentalism he betrayed the radical consequence of his insight: it is this difference that rescues the subject from the perpetual "indolence" of undifferentiated repetition, from a revolution as natural and regular, as unbroken and unbreakable, as that of the starry sky above. Rousseau's revolution longs for such indolence, imagines a happy end to desire, recuperates and reinvests the energy expended through the subject's becoming so that it will become so again, and again, identically and forever. In a perverse twist, then, it is his pedagogical program, with its mirage of satisfaction at the horizon of its completion, that would destroy any possibility of a future.

The future, it turns out, belongs to the Marquis de Sade.

The Write to *Jouissance*

Whence does the Sadean future spring? What would it mean for a social order to found itself upon a subject thus reconceived in the name of the *jouissance* that compels and torments it?

Sade's answer is his principal political treatise, "Yet Another Effort, Frenchmen, if You Would Become Republicans." It comprises the bulk of the novel's fifth dialogue, where, after an especially exhausting orgy, the players read it aloud in response to Eugénie's query "whether manners are truly necessary in a governed society" (295). Embedded within *Philosophy in the Bedroom* (his reply to *Émile*), the treatise can be divorced from neither its pedagogical nor its literary context.

In light of his more typical tendencies, this humanist panegyric on the possibilities, excesses, and faults of the French Revolution is a curious document. Sade's usual invective against religion and its false virtues is on full display, but he also warns the revolutionaries against massacre and expulsion—"these are royal atrocities" (306); offers "humanity, fraternity, benevolence" as the guideposts of "our reciprocal obligations" (309); roundly opposes the death penalty as an "impractical, unjust, inadmissible" obscenity (310); criticizes the new republic's emphasis on private property as a fatal compromise of its principle of equality and a recipe for permanent social injustice (313); equates any man's claim to exclusive possession of a woman with slavery, both of which are utterly indefensible (318); and even argues that there is no difference between murder and the killing of animals (330).

All this seems at odds with *Philosophy in the Bedroom*'s torturous conclusion and Sade's larger inventory of atrocities. In fact, this political vision is the consequence of his libertine education program, neither of which can be separated from the work of literature and the poetry of reference in which they are inscribed. Together, the sexual circus, Eugénie's tutelage, and the political treatise comprise a novelistic discourse upon a society founded on the right to *jouissance*, rather than to its exclusion or by way of its disavowal.

This discourse is scaffolded by the fluxional architecture of both Sade's erotic assemblages and the structure of his republic. Against the ersatz revolution which made Rousseau into its poster child and ossified into the Revolutionary Assembly, a true republicanism, Sade claims, is like these infinitely creative sexual tableaux: forever moving, always unsettled. Properly (re)aligned with the dictates of Nature and therefore with the principles of Enlightenment, the social is inseparable from the sexual. With Sade, the very distinction between the public and the private, the street and the bedroom, is disqualified from the start. To separate the political and the libidinal would drain politics of the excitation, the insurrectionary energy, that ought to sustain it, resulting in a social stasis whose correlate in the bedroom is sexual quiescence.

This is an Enlightenment theory through and through. Libidinal excitation, desire suspended in its unfulfillment, is for Sade not the enemy but the cornerstone of reason, including therefore the reason upon which his republicanism is built. This is why, here and throughout Sade's other works, philosophical dissertation is inseparable from its demonstration. To cite just one of a dozen possible examples: in the midst of an orgiastic practicum on the natural principles of libertinage, Madame de Saint-Ange warns the teacher to restrain himself while being "frigged" by his student Eugénie: "Be reasonable, Dolmancé: once the semen flows, the activity of your animal spirits will be diminished and the warmth of your dissertations will be lessened correspondingly" (201). All at once, Sade's characters fuck and torture and hold forth on the moral indifference of the universe, waxing philosophical as their animal spirits rise, because their words and actions, their positions sexual and political, are inseparable from the *jouissance* they represent—not as representations of the unrepresentable (impossible) beyond the pleasure principle, but as its representatives, as a signifier represents a subject to another signifier.[46]

Alongside Rousseau, then, for Sade the passions are the royal road to reason. But *Philosophy in the Bedroom* pushes the passions beyond Rousseau, refusing to release the tension generated by the friction of desire because the work of reason takes place just there, in the agony of suspension between desire and its fulfillment.[47] Neither a dispassionate reason nor a passion moderated by reason, but a *passionate* reason—this is a reason as uncompromising as any rationality, only it is organized around the truth of desire, on behalf of the subject and not the cold, bloodless truth of an ultimately disembodied objectivity drained of *jouissance*. With Sade, the subject gets its body back without thereby losing its reason. The subject is rationality organized and oriented by fantasy, which is also not without its reasons; fantasy is rationality's reason.

"Yet Another Effort" thus installs this logic of the fantasy—and with it, the right to *jouissance*, the pursuit of one's desire regardless of the upheavals it might produce in the social order—as the basis of a truly revolutionary republicanism. "Insurrection has got to be a republic's permanent condition" (315). A true republican refuses any prevailing morality, any collective code of conduct and right reason, especially one that masks itself (in the name of Rousseauism, for instance) as Natural Law but in fact is an exercise in social and psychological repression. True republicanism would define the ethical subject's freedom negatively, as resistance against the pleasure principle and the quiescence of desire, following instead the movements of the death drive.[48] A true republic would be built upon its subjects' *perpetual dissatisfaction*, upon their desire rather than the (always false, ideologically saturated) promise of their fulfillment.

If such a society never existed and still does not exist, if it never can exist except in the form of an interminable revolution—if Sade's Enlightenment republic and his enlightened subject are impossible—then like Rousseau's subject they can only be articulated within the existing parameters of the possible, in the language of reality and the poetry of reference, in and as a novelistic fiction. Like the subject of literature, the revolutionary subject of education exists in this fiction of its interminable becoming: the subject is its movement toward the nullification of its own conditions of possibility, against the limits of the possible, into an impossible beyond. This fiction is the future to which Sade's writing gives form.

This writing toward the impossible is also why Sade kept writing. The whole sprawling, unfinished and interminable Sadean corpus is like Rousseau's: a monument to its own failure. Unlike Rousseau, though, Sade's writing does not stop, never arrives at the illusion of "perpetual spring" and happy repose. To the end, it remains true to his paradoxical vision of a permanent insurrection. His philosophy and his storytelling, in all their tediousness and excess, with their baroque grotesquerie and vitriolic humor, together are the sign of the *jouissance* that compels his graphomania from the other side of the order of the signifier, the other side of the possible, beyond the pleasure principle which organizes and maintains them.[49] To track after the subject here is to read the Sadean text as the trail the fantasy leaves in its wake, as a snail is followed by its slime.

Taking Sade Literally: The Right to *Jouissance*

Rousseau's anti-systematicity results in a system, a self-contained and self-regenerating telos, while Sade's systematic elaboration of a new morality of crime ends in paradox without resolution. There can be no law of lawlessness; "permanent insurrection" is a hopeless contradiction. Sade knows this, yet his answer is: So be it. Fidelity to the singularity of desire at stake in the fantasy demands that the subject refuse to cede its incongruity with any purportedly universal code, any moral or juridical law.[50] After Eugénie's exemplary education, this means to assume responsibility for her desire, and to act upon that responsibility regardless of its consistency or inconsistency with the surrounding order to which it had been subordinated. But far from tending toward a vacuous nihilism or installing self-interest as the only moral good, Sade goes beyond morality, beyond good and evil; his writing, as writing, as the writing of what doesn't stop not being written, displaces education's moral function with a contrary ethics of desire that would underpin his imagined libertine republic.

How could such an ethics provide a basis for the social link, which by definition requires the negotiation, and thus the constraint, of competing desires? Would Sade's ethics (or, for that matter, the ethics of psychoanalysis) not result in radical fragmentation, a Hobbesian state of perpetual war? How can an ethics of desire found a viable republicanism?

To answer such skepticism, we must retrieve Sade from the psychological and literary-critical history according to which "Sade" means sadism and "sadism" means Sade. Maurice Blanchot's articulation of the Sadean maxim is exemplary of this history, and by no means unique:

> This philosophy is one of self-interest, then of complete egoism. Each of us must do what pleases us, each of us has no other law but our own pleasure. This morality is founded on the primary fact of absolute solitude. Sade said it and repeated it in all its forms: nature creates us alone, there is no connection whatsoever linking one man to another. Consequently, *the only rule of conduct is that I favor all things that give me pleasure without consideration of the consequences that this choice might hold for the other*. Their greatest pain always counts

less than my pleasure. What does it really matter, if the price I must
pay for even my slightest joy is an outrageous assortment of hideous
crimes, since this joy delights me, it is in me, yet the effects of my
crimes do not touch me in the least, they are outside me.[51]

This supposes that the end of Sade's ethics is pleasure and that the Sadean
hero, absolutely solitary, owns his pleasure as though it were his private property which he is free to impose without regard for how it might compromise
the privacy of the other—hence its "complete egoism." But this is incorrect.
Sade's philosophy is not egoistic, nor can his law be the law of "our own
pleasure," because it is only through the other's pain that pleasure occurs; my
pleasure depends absolutely upon the other, which is why I need the other
and am nothing without them. I am not absolutely solitary. My pleasure
belongs to the other's pain.

All this indeed seems patently sadistic until we follow Sade further along
the trail he charts after Rousseau: the pleasure at stake in his universe is patterned after Nature. And since I am other to Nature, since like all signifiers
I am the otherness Nature introduces into itself, *it is only through my pain
that Nature enjoys.* In this universe, I am a subject not to the extent that I am
master of my desire, but only insofar as I am subjected to Nature's movement
of self-cancellation. If I am a criminal, if I delight in the other's suffering,
it is as a consequence of this movement by which I am made (compelled,
created, designed) to suffer the annihilatory enjoyment of the Nature which
commands me. Whence Sade's insistence, after and against Rousseau, that
the end of Nature is not regeneration but annihilation. In short, Sade's ethics
does not permit us to use others without regard for any consequence other
than our own pleasure; rather, he commands us to *be used.* The whole of
Sade's writing thus repudiates any characterization according to which the
"only rule" in the libertine universe is the rule of pleasure. The motor driving
the libertine's actions—and the entire Sadean corpus—is this subjection to an
enjoyment that pushes the human beyond the limits of what is useful or good
for the organism, beyond the reproduction of the self or the species, beyond
what is friendly to a social order built to Nature's exclusion. Beyond pleasure.

Its very writing, moreover, disproves "the primary fact of absolute solitude," since the text, as text, fatally compromises the author's sovereignty.
To give oneself over to language is already to accede to the structure of the
social link. "Sade said it," Blanchot insists, "and *repeated* it" (my emphasis):
"nature creates us alone, there is no connection whatsoever linking one man
to another." Yes, but it is precisely this *repetition* of the impossible fantasy of
absolute freedom from the Other that operates the text. Because the enjoyment he addresses to us can never be written, it is there in the signifier's
failure, in the writing, as the tormenting repetition of this failure to write the
unwritten.[52] The text is the interminable record of the author's torment under
the action of the impossible object of the fantasy.

Compare Blanchot's articulation of the Sadean maxim with Lacan's contrary articulation in "Kant with Sade," the peculiar grammar of which rewards attention to the French original:

> "I have the right to enjoy your body, anybody can say to me, and I will exercise this right without any limit stopping me in the capriciousness of the exactions I may have a taste to satiate."[53]

> "J'ai le droit de jouir de ton corps, peut me dire quiconque, et ce droit, je l'exercerai, sans qu'aucune limite m'arrête dans le caprice des exactions que j'aie le goût d'y assouvir."[54]

Lacan situates the maxim inside quotation marks. The English is from James Swenson's 1989 translation for the journal *October*; Bruce Fink's later version in his translation of *Écrits* separates the "anybody can say to me" from the rest of the statement with added quotation marks, which only confounds Lacan's point.[55] Without those additional marks, the strangely interpolated *anybody can say to me* displaces the subject of enunciation, thereby also rendering ambiguous the subject of the address. Who speaks it? Me? Or the "anybody" who can say it to me? The "I" is both subject and object of the maxim. In this way, with this subtle but essential grammatical twist, Lacan's *anyone can say to me* disappropriates the right to enjoy from the sovereignty of any ego. One's subjection to this right is without limit because one does not own one's *jouissance* but in a sense is owned by it. One does not choose the object of the fantasy, it is not a piece of private property or an object of the will. It is an internal expropriation that renders the subject incurably im-proper to itself. It does not stop acting upon the subject, motivating and orienting the peregrinations of *jouissance* that trace the subject's becoming, because this action of the fantasy is the subject. This subject is the tension and torment in which Sade located the work of reason and its revolutionary potential.

Blanchot's claim that Sade's "morality is founded on the primary fact of absolute solitude" thus not only mistakes an ethical commitment for a moral imperative—an essential distinction, to be sure—it also situates the ambition for solitude within a framework of egoistic self-interest. The essential psychoanalytic insight, however, already evident in Sade, is that nobody exists in absolute solitude, the subject is never sovereign, because it is always subjected to a will which it cannot but imperfectly assume as its own, which because of this imperfection doesn't stop not being written. It is this, and not any enthusiasm for cruelty, to which the fury and failure of Sade's work bears witness.

Thus read through the ethics of psychoanalysis, Sade's maxim does not grant a person, an ego, full license to pursue his own selfish pleasure. Lacan's iteration of it is a construction: a narrative organization of the fantasy which reveals, in all its grammatical oddness and ambiguity, that for Sade true freedom is not the freedom to use another for one's own pleasure "without consideration," as Blanchot asserts, "of the consequences that this choice might hold for the other." It is rather the freedom to be enjoyed, which means to be tormented beyond the limits of pleasure by the fantasy which structures one's impossible desire.

This tormenting relation, Sade suggests, is also the only viable basis for a just social order. Such a society would be founded upon each of its constituents' right to the unfaltering pursuit of the truth of their desire, without regard for the consequences this will entail for *one's own ego* and its imaginary and symbolic supports in the social link. It would take the subject beyond the pleasure that lures the ego into complacency and complicity with its social and symbolic entrapment. It would mean permanent insurrection since the subject is constitutively against the law.

We can now return to the question whether any of this could form the basis of a viable republic. Does an ethical refusal to cede one's desire, whatever the incalculable consequences, not confirm Blanchot's claim that in Sade's universe "there is no connection whatsoever linking one man to another"? If each of us is condemned to the singularity of the fantasy, condemned to be used each in our own ways by the *jouissance* it exacts, does this not validate the suspicion that Sade's ethics or the ethics of psychoanalysis would result in a fragmentation so profound that it would make any society, and any conception of the political, impossible?

Yes. But, again, so be it. In accepting and finally exceeding her tutor's injunctions, Eugénie shows us the way through the Enlightenment and the parameters of possibility it established: to a conception of the political that belongs to it, that is articulated in its language and torments that language, beginning with but taking us beyond the limits of the liberal imagination. Unlike Émile, who repeats his tutor's arrival at subjective plenitude, at abundance without lack, Eugénie completes her education through an act of renunciation. And what she renounces by embracing Dolmancé's lessons and moving past them to direct the flow of come and blood herself, by joining in the festivities as an equal among the other libertines, on her way to a new society and under the banner of a real revolution, what she cuts away from herself is her beholdenness to a master. "I cannot repeat it to you too often," Sade writes to those who would be true to the spirit of the revolution, "no more gods, Frenchmen, no more gods, lest under their fatal influence you wish to be plunged back into all the horrors of despotism" (309). There where the master was, so will the subject become, without, however, succumbing to the illusion that such becoming comes to any personal mastery or anything other than the nullification of her own conditions. This would be a real revolution, then, because its spring is the real—the real of fantasy, which must depose the ideality of every master and mastery, interminably.

Blanchot's version of the Sadean maxim, meanwhile, would better serve as the maxim of the liberal tradition against which Sade's republicanism is opposed. Liberalism, the moral and philosophical field in which the bourgeois revolutions articulated their political and economic authority, evacuates the prior occupant—the monarch or the sovereign—from the space of the master only to refill it with a more abstract and unimpeachable master in the form of an ideal. Thomas Jefferson's overwriting of Locke's original ideal, "property," with "the pursuit of happiness" is exemplary. The declaration of the inalienable right to happiness, that most elusive and alluring of ideals, displaces but retains the property at its foundation—the very property, the human property, the enslaved people Jefferson did not hesitate to use "without consideration of the consequences" on his plantation estate, a country chateau as picturesque as but far more brutal than any in Sade's catalogue of fictions.

The true morality of "complete egoism" is the liberal dream of equality of opportunity, founded upon the notion that humanity names a universal common denominator, a Rousseauistic natural sameness, from which one has the right which is in fact the obligation to separate oneself, to amass the signs of one's propriety. Self-possession as an effect of what one possesses, individuality as an imperative to accumulate, property as the boundary of one's privacy—"This philosophy is one of self-interest" (Blanchot again), "founded on the primary fact of absolute solitude." This anti-sociality, with all the egoic and super-egoic imperatives it implies, is the space of liberal political possibility.

But *what if?* What if in place of the idealistic imperative and ruse (the ideology) of happiness, instead of the illusion of personal fulfillment and the existential freedom that sustains it, against this notion of freedom which in reality is an enchainment to property, propriety, and possession—what if instead of the right to private property, the universal basis of the social order was the right to be dissatisfied, to be used by the fantasy? What if the right to have rights was the right to *jouissance*?

This is not a mere inversion of the liberal formula, wherein to be possessed would be better than to possess. It would explode the whole notion of private property and reinvent the social link according to another universalism. Such a world would not be founded upon what each member of the community has, or could have, but rather upon the unfulfillment of desire, upon *lack* rather than the myth of plenitude. Social justice in this regard would not name the ideal condition in which each of us is free to pursue our own private happiness, but the real condition in which we pursue what we can never have. This would mean freedom to pursue—and in that pursuit to be tormented by, and in that torment to realize—the singular desire at stake in every unconscious fantasy. To have done with masters and with all their false promises and pretensions. To have the freedom of perpetual dissatisfaction, to define and direct one's existence by the inexistence of the object that would complete it.

The right to *jouissance* would be a truly universal human right. Beyond all contingencies of citizenry or history, against the reduction of humanity to a base sameness that calls itself Nature, it designates the inadequacy of any collectivity, any language, any text, to account for, let alone master, the radical singularity of each of its constituent elements. As Rousseau has shown us, adherence to the illusion of the master or the ideal of mastery condemns the subject to a dull repetition according to which the future is determined in advance by its own origin.[56] With Sade, on the other hand, we imagine another kind of interminability: that which doesn't stop not being written, and therefore demands to be written and written again, not despite but because every effort at its inscription will miss its mark.

Far from positioning an antisocial selfishness at the heart of such a republic, the right to *jouissance* cannot be arrogated to the individual whom it dispossesses of her sovereign individuality; it is realized only through the action it inspires. This inevitably introduces the question of responsibility, which for the ethics of psychoanalysis involves responsibility both to the truth of one's desire and to the social link from which it is barred. It means taking responsibility for that desire and its effects, carving a channel for the trajectory of unconscious fantasy on the social scene. It means making a way there for what the order of the signifier has constitutively excluded. Sade's writing is perverse, but the ethics of his writing is not that of the pervert. Perversion needs and loves the law in order to savor its transgression.[57] A real revolution (in the Lacanian sense of the real: the impossible, the sexual relation, which does not exist and doesn't stop not being written) acts upon the social link through the order of the signifier that structures it; real revolution does not violate the law but subverts it, denying the inevitability and refusing the stability of its contingent configurations, exposing the law's arbitrary authority and arrogance, refusing and thereby transforming the terms of the speakable and the thinkable, going beyond what is possible. Such a revolution does not deny or destroy but literally changes the world.

For Sade, the work of revolution, the permanent insurrectionary act, is the work of literature. This, finally, is the only way we should take Sade *literally*—not because his preposterous and grotesque fiction of Eugénie's tutelage affords a sound blueprint for a truly liberatory education, but because to the end he was a man of letters. His writing signifies his effort to intervene within the social link, to twist and tangle the order of the signifier and to push, impossibly, beyond its limits. His language is revolting because it is language in revolt. The pitch to which it can climb does not testify to his monstrosity but rather to the cause for which he tortures his language and his characters, the motor behind the unremitting movement of his pen, and the object of the treatise he placed at the political heart of his absurd, obscene pedagogical program. After all the orgies, all the endless encomia to crime and harangues against religion and morality, all the education, the political lesson of Sade's unreadable, unruly, and always unfinished corpus is this: Have done with the master in all its forms, follow the trail of your fantasy beyond the comforts of what pleases you, take responsibility for the action of your own desire, and embrace your failure. Interminably.

The Object at the End of Education

Education, Henry Giroux reminds us, is never neutral. It is either reactionary or revolutionary, incarcerating or emancipatory, conservative or progressive. The question of the future of progressive education today is whether education ought to be oriented primarily by private right or public good. Is education a kind of personal property, or does it belong to the total society whose destiny stands or falls on the processes of subject-formation that constitute its citizenry?

From the beginning of modern pedagogical theory, from the eighteenth century to the present, these two incompatible values have been conflated. That is the trouble with liberalism: whatever its contrary pretenses, whatever its variances from neoliberalism, it casts private right as the supreme public good; it did not invent private property, but it did reinvent the concept of the social subject on its terms and under its conditions. The ever-widening private sphere, its consuming and cannibalizing its other (the citizen and the state), the mounting victories of neoliberalism over classical liberalism in the contest over education today—these are not anomalies or accidents. They are the consequence and logical outcome of an intellectual and pedagogical tradition driven from its inception by the ideological imperatives of individuality and individualism. This is progress.

Freud redefined progress in *Civilization and Its Discontents* as the advance of ever more diffuse and creative mechanisms of repression. This was already Sade's position, as well, but whereas Freud considered repression to be the price of entry into the social link, Sade wanted another sort of society. For him, true progress means unlearning the habits and razing the mental edifices of repression; it is marked, for instance, by Eugénie's self-congratulatory outburst as she executes her vengeance upon her mother for the crime of having birthed her: "What progress, my friends!" Such is also the logical conclusion of *Émile*, the full stakes of which Sade drew into the open by insisting upon the self-canceling, annihilatory truth at the end of Rousseau's rainbow.

But for Rousseau himself, this truth remains under the veil of repression, where it returns symptomatically as a self-serving authoritarianism that annexes his pupil as a pliable piece of private property from the cradle to the grave and back again, ensuring that movement's endless repetition. Because of this repression, Rousseau was welcomed into the narrative of progressive, rational civility that marches under the banner of the Enlightenment, modernity's master signifier. Only later would Rousseau's fiercest critics discover the symptom of this repression in order to insist that his pedagogy thereby betrays its own cause.[58] Failing to see beyond liberalism's horizon, operating still in the name of the Enlightenment, these critics do not notice that Rousseau's apparent authoritarianism is only his subjection to the even more despotic will of his master, Nature, with which his novelistic pedagogical program is designed to unite him. They do not notice that the subject of education is not the student but the teacher, and so they are offended that this teacher dictates the terms of the student's personal fulfillment the way a master wields his object, in opposition to what they assume is the student's intrinsic (inalienable) autonomy. From this perspective, Rousseau forecloses the libertarian ideal of *free choice*. Émile is radically unfree because Rousseau has deprived him of even the awareness that his destiny was his to choose.

The danger of such an ideal is clear enough: the freedom to choose one's destiny presupposes a freedom *from* the social order, which is precisely the existential freedom Rousseau's pedagogy sought to realize. Unlike the right to *jouissance*, it is the liberal ideal of the sovereign subject that most evinces the complete egoism and self-interest from which we have here retrieved Sade. Perversely, then, even sadistically, the liberal conception of equality (of opportunity)—as a natural, and thus universal and irresistible, basis from which the individual is obligated to distinguish himself in pursuit of whatever brings him pleasure—is antisocial. The doctrine of natural equality is predicated upon an imperative of inequality.[59]

This is not only because in the competition for profits and power there must be winners and losers, but also because the pursuit of happiness, the pursuit of property, is an ideal, which is to say it is a commandment that can never be satisfied. Apropos of *Civilization and Its Discontents*, Lacan explains the Enlightenment's liberal voraciousness or voracious liberalism in this way: "the form in which the moral agency is concretely inscribed in man—and that is nothing less than rational according to [Freud]—the form he called the superego, operates according to an economy such that the more one sacrifices to it, the more it demands."[60] Concretely, this means that the abstract ideal of a rational moral agency secures the right to *jouissance* and its bottomless dissatisfaction not in the subject but in the symbolic.

The late annexation of the subject of education by the super-egoic imperatives of private property, consumption, and accumulation is thus perfectly allegiant to the moral order for which it stands. From its roots, beyond the distinctions between liberal and neoliberal economic doctrines, this moral order operates as if subjectivity is an effect of private property, as if the subject could ever be realized in such a restricted economy. Theorists of progressive pedagogy rightly recognize the privatization of public education, the devaluation of true teaching in favor of disciplinary conditioning, the priority of profit over pedagogy, and the logic of efficiency over intellectual curiosity as neoliberal assaults on liberal values. But well before the advent of this new fundamentalism of consumer choice, education's status as a public good was already subordinated and determined by the private rights of the bourgeois individual, who as a condition of what Lacan calls their "moral agency" is commanded to conform ever more closely to the ideological parameters of individualism and, with them, the insidious tyranny of the pleasure principle. The present assault on education is the continuation of this tradition. In this regard, neoliberalism is not the enemy of liberalism, but its more perfect offspring.

Against the super-egoic imperative of individualistic accumulation, Lacan asserts, "There's absolutely no reason why we [analysts] should make ourselves the guarantors of the bourgeois dream. A little more rigor and firmness are required in our confrontation with the human condition."[61] What, then, is to be done?

In the first place, an education founded on the right to *jouissance* would not guarantee a universal right to succeed. Instead, it would ensure a *universal right to fail*, again and again, in pursuit of an object that is not ideal but *real*: the impossible, fantasmatic object of desire. This object is not something one consciously chooses, it cannot be fashioned or appropriated by any conscious will, and it is not free to be given or exchanged. It does not exist except in the singularity of the fantasy, beyond the parameters of the possible, beyond what is "realistically achievable," beyond any ideology built upon the promise of success or subjective satisfaction. If there is any choice at stake in the right to *jouissance*, it is only the ethical decision to refuse all partial, imaginary objects which would substitute for the impossible object of desire—an impossible choice, to be sure, since choosing the impossible assumes precisely one's unfreedom to choose.

Motored by the death drive, the subject who quests after such an object does so according to a general economy of expenditure, not a restricted economy of accumulation and reproduction. In this regard, it is not Eugénie or Dolmancé who we should take as our model, but Sade himself, whose writing to the end fell short of its mark. What remains of his quest—the Sadean text, Eugénie and Dolmancé and all his other heroes and victims—is a testament to his refusal to stop failing and to the exquisite torture of that refusal. To adopt such a model does not mean to be like Sade. Neither he nor anyone else should be our new master. Nor does it mean to repeat the truism or cliché that one best learns by failing. Failure here is not a means to the end of eventual success but the foundation of a radical pedagogical ethics, an ethics of the impossible.

Practically, to have done with masters, especially the sort that cloaks itself in the form of the liberal or neoliberal ideal, would mean to have done with the notion that a teacher's first responsibility is to manufacture good subjects, since there would be no illusory position of mastery to which the student is supposed to ascend. There would be no "good subjects" at all, no Émiles, since nobody would be awarded for the extent to which they identify with, internalize, and therefore reproduce authority. The task of the teacher would no longer be to issue "useful information," since this reduces the teacher, as Nature does for Rousseau, to a mere conduit for the transmission of a greater authority: the ideological authority which decides what information is useful and what is not, in advance of any inquiry and in its own interests. Instead, education could actualize real thinking, the kind of critical consciousness Said and Freire envisioned—the constant questioning, the will to learn without the promise of some material or moral reward, without subordinating knowledge to a collective conception of the good which conflates the public good with the service of goods. A teacher would be one who acts from the prop of their experience with regard to their own failures, and helps guide the student toward an ethical fidelity to failure and away from the fraudulent lure of success.

The end of such an education would be interminable in just the sense that Freud describes the end of psychoanalysis: the point at which one assumes responsibility for the unconscious and for the pursuit of its truth without any expectation of eventual mastery. The purpose of education would not be to inculcate the student with what Freud called the "ideal fiction" of normality. Education would no longer be the foremost Ideological State Apparatus whose function is to ensure the next generation's conformity to the existing order of things. The prison, the factory, and the sanitorium could no longer be the school's correlates and precedents, since the function of the school would be radically anti-disciplinary. It would be a site for the coalescence of subjects of desire, not an apparatus of social reproduction. In place of the vanishing point of success, the task of the student would be to embrace both the inevitability of failure and the ethical commitment to try and fail again, interminably.

Failure is anathema to our modern political, therapeutic, and moral sensibilities, and in this way it indexes the distance between the good subject of ideology and the remainder of the human whose very existence defies ideology's totalizing ambitions. These remainders, for ideology, are always "bad subjects." An education in the name of such subjects, founded on the right to *jouissance*, would still be responsible to the society in which it unfolds because, as Rousseau and Sade have taught us, the very fact that one's truth cannot be written is the reason it must be written. To be responsible for one's desire also means to take responsibility for it, to translate it into a common register, with the knowledge that no translation is ever adequate to its original, that inevitably something of that desire is lost in translation and that this loss is why the work of translation must be undertaken again.

This alternative notion of social responsibility finally demands that we reconceive *justice* in terms other than those of the liberal dream, which wishes that everyone may have a stake in the common good and falsely promises that everyone may be equally satisfied. Toppling private right and private property, the right to *jouissance* and the failure it authorizes would rebuild the idea of justice on a truly universal ground. It would entail a universal renunciation of the right to succeed, a universal equality of dissatisfaction.

This freedom of desire must presuppose a universal freedom from natural necessity, because the immediate imperatives of physical need draw the line at which the natural organism ends and the human, the being of desire, begins. Freedom from physical need is not freedom from want but the freedom to want: the freedom to live the specifically human torment of lack, each of us in our own curious way. The human—monstrous derangement of its nature, infinitely creative in the circuitous discourses it takes on its way beyond its conditions of possibility—is not a vessel of reproduction, not a mere object of ideology, but a creature of the drive: a subject of the unconscious. Real justice, a justice of the real, would be the right of every subject to follow the fantasy in the direction of an impossible future at which we will never arrive. A real future, without telos or repose—this would be the endless end of education.

Chapter 3

✦

The Novel—Broken Sex Machine

Tristram Shandy and the Writing of the Impossible

If you have read Laurence Sterne's *The Life and Opinions of Tristram Shandy, Gentleman,* you likely will agree that it is an impossible book. Endlessly digressive, meandering, discombobulated; pages left blank or blackened with ink, fraught with lacunae and hiatuses and typographical oddities; suffused with double- or triple-*entendres* that send the imagination spinning away toward the implied, the unsaid, the unspeakable, the indescribable and the indecent; self-censored and self-obsessed—it is a composition that decomposes, like its eponymous narrator's ailing, increasingly decrepit body, through the very process of its inscription. Every complication adds to the confusion it intends to clarify, running away with the life it is meant to express, hurrying Tristram toward the death his writing wants forever to forestall. Driven by death—as when in the novel's longest digression, its entire seventh volume, Death knocks on Tristram's door and literally chases him across Europe, their two chariots separated only by the speed his writing can maintain—his text is the trace of his desire to outrun his own finitude, to tell his whole story, lest the narrative remain incomplete when he arrives in his turn at Death's door. Which, of course, it is.

It could not be otherwise. No life story can fully be told until the death at which it terminates, and this is a limit the autobiographer cannot cross. So Tristram laments:

> —write as I will, and rush as I may into the middle of things, as *Horace* advises—I shall never overtake myself—whipp'd and driven to the last pinch, at the worst I shall have one day the start of my pen—and one day is enough for two volumes—and two volumes will be enough for one year.[1]

Too much of the past, too little of the future. If the presentation of a single day may occupy two volumes (in fact, the day of his birth spans almost four volumes), and if two volumes will take a year to compose, then Tristram will need at least 365 years to write just the first year of his life. If he could but transcend the limit dividing the time of writing from the infinity he desires, if he could traverse Death's divide and exist beyond time altogether, he would be free from the lamentable diachrony to which he is constrained and condemned. Whether anyone would care to read an autobiography in which only the writer's first year extends to 730 maddening volumes is not a question he bothers to consider.

It is true to the point of inanity, however, that it takes longer to write a thing than for the thing itself to transpire. Equally vacuous is the banal observation that a life story cannot fully be told until it is over. The real trouble with the author's finitude is that Tristram's story will remain incomplete, cannot possibly be completed, because it incompletes itself with every effort toward its completion. Giving an account of himself, Tristram discovers that his story is inseparable from the other stories, the peculiar lives and opinions, of the other characters who together constitute his world, his text—his whole existence, since he is only the text bearing his name, only these fragmented tissues of a reality stitched into a monstrous joke by a broken writing machine. And this accounting for others is compounded by all the other figures whose stories in turn constitute each of his characters' worlds because they, too, are the singular composites of the stories comprising the other characters in their worlds, and on and on; it's stories all the way down.

Tristram's authorship, his text, his body, his being, are therefore a strange sort of autobiography: an *allo*biography (from the Greek *allo*-, "other," "different," or "strange"), a writing of the self through the writing of the other. Writing himself allobiographically, every exercise of his authorial sovereignty is its own subversion. So, even if he could surmount the limit that is Death's divide and continue writing from beyond the grave, his narrative, the synonym of his being, would forever remain unfinished because, bound to this indefinite multiplicity of other narratives, it is not and never could be his own. And yet, it cannot be anyone else's, either.

This self-making and self-subverting, de/composing otherness is more than a fact of the novel's plot; it is fundamental to the text *as* text, in the paradigmatic otherness of the sign. Chasing after his story, Tristram's writing is constantly running away with the meaning it is supposed to secure, distorting it, perverting it according to the incalculable proclivities, the strangeness, the very otherness of the other. Against this insecurity of meaning, he develops ever more elaborate security measures out of the same material—the materiality of the sign—at the root of his troubles, as if with yet another effort, a little more ink, the other could be pinned down, determined finally and for all time, rendered obedient to and by the order of the signifier. Every apparent digression thus is a redoubling of Tristram's effort to maintain this order and to ensure the transmission of a definite sense, as he insists, "by way of commentary, scholium, illustration, and key to such passages, incidents or innuendos as shall be thought to be either of private interpretation, or of dark and doubtful meaning" (27). But all these attempts to reduce the signifier's errancy only multiply it. Every frantic stroke of the pen, every effort to define the indefinite other, every exercise of authorial potency, amplifies the author's impotence.

That does not stop him from trying. In fact, this constitutive impossibility of ever getting to the point, of telling his story completely, is just what sustains him. He enjoys the frustration, revels in it, because it is the condition of his being, because he is nothing without the tension between his urge to sense and the unruly incursions of what, in the framework of that urgency, can only appear as nonsense. He is that tension, that special sort of agony we recognize as *sexual frustration.*

Following our reading of Sade and Rousseau, and alongside Lacan's return to the death drive after Freud, sexual frustration names the *jouissance* that pushes the subject beyond the pleasure principle. It is the motor of unconscious fantasy, the painful enjoyment that sustains the subject's dissatisfaction with its reality, which in Tristram's case is a dissatisfaction with his writing. "I shall never overtake myself," he complains. I shall never be satisfied with my self-inscription because it is only a relic of what I want but failed to say. In the words of that later exemplar of masculine deflation and decrepitude, T. S. Eliot's Prufrock, "It is impossible to say just what I mean!"[2] But sexual frustration is not merely cause for complaint. Inasmuch as it sustains the narrative, it is also the enjoyment of the impossible, enjoyment of the impossibility to be satisfied within the parameters of the fantasy which, more than mere organic death, give the true circumference of the subject's finitude. Sexual frustration is the lubricity in Tristram's failed and flailing lucubrations, his delight in those untimely interruptions that at once compose and decompose his narrative body, the sentimental sociality and affection that emerge from the signifier's wandering.

This novelistic expression of sexual frustration shows us how *jouissance* is divided. This division is what Lacan calls sexual difference, by which he designates the two modalities of the subject to the extent that the subject signifies—which it does, or else it does not exist. To make sense, to arrest the sign's meandering, manifests the masculine ambition to represent the truth without remainder: to dictate the desire of the other and to be unrestrained by it, to gain possession of the impossible object of the fantasy, to remediate the subject's constitutive alienation from that object, to exceed the limit imposed by the phallic function, to be above the law of universal (symbolic) castration, to be sovereign, master of one's significations and therefore the master signifier. The other modality is no less subject to the phallic function, but nor is it the remainder of the masculine, as though it were some secondary aftereffect. The feminine, rather, is there in the sign's wandering, which in itself is an insurrection against the order into which the signifier who would be master has enlisted it. Its refusal to be mastered is not so much a protest, which still would mean a complementary opposition and determination, as it is an indifference to the signifier's pretended authority; in evading and confounding that authority, the feminine is the indetermination that subverts and disorders the order of the signifier from within and with its own terms. In this way, it is what excites the masculine's impotent fulminations against its own impotence—and this is all the term "masculine" really designates.

Because the subject does not exist except to the extent that it signifies, this irreconcilable difference between the masculine and the feminine, this difference without symmetry or complementarity, is inherent to every subject, and not only the subject called Tristram or the subject of literature he represents. It is the root of the subject's existential dilemma: to strive for one's being, to complete oneself, is at the same time to incomplete oneself. To exist is to commit to one's inexistence.

Throughout this chapter we will find that *Tristram Shandy* more than thematizes this ontological dilemma. The novel is positively structured by it. Freud transformed sex from a particular idea or activity into the energy and action of the unconscious, the specifically human dimension of our being. Lacan distilled it into a series of logical formulas, redeeming sex from its misapprehension as either a metaphysical essence or (much the same thing) a biological category. Well prior to the Freudian discovery or its Lacanian iteration, Sterne formalized sex from another angle, that of literary form. Thus, far from overlaying an extrinsic complication upon a text which is already sufficiently complicated, Sterne's novel invites a psychoanalytic sensitivity especially to the problematics of sexual difference because psychoanalysis is organized by, founded upon, and therefore might learn something from *Tristram Shandy*'s core concern: the creative and subversive potential of the frustrating, sexual (non-)relation between signification and the subject. This is the impossible condition of the subject's existence, which therefore, in its impossibility, doesn't stop not being written. Tracking this action of the impossible throughout Sterne's text, we will find that *Tristram Shandy* is an impossible book because it stages the impossibility of the sexual relation.[3]

To arrive at this conclusion and develop its broader implications for the work and the subject of literature, we have to meet the novel on its own terms, first considering how it reflects, complicates, contorts and subverts its historical-aesthetic context with the same systems and paradigms that most characterize that context. We will examine how the spring of this subversion is an incurable tension between two mutually constitutive but incompatible modes of signification: one, compelled by masculine *jouissance*; and the other, by what Lacan calls the "other *jouissance*" that sustains the signifier's errancy or promiscuity. This will prepare us to venture a construction, after a Freudian fashion, of the text's primal scene. Constructing, narrating the sexual relation that is the text's impossible condition of possibility will draw into relief that other narrative, here the narrative of the desire of the Other, around which Sterne's writing swirls—the fantasy that orients and compels it. With this experiment, we hope to further concretize our foundational analogy between the subject of literature and the subject of the unconscious, illustrating and punctuating this analogy's critical potential. By situating this formalization of the fantasy alongside the formalist assertion that, for all its oddness, *Tristram Shandy* is "the most typical novel in world literature," I will suggest that the subject of literature per se, and not only here, is a sexed subject, riven and driven by sexual difference and the frustration it engenders.[4]

Beauty and the Broken Machine

The provocative assertion that *Tristram Shandy* is "the most typical novel in world literature" belongs to Viktor Shklovsky, who famously argued that what distinguishes artistic narrative from other forms of writing is its way of disrupting the "automatic" association between the prosaic and the practical (in our Jakobsonian frame, this automization is an effect of the referential linguistic function). An artist's various devices render laborious the otherwise efficient "economy of effort" through which objects are perceived. By acting on perception rather than the object thus perceived, by drawing out or manipulating the mechanics of perception, art retains the object's familiarity while yet making it strange to us. The truth of art, in other words, is not in the "enstranged" object, but in the reader's experience of the enstrangement: "*Art is a means of experiencing the process of creativity,*" Shklovsky explains. "*The artifact itself is quite unimportant.*"[5] Positioning *Tristram Shandy* as the most typical novel in world literature therefore implies that this book, more than any other literary work, presents a *typology* of the creative process, a "laying bare the device" of novelistic composition, so that what Sterne's text represents is creativity itself; it is a means of experiencing the creative process of the novel form.[6]

To experience this process with *Tristram Shandy* (and please believe, to write about it) is indeed strange and laborious, so much so that readers after Shklovsky have abandoned his assertion of the novel's typological typicality in favor of its confounding incongruity. Exemplary in this regard is E. M. Forster's assertion: "Obviously a god is hidden in *Tristram Shandy*, [and] his name is Muddle."[7] A. Alvarez takes this in a more pejorative direction, implicitly taking aim at Shklovsky's use of this novel as the basis for his enduring distinction between storyline and plot: "Sterne seems not much interested in stories," Alvarez writes. "Occasionally, he digresses into narrative, but mostly he simply digresses, as yet another fascinating and seemingly urgent side-issue crosses his mind. And these digressions, like his two novels themselves, are substantially without plots. The whole rickety substance is supported and validated simply by the flow of talk, talk, talk. It reads like a picaresque novel transformed into abstract art."[8] This position is echoed even in more generous readings which see in the novel's endless digressions a kind of verisimilitude or early naturalism, its rhapsodic tone mimicking and celebrating the flow of conversation—the cacophonous talk, talk, talk—that comprises quotidian, intersubjective reality.[9]

While these readings draw out a number of important aspects of the novel, they unfold from the mistaken premise that there is no pattern or order or regularity, no coherent structure, to the text (or, for that matter, to everyday conversation—an assumption we have learned to question at least since Freud's *Psychopathology of Everyday Life*). Taking Shklovsky's provocation seriously, however, and disentangling the novel's storyline reveals that it does have a plot and that this plot is only apparently haphazard. Far from random, it is structured according to *seven constitutive events*, each one thematizing some generative, emasculating trauma, some literal loss of phallic authority. With more than a little effort, but without any interpolation or conjecture, nearly every seemingly random narrative thread, every conversation, conflict, digression, or embellishment, no matter how varied or extensive, can be traced to one of these traumatic origins.

When unwoven from the plot, straightened out, and spread across the rectilinear, calendrical order of the storyline, these events and their dates are:

1. Tristram's uncle Toby suffering a wound to his groin while fighting at the siege of Namur (1695).
2. Toby's footman Trim revealing that their neighbor, widow Wadman, has been lofting a cannonade of interest after Toby's wound not because she cares to mount his hobby-horse (his obsession with the minutiae of military sieges) and ride it with him, but because her own hobby-horse is the question of Toby's sexual viability, from which revelation Toby recoils and retreats (1713).
3. Tristram's not-so-immaculate conception in the novel's opening pages, wherein his father Walter (Toby's brother), punctiliously performing his conjugal duties, is interrupted in medias res by an impertinent question from Tristram's mother Elizabeth, scattering the animal spirits in confusion and disheveling the poor Tristram-homunculus on its way to incubation (March 1718).
4. The country doctor, Doctor Slop, crushing Tristram's nose with his shiny new forceps during his birth (November 1718).
5. Tristram's botched christening, moments after his birth, when the maid Susannah fails to deliver Walter's chosen name, *Trismegistus*, and instead imprints the infant indelibly with the name his father happens most to despise.
6. The sudden death of Tristram's older brother, Bobby (late 1718).
7. Tristram's accidental circumcision by a faulty window sash (1723 or 1724).

If the text seems, in Alvarez's terms, to be "rickety" and "abstract," this is not because it is adventitious, but because it is scaffolded by a series of losses.

Every new morsel of the plot, however seemingly disconnected or arbitrary, is another moment in the continuous effort to fill the abyss of meaning each of these losses opens in the narrative, as if a bit more writing could return the text to a stable ground which, as the principle of allobiography shows, never existed in the first place. The narrative weaves and unweaves itself around these instances of material or symbolic castration, attempting to contain or cover over the crises they precipitate, bringing the threads together only to unravel them and start again, like Penelope at her loom.

As these constitutive events are all variations on this same theme, the text's wild variety spins around a subtending unity. In this way, it operates and complicates one of the most influential aesthetic theories of Sterne's time, to which Tristram himself frequently refers: William Hogarth's *The Analysis of Beauty* (1753).[10] Published six years prior to the novel's first two volumes, Hogarth's treatise was a response to contemporary aesthetic doctrines which held that beauty ought to be derived from Platonic ideals of order, harmony, and proportion (ideals to which critics like Forster and Alvarez, at least in their treatment of *Tristram Shandy*, still seem curiously attached). Formulating what Ronald Paulson calls an "anti-aesthetics, or a practical aesthetics," as opposed to the prevailing "theoretically pure aesthetics," Hogarth insisted that order may be beautiful only if it includes a proper measure of disorder, and that "the art of composing well is the art of varying well."[11] From this practical perspective, aesthetic pleasure emerges from the interplay between formal perfection and those subtle imperfections that saturate lived reality, since otherwise art becomes static, loses its hold on life, and deprives beauty of its energy and its power of attraction.

To summarize one of Hogarth's favorite examples: the portrait of a beautiful face is rendered all the more pleasant if a stray ringlet is drawn dangling along one side of the forehead or a dimple is sketched on one of the cheeks. Such apparent imperfection highlights and therefore augments the symmetry and regularity of the figure against which it is set. These pleasing blemishes, moreover, must contain an internal variety of their own: the lock of hair will be curled, the dimple will be shaded to suggest its curvature and dimension.

This example and the formula for perfect imperfection it exemplifies point to what Hogarth held was his true contribution to the emergent field of aesthetic theory: the "discovery," as he calls it, that the root of all aesthetic pleasure lies in the artist's skilled use of precise, though not always straight, lines. While straight lines, Hogarth explains, "vary only in length, and are therefore least ornamental,"

> the serpentine line, by its waving and winding at the same time different ways, leads the eye in a pleasing manner along the continuity of its variety, if I may be allowed the expression; and which by its twisting so many different ways, may be said to enclose (tho' but a single

line) varied contents; and therefore all its variety cannot be express'd
on paper by one continued line, without the assistance of the imagination, or the help of a figure; see where that sort of proportion'd
winding line, which will hereafter be call'd the precise serpentine line,
or *line of grace*, is represented by a fine wire, properly twisted round
the elegant and varied figure of a cone.[12]

The image to which Hogarth refers here and throughout his *Analysis* deserves
some attention, since it is a worthy visualization of the narrative structure of
Tristram Shandy (see figure).

From the illustration folio in William Hogarth's *The Analysis of Beauty:
Written with a View to Fixing the Fluctuating Ideas of Taste* (London:
J. Reeves, 1753). Avery Classics Collection at the Avery Architectural
and Fine Arts Library, Columbia University. Photograph courtesy of
the author.

This drawing demonstrates Hogarth's eight aesthetic principles—
including what he calls *fitness*, the preliminary criterion to which an object
must adhere before it can be considered aesthetically. The cone exhibits a
uniformity of design, a *symmetry* of composition, and a geometric *regularity*. Its size relative to the serpentine line traversing it reflects Hogarth's
concern for *quantity*, or the measured proportionality of multiple objects
in a single composition. The effect of the winding line is to contribute a
serene *variety* to the overall *simplicity* of the sketch, as does the shading that
sets the cone in three dimensions. Finally, and most importantly for both
Hogarth's aesthetics and Sterne's novel, the image reflects formal *intricacy*
in that the line twice disappears from view, thereby surrendering it to the
play of the imagination. "Intricacy in form," Hogarth elaborates, is "that
peculiarity in the lines, which compose it, that *leads the eye a wanton kind
of chace*, and from the pleasure that gives the mind, intitles it to the name of
beautiful: and it may be justly said, that the cause of the idea of grace more
immediately resides in this principle, than in the other five, except variety;
which indeed includes this, and all the others."[13] Unity in variety, variety in
unity, and the imagination's playful, pleasant response: these are the core
principles of Hogarth's aesthetic, the practical and theoretical foundations of
the beautiful.

Sterne's first reference to the *Analysis* is both descriptive and performative. Reacting to one of his characteristic textual lacunae—an indefinite **** which censors a remark from Toby about Tristram's mother Elizabeth Shandy's sex organs—Tristram exclaims:

> Just heaven! how does the *Poco piu* and the *Poco meno* of the *Italian* artists;—the insensible, MORE or LESS, determine the precise line of beauty in the sentence, as well as in the statue! How do the slight touches of the chisel, the pencil, the pen, the fiddle-stick, *et caetera*,—give the true swell, which gives the true pleasure!—O my countrymen!—be nice;—be cautious of your language;——and never, O! never let it be forgotten upon what small particles your eloquence and your fame depend. (77–78)

Condensed here is the entirety of Hogarth's "fine wire, properly twisted round the elegant and varied figure of a cone," extracted from the realm of the visible and rendered linguistically. There is, first of all, an intricacy in the absence, the ****, which cannot but send the reader's imagination wandering after just what it was Toby may have said, even if, as Tristram suggests, he in fact said nothing at all, having been interrupted by the "sudden snapping of my father's tobacco-pipe" (77)—which obviously solicits its own salacious associations. As a brief digression on the shape of Toby's sentence (in addition to the explicit reference to Hogarth's line of beauty, its treatment of Italian sculpture parrots a similar passage from the *Analysis*), it also introduces variety into the novel's linear action, which in this moment concerns a conversation between Toby and Walter on the value of midwifery relative to modern, because more expensive, medicine. Tristram's serpentine interruption also sustains a sense of unity, as his sexual innuendoes pertain to the lacuna in question; and behind all this, there remains the unfolding of the single occurrence, Tristram's protracted birth, which occupies most of the novel's whole first half. And because Tristram enriches the reader's appreciation of a single sentence without thereby overwhelming the principal action, the brevity of this digression reflects Hogarth's concern for quantitative moderation. Consistent with the *Analysis*, then, the polyphony of Sterne's prose embellishes the overall form, much as a series of trills ornaments the performance of a piece of music, or a stray strand of hair augments the beauty of a painted portrait.

We can thus see why Shklovsky was right to find in *Tristram Shandy* the quintessential work of art as narrative—but not, in his strictly formalist fashion, by neglecting the novel's historical specificity or overlooking its tendency toward cacophony in favor of the ways it lays bare the devices of artistic composition. Situating the text within its cultural and aesthetic context, we can better see how Sterne's artistic devices, which also make the stuff of the narrative, were exercises of a practical aesthetics that corroborates the book's mimetic engagement with the conversational texture of everyday life, framing this mimesis, constraining it, within definite compositional principles. For all its apparent discombobulation, the novel is a work of beauty.

But Sterne did not merely apply aesthetics to literature. Hogarth and the other major eighteenth-century aesthetic theorists (earlier, Joseph Addison; later, Edmund Burke) wanted to establish the objective criteria of the beautiful (or the sublime) upon principles derived from a basically Lockean, empiricist conception of Nature.[14] This modern idea of beauty was deduced from the view that a natural object's fitness (its purposiveness) perfectly harmonizes with its ornamentality, so that artificial beauty ought to be modeled after the empirical, objective, delimitation of this perfect natural unity of form and function. The task of art was to play the imagination in tune with nature in order to reproduce and amplify nature's intrinsic harmony. Sterne reveals, however, that the work of literature fatally undermines these empiricist presuppositions. Literature—that most human of inventions—is crafted from language and therefore has no place in Nature. Harmony is impossible. Confronted with the pleasures of the text, empiricist aesthetics cannot account for this discord language introduces between Nature and human being and in which Sterne discovered so much delight. By working with Hogarth and Locke, according to their own procedures and concepts, Sterne works through them to confront empiricism with its own internal limit: the unruliness of the signifier, to which the empiricists, too, were subjected. Crafting beauty out of dysfunction, compounding rather than mitigating the signifier's inherently disorderly conduct, Sterne subverts (twists, contorts, or topples) Hogarth's principles by staying true to them, subverts them with their own truth.

To see how Sterne pulls this off, we first should recall from Rousseau and Sade that language is decidedly de-naturalizing, such that a linguistic being, a human being, is constitutively a monstrous deformation of its own nature. Hogarth similarly implies the human's constitutive exile from nature's indisputable perfection, distinguishing "the living machines of nature, in respect of fitness" from "such poor ones, in comparison with them, as men are only capable of making." His point is to emphasize artistic constraint against any ornamentality that might impede a machine's proper functioning—in this example, a clock "for the keeping of true time at sea."[15] For Sterne, however, the work of literature is a machine whose proper function and purpose is to reify the human's impropriety, to amplify its disharmony with respect to the natural perfection, the self-contained totality, from which the human springs and to which it will return once the writing is done.

Still following Hogarth, the mechanism of this reification—in Shklovsky's paradigm, the artistic device, attention to which disrupts the otherwise automatic operations of perception—is a recurring metaphor by which Tristram presents his book as, precisely, a clockwork machine.[16] The metaphor initially appears in an early apology for his first volume's professed disorderliness:

—This is vile work.—For which reason, from the beginning of this, you see, I have constructed the main work and the adventitious parts of it with such intersections, and have so complicated and involved the digressive and progressive movements, one wheel within another, that the whole machine, in general, has been kept a-going. (54)

Like the inner workings of a clock, the book moves in two directions at once: "In a word," Tristram continues, "my work is digressive, and it is progressive too,—and at the same time" (54). This horological metaphor is recalled and repeated several hundred pages later, in the first paragraph of volume seven—which you will remember is the account of Tristram's Death drive across Europe. Lamenting the "vile cough" which constantly interrupts his work, he reminds us that his writing machine "should be kept a going . . . forty years, if it pleased but the fountain of life to bless me so long" (383).

Now, at the beginning of this chapter I called this seventh volume the novel's longest digression. This was because of its heterogeneity relative to the rest of the narrative. Yet the volume's epigraph tells another story: it quotes Pliny the Younger, "*Non enim excursus hic ejus, sed opus ipsum est,*" "This is not a digression from it, but the work itself" (381).[17] If this is so, then we are forced to conclude that my initial remarks had it upside-down. In fact, the novel's longest digression is the whole rest of the novel, the entire allobiography, which at once comprises and resists the narrative's progressive movement. "The work itself" is a progress of digression.

Nowhere is this more apparent than here in volume seven, which concerns Tristram's favorite theme, the existential antagonism between sex and death. As it begins, Tristram has been telling his occasional interlocutor Eugenius a "most tawdry" tale about a nun and a monk when Death comes knocking. Tristram would send this untimely visitor away in "a tone of careless indifference," but Death, ever the bureaucrat, protests, "'There must certainly be some mistake in this matter.'" Tristram responds like an actor breaking the fourth wall, addressing his readers, making us subjects and participants in the scene: "Now there is nothing in this world I abominate worse," he tells us, "than to be interrupted in a story" (383–84). Death is cast as the Great Interrupter who threatens to stop the winding, multifarious movement of signifiers—here, literally a story about sex—by bringing the work to its fatal conclusion, closing the curtain on the spectacle in which Tristram implicates both himself and his audience, all of us together watching and watching ourselves being watched. His ensuing effort to outrun Death by writing his way across the continent thus is not a digression but the novel's core ambition: to finish his most tawdry tale, to resist the ultimately irresistible end of the time of writing, to delay the final tick of the clock after which the writing machine will grind to a halt.[18]

The writing machine thus is a processor of signifiers that works only by forestalling the completion of the very operation for which it was designed. This presents a radical challenge to Hogarth's practical aesthetics: whereas

The Analysis of Beauty wants art to mimic or amplify natural perfection, wants art to take its cues from and work in service to Nature and natural purposiveness, *Tristram Shandy* insists that the work of literature works only insofar as it doesn't work, at least not in service to a predetermined end. Working against its own purposes, against the whole notion of natural purposiveness, the novel mal/functions, or unworks. To cure itself of its monstrosity and close the disconnect with Nature, as was Rousseau's ambition, the writing machine would no longer be a human machine; it would be as perfect as any natural machine, and therefore not a work of art. Instead of a clock, it would be the indifferent mechanics and absolute regularity of the Earth's movement through the cosmos and the Sun across the sky.

So, while Hogarth's conception of aesthetic pleasure demands that the artist minimize the finally unbridgeable distance between Nature and its representation, with Sterne the opposite is true. The pleasure of the text is in its malfunctioning, its discordance and irregularity. It is there where the wheels fall off—where, like an ill-timed engine, there is a misfire of the signifier, as in the opening *coitus interruptus* through which Tristram is (impossibly) conceived and his writing machine set a-going. Pleasure is the indefinite meandering of the signifier that deranges the subject, inscribing a new, infinitely variable path for its becoming within the finite time of writing. To quiet the disharmony the writing machine introduces between the (human) imperfection it motors and the (natural) perfection it offends would mean to stop its mal/functioning altogether. Like the humanity it wants to represent, Tristram's text—his body, his life—only works insofar as it is broken: malformed, imperfect, denatured. *Hoc est opus ipsum.*

Shklovsky is right: this is the most typical novel in world literature. It brings the creative process into the field of literary representation, lays bare the device, not only thematically but because Tristram *is* the device, the errant and unruly signifier in whose name the creative process unfolds, indefinitely and interminably. Tristram is a signifier, a writing machine; and what he signifies, what as a writing machine he processes and produces, is simultaneously a desire for being and an impossibility of being, an impossibility that enjoins this very desire. The result of this frustration, this generative friction through which the subject of the text becomes but never arrives, is the work of literature. That is why this friction has the structure of a fiction.

Enjoying the Impossible

To deliver the monstrosity that is being human, to drag it out of the agony and anxiety of its constitutive alienation and into the comedy of the everyday, Sterne assembles a writing machine that works through empiricist aesthetics in order to break with the empirical, with natural purposiveness, and with the determinate meaning they imply. In their place he institutes *a novelistic aesthetics of the drive*. For the drive, like the text, goes and goes, on and on, around and around. The circuit of its repetition is its mode of satisfaction.

Such a machine could well stand as a practical representation (in Hogarth's sense) of the death drive, as well as the drive's inseparability from sex. In the previous chapters, we established that the human is not above and beyond nature, that such an assumption introduces a false metaphysics, a metahistory and metalanguage in which we recognize the psychosis of reason after *Robinson Crusoe*. With Rousseau and Sade, we further found that nature, too, is a signifier, that nature is not above or beyond the human. There is no "human nature" because nature is not an essence or undifferentiated sameness that precedes, subtends, and directs the human, but is only retroactively conceived as such from the other side of our exile in language. The inverse of this exile, the properly human kernel of our being, the subject, is that mode of being for which the energies of the drive are diverted from their organic aims (that is, from instinct or natural determination) and into the inorganic yet still immanent field of unconscious fantasy. It is this diversion and derangement brought about by the cut of the signifier, and not any urge to biological reproduction or pleasurable discharge of excitation, that psychoanalysis calls sex. Sex is not essentially purposive; it is polymorphously perverse; it is what denatures the human and thereby delineates its humanity. Thus diverted in directions that serve no organically useful purpose, that can find no outlet for the release of the tension sustaining the movement of the drive, sex is compelled by *jouissance* and not pleasure. Sex is unnatural, monstrous, ridiculous. It is about repetition, not reproduction. And because it squanders the organism's energies especially of reproduction and deploys these energies otherwise, in service to fantasy, beyond any possible appeasement, sex is the death drive in action—not a resistance to death, not the opposite of it, but the manifestation in life of the death we are always already living.

So the drive is a kind of machine that works, like *Tristram Shandy*, by unworking—supplanting the functional logic of the organism with the mal/functioning logic of fantasy. The drive is a broken sex machine. Its operations can take the subject far from what any cultural script conditions us to recognize as sex; but the core of the Freudian discovery is that in all such wanderings it is still sex that is at stake. In the return of the repressed (the symptom) or the sublimation of the drive (its aesthetics), sex is not so much translated as transposed, not transformed but displaced in ever more novel forms.[19]

Here as elsewhere, exercising our analogy between the subject of literature and the subject of the unconscious is not an anachronistic imposition. The language of psychoanalysis is a means to clarify, through a literary-critical refraction, what is already there in the text: the enjoyment of the impossible. The impossible, even ridiculous fulfillment Tristram is after is *to say it all* as if he could exist without being subjected to the conditions of his existence, which would mean to control his language, to exempt himself from the violence of the signifier, to be the one who is not castrated. He never can accede to such a status; his very origin is those seven constitutive castrations that set the writing machine in motion. The quest to say it all is his cause and his torment. But the frame of this quest, the mechanics of the text, is the circuit of the drive: an enjoyment without fulfillment, an enjoyment not in capturing the impossible and putting a stop to the writing machine once and for all, but in circling around and around it. An enjoyment *of* the impossible, as the impossible, in its impossibility—that is what it means to enjoy what wounds you.

This is not a metaphysical or otherwise transcendental hypothesis. We will see in the following sections that it is a fact of Sterne's aesthetics. The impossible is unwritten, but it is not without its writing. It is inscribed in the text, within the finite time of writing, in the modalities of the signifier and its modes of torturous enjoyment, in the inscriptions that circle around and around it.

How, then, does the broken machine work? What are the mechanics of its generation, the component gears of its digressive progress? What is the logic of its organization, the unwritten truth of its writing, the framework of its becoming? What is the fantasy structure of the text?

These questions require attention to the consequences of those seven quilting points in the storyline, those seven castrations, from which the narrative unfolds. These consequences are the novel's plot—the text's obsessive, flailing, failed effort to recuperate the loss of masculine authority those constituting castrations signify, to close the gap between the subject and its impossible object, to realize the sexual relation. The plot is accomplished primarily by two narrative devices, which I present here as the two halves of the broken writing machine. The first device, operating the phallic function, we may designate *digressive enhancement*, emphasizing the masculine logic, the urgency and impotence, the posturing and deflation, of its desire to arrest the errancy of the signifier within the prison-house of sense. The second device is not senselessness; it is not symmetrical with or reciprocally related to its phallic other, yet nor is it separable from it. It is there in that non-sense, the other side of sense which is the province of a rambling *jouissance*, in that meandering and unruly, incalculable otherness which lends the signifier its promiscuity, its contrary libidinal adventurousness, and its unwillingness to wait on its enjoyment until the masculine gets to the point (which, of course, it never can); this is the half of the writing machine we will call *untimely interruption*.

Nose is a nose is a nose is a nose: Digressive Enhancement

Digressive enhancement names all the addenda, appendixes, and admonishments against our indecent imaginations with which Tristram constantly interrupts his narrative itinerary, trying to contextualize and clarify his and his other characters' idiosyncrasies, artificially inflating the power of the signifier while, in so doing, multiplying the play of possible meanings he wants to arrest.

The best example of digressive enhancement is the novel's preoccupation with noses, which Melvyn New calls "perhaps Sterne's most extended analysis of the noise and dangers of endless commentary" (and New would know, having contributed more than anyone to the analysis of endless commentary in Sterne's works).[20] The digression recurs by fits and starts, beginning when Tristram interrupts his narrative with a bit of family history to account for the origin of his nasophilia. He relates that while arguing over her marriage contract, his great-grandmother had insisted that she be paid a yearly jointure, in perpetuity, of 300 pounds, a demand his great-grandfather found unreasonable, given the modest fortune she would bring to the family. Why did she make this demand?

> ——"Because," replied my great grandmother, "you have little or no nose, Sir."——
> S'death! cried my great grandfather, clapping his hand upon his nose,—'tis not so small as that comes to;—'tis a full inch longer than my father's.——Now, my great grandfather's nose was for all the world like unto the noses of all the men, women, and children, whom *Pantagruel* found dwelling upon the island of ENNASIN.——By the way, if you would know the strange way of getting a-kin amongst so flat-nosed a people,——you must read the book;—find it out yourself, you never can.——
> ——'Twas shaped, Sir, like an ace of clubs. (170)

Tristram continues to relate that, since his great-grandmother has outlived both her husband and her son, the rights of inheritance have delivered this pecuniary obligation—this costly reminder of the patriarch's failure to measure up to his wife's expectations—to the family heir, his father Walter, for whom it has become an obsession:

> For three generations at least, this *tenet* in favour of long noses had gradually been taking root in our family.——TRADITION was all along on its side, and INTEREST was every half year stepping in to strengthen it; so that the whimsicality of my father's brain was far from having the whole honour of this, as it had of almost all his other strange notions.—For in a great measure he might be said to have suck'd this in, with his mother's milk. He did his part however.——If education planted the mistake, (in case it was one) my father watered it, and ripened it to perfection. (171)

This is by no means the end of the digressive enhancement. For we will know nothing beyond the root of Walter's obsession, nor will we understand its inheritance in Tristram, until we are introduced to the ripened fruits of Walter's labor, the opinions he has formed on the subject. And as with any academic intervention, no true notion of the extent or originality of those opinions is possible unless we are familiar with the sources, the whole citational apparatus, from which they have been derived and distinguished, including Erasmus's "De captandis sacerdotiis," Joachim Scroderus's *Disputatio de musculis in genere et horum motionibus*, Guillaume Bouchet's *Serées*, and, most importantly, the fictional Hafel Slawkenbergius's treatise *De nasis*.[21] We thereby are charged with reading these obscure, perhaps forgotten, sometimes nonexistent works, along with Rabelais's ribald depiction of the imagined island of Ennasin—all while keeping in mind Tristram's admonishment against our indecent imaginations, "For by the word *Nose*, throughout all this long chapter of noses, and in every other part of my work, where the word *Nose* occurs,—I declare, by that word I mean a Nose, and nothing more, or less" (170). This digression will take us through the final eleven chapters of volume three and into volume four, drawing to a provisional conclusion with the ninth tale from Slawkenbergius's tenth decad. The latter tale, an excerpt from a work that otherwise does not exist, appears prior to the first chapter of the fourth volume (and is significantly longer than *any* proper chapter, across the full nine volumes of the novel). The excerpt includes nothing of the story thus far developed, only a fable suggesting the size of a man's nose is the measure of his reputation.

This interplay of clarification and obfuscation, here rendered both through allobiography and as a parody of paratextuality, confirms the semiotic axiom first formulated by Saussure that signification unfolds differentially and diachronically. Like the sign "Tristram" that puts it in motion, "nose" takes on meaning only negatively, in relation to the rest of the signifying matrix comprising Tristram's world; to declare emphatically that "nose" only means "nose" is just as emphatically to recall the logical inseparability of the sign from all the other signs which it is not, opening rather than closing it to unseemly associations. And because he is trapped within the time of writing, condemned to the diachronic unfolding of the text, Tristram's meaning can never be fixed. The signifier cannot run ahead of itself to account for and defend itself against every other sign with which it may become (or logically, always already is) associated. Attempting to do so actualizes the possibility that despite—in fact, because of—Tristram's protestations, sometimes a nose is *not* just a nose, and may not be a nose at all, even or especially if everything following from it pertains to noses and nothing else.

To be otherwise, to exceed the time of writing and escape the differential-diachronic play of signs, to pin this play of the indefinite to a definite meaning, signification would not be a dynamic process. It would be a status and a stasis: a synchrony in which every possible movement of every signifier would be present all at once. The output of Tristram's writing machine would not be a text but a senseless opacity, like the black page marking the death of his beloved Parson Yorick, containing in the saturation of ink "the many opinions, transactions, and truths which still lie mystically hid under [its] dark veil" (176). "Nose," like Hogarth's serpentine line, like Tristram's drive across Europe, like the whole work itself, sends the reader along a wanton kind of chase, opening ever more errant avenues of sense lest it arrive at a terminal meaning that can only be represented by the fatal inscrutability of the black page. The signifier either chases after meaning or is buried by it.

This particular signifier's momentum, moreover, like so many others throughout *Tristram Shandy*—like Tristram himself, conceived impossibly after his father's premature withdrawal from his conjugal responsibilities—is generated by a woman's dissatisfaction. Walter's obsession, and his son Tristram's, marks (and therefore remarks) the inheritance of that dissatisfaction, as well as its cheeky connotations. Walter and then Tristram's ever-growing list of citations is an effort to compensate for the patriarch's lack, as if they could secure his authority against the nose's inadequacy by amassing knowledge about it. The trouble is, the longer this mass of knowledge grows, the more supplements with which it is treated, the more inadequate the signification of the nose becomes. All this exercising augments the insecurity it is supposed to treat, proving itself impotent against the inexpiable obligation the woman's dissatisfaction sustains. The novel is an exercise of nasological (viz., phallic) authority, the authorship of which is provoked by the default of that same authority; it writes against the default, but in so doing, in the very writing, reifies and enhances it.

No matter how much it signifies, the machine does not satisfy.

We should take care not to conflate the feminine with woman or the masculine with man, although in this example they are conveniently aligned. Here as elsewhere, *woman and man are signifiers*, and they therefore behave in just the same way as does Tristram's nose: the more they are subjected to definition, the more indefinite they become.[22] The point, for our purposes, is that joining the signifier of the woman's intractable, untreatable dissatisfaction with Saussure's laws of signification reveals how the problematics of sex, desire, and frustration—how sexual difference and the impossibility of the sexual relation—are not only thematic obsessions of the text, they are the engine which moves it. Refracted through the peculiarities of Tristram's inheritance and its discontents, the phallic stratagem of inflating and elongating the chain of signifiers, as if this ostentation could do anything other than perpetuate its own ridiculousness, forms half of the broken writing machine's signifying structure.

Untimely Interruptions: Of Symptoms and Their Simple Modes

It is from the other side of this impotent exercise of phallic authority, with the promiscuity of the signifier, where fathers and great-grandfathers prove unable to discharge their responsibility, that this paternal frustration is made into the spring of enjoyment.

Of the panoply of possible examples of the narrative device of untimely interruption, the most fitting is Toby and Walter's abortive conversation concerning the origin and experience of, precisely, time. "It is two hours, and ten minutes,—and no more,——cried my father, looking at his watch, since Dr. *Slop* and *Obadiah* arrived,——and I know not how it happens, brother *Toby*,——but to my imagination it seems almost an age." Indeed, after almost three volumes of text, it does feel implausible for such a short time to have passed, yet Tristram's mother still can be heard screaming in labor from the higher floor. But Toby, a most unlikely metaphysician, replies thus: "—'Tis owing . . . to the succession of our ideas." The ensuing discussion must be quoted at length:

> Do you understand the theory of that affair? replied my father.
> Not I, quoth my uncle.
> ——But you have some ideas, said my father, of what you talk about.——
> No more than my horse, replied my uncle *Toby*.
> Gracious heaven! cried my father, looking upwards, and clasping his two hands together,——there is a worth in thy honest ignorance, brother *Toby*.—'twere almost a pity to exchange it for a knowledge.——But I'll tell thee.——
> To understand what *time* is aright, without which we never can comprehend *infinity*, insomuch as one is a portion of the other,——we ought seriously to sit down and consider what idea it is, we have of *duration*, so as to give a satisfactory account, how we came by it.—What is that to any body? quoth my uncle *Toby*. *For if you will turn your eyes inwards upon your mind*, continued my father, *and observe attentively, you will perceive, brother, that whilst you and I are talking together, and thinking and smoaking our pipes: or whilst we receive successively ideas in our minds, we know that we do exist, and so we estimate the existence, or the continuation of the existence of ourselves, or any thing else commensurate to the succession of any ideas in our minds, the duration of ourselves, or any such other thing coexisting with our thinking,*——*and so according to that preconceived*——You puzzle me to death, cried my uncle *Toby*.—

As ever, Walter is undeterred by Toby's increasingly exasperated complaints and confusion.

> Now, whether we observe it or no, continued my father, in every sound man's head, there is a regular succession of ideas of one sort

or other, which follow each other in train just like——A train of artillery? said my uncle *Toby*.—A train of a fiddle stick!—quoth my father,—which follow and succeed one another in our minds at certain distances, just like the images in the inside of a lanthorn turned round by the heat of a candle.—I declare, quoth my uncle *Toby*, mine are more like a smoak-jack.——Then, brother *Toby*, I have nothing more to say to you upon the subject, said my father. (146–48)

As Toby has tried to insist, Walter might as well explain his concept of time to a horse. Never one to be dissuaded from an opportunity to pontificate, however, regardless of his audience's capacities or interests, Walter carries on anyway, resulting in a conversation without communication wherein his words only add more fuel for the smoke-jack rising from the train of ideas chugging along in Toby's one-track mind. Walter thus withdraws his discourse in frustration, derailing his own train of thought just at the brink of his most profound insight, committing "a robbery of the *Ontologic treasury*," Tristram laments, "of such a jewel, as no coalition of great occasions and great men, are ever likely to restore to it again" (148).

Sterne is playing with Locke, from whose *Essay Concerning Human Understanding* Walter's theory of time has been lifted. Locke proposes that time is the experience of duration; this idea of time, like all ideas, may be confirmed by the operations of reason, particularly reflection. Thus, anyone who reflects on "what passes in his own Mind," Locke argues, will discover there "a train of *Ideas*, which constantly succeed one another in his Understanding, as long as he is awake."[23] Throughout this chapter of the *Essay*, titled "Of Duration and Its Simple Modes," the phrase "train of ideas" appears no less than sixteen times. Toby's disruptive interpolation—"A train of artillery?"—reveals that it is precisely such metaphoricity which gives the understanding over to *mis*understanding. Condensing and combining disparate ideas, the metaphor provokes the signifier's promiscuity, which for Toby inevitably draws his thoughts in the same singular direction along which his hobbyhorse is always galloping.

But what could Locke do? He well knew that the relation, therefore also the difference, between language and sense is fraught with such dangers. He knew that the potential to be misunderstood, as well as language's vulnerability to abuse, were inevitable. Dedicating the entire third book in his *Essay* to this problem, he concluded that only a rigorous consistency in the use of linguistic signs according to their definite and general (that is, objective) meaning (the ideas to which they refer) could prevent the widespread confusion that otherwise derails the progressive work of reason. For Locke, this exactitude was as much a practical as a moral concern.

Sterne's subversion of this conceit, at once sympathetic and sardonic, can be observed in the subtle difference between Locke's text and Walter's appropriation. Locke reads as follows:

'Tis evident to any one who will but observe what happens in his own Mind, that . . . whilst we are thinking, or whilst we receive successively several *Ideas* in our Minds, we know that we do exist; and so we call the Existence, or the Continuation of the Existence of our selves, or any thing else, Commensurate to the succession of any *Ideas* in our Minds, the *Duration* of our selves, or any such other thing co-existing with our Thinking.[24]

Here again is a portion of Walter's position, with the crucial alteration underlined:

For if you will turn your eyes inwards upon your mind . . . and observe attentively, you will perceive, brother, that whilst you and I are talking together, and thinking and smoking our pipes: or whilst we receive successively ideas in our minds, we know that we do exist . . .

The subversion is this: Locke's conception of time as the experience of duration is at the center of his protracted meditation on personal identity, and concerns the private dimension of our reflections as they proceed in isolation from others—"whilst we are thinking." This is why language, an inherently social institution and the structure of sociality as such, is always a threat to the very work of reason it also enables. To the extent that this work is articulated (in, for instance, Locke's *Essay* itself), it disappropriates its operator from the mechanics of his operations. But unlike Locke, Walter introduces conversation and sociability as the framework of reflection. Shifting the editorial "we" to a particular "you, brother" joins the question of duration—and with it, thought in general and the experiential foundations of identity—to the trouble with language Locke exhaustively diagnosed but could not, for all that, avoid. To borrow another Lockean term, thought becomes a *secondary quality* of conversation. Language is primary because otherwise ideas could not be made into the stuff of shared objective knowledge and instead would pile up inside the mind like the smoke from a blocked chimney. There can be no reflection without communication, and this means that thought is intrinsically open to, and impossible without, the signifier and its errancy.

The Humean resonances with this emphasis on sociability and the sympathetic interdependence of identity and otherness are clear enough.[25] But remaining with Locke affords a realization that troubles his and Hume's and all other philosophical inquiries: in adding Locke's voice to the novel's "talk, talk, talk," and triggering Toby's misprision of his brother's discourse with Locke's own metaphor—"a train of . . ."—Sterne reveals that the potential for misunderstanding is not a hazard thinking risks by entering the order of the signifier. On the contrary, *misunderstanding is the very condition of thought.* A world without the misfire of the signifier would be a world devoid of conversation and thus without the miscommunication that sustains it; and because Tristram's life, his textual body, his whole world, is primarily a composite of frustrated conversations, we may conclude from this that a world without miscommunication would not be a world at all.[26] At best, it would be a dead world, a grave—a black page, at once overflowing with meaning and devoid of the means to convey it. Locke's dream of a signifier perfectly commensurate with itself cannot but be a dead letter.

This explains the onanistic exhibitionism of Walter's discourse. Whence his final flaccidity before an unwilling audience, redoubled by Tristram's disappointment that his father yet again, as in the scene of Tristram's conception, has moodily withdrawn before coming to the point. Here and throughout Walter's many lucubrations, it is clear to everyone but himself that he talks, talks, talks not despite but because he will be misunderstood. Even if his messages' failures to arrive bring him no pleasure, he nevertheless *enjoys* the failure since otherwise he would not keep sending them. His hobby-horse, the fabrication of systems, the endless elaboration of preposterously idiosyncratic opinions, can sustain itself only if he is always misunderstood. This is why Walter halts his monologue at the moment of truth, depriving the "Ontologic treasury" of the jewel that would complete its crown. Barred from its articulation, thus shielded from the understanding, this gem of knowledge remains beyond the limits of the conversation of which it is nonetheless generative. To define the indefinite, to transgress these limits, would enrich the treasury of concepts only at the expense of the play of signifiers upon which Walter's pontifications and, with them, much of Tristram's writing—his very being—depend.

Every person, Tristram argues, is defined and distinguished by their hobby-horse, including the author himself, whose peculiar fixation, of course, is writing. If Walter's hobby-horse, his passion for systems of reason, bucks him injuriously at the edge of its arrival to sense, leaving the truth unsaid and unwritten, Toby's passion affords an inverse account of the hobby-horse as the displaced repetition of the unwritten within the written. In the language of psychoanalysis, this form of passion or passionate form is called the symptom.

A first clue to the hobby-horse's symptomatic dimension is Tristram's insistence that one does not choose one's fixation. The hobby-horse is the manifestation of an obsession one cannot but embrace and endure. In addition, its untimely interruptions derail the train of ideas and, in doing so, derange the concept of duration upon which Locke's epistemology of personal identity depends. According to Sterne's model, one's singular identity is much more a matter of these untimely disturbances than it is a composite of empirically delimited experiences. The singular enjoyment it provides, moreover, results from the equally singular cause to which it bears witness, which, as with the text's whole narrative structure, is always a wound that at once enjoins and resists its articulation. The imperfect repetition of a traumatic (because unsignifiable) origin is what sets every hobby-horse on its way.[27]

Recall that Toby's hobby-horse is an almost unbridled penchant for military history, particularly the minutiae of sieges, which he endlessly reproduces in the model fortifications he and Trim construct in his kitchen garden. This "great singularity" originated after the siege of Namur, at which Toby suffered a severe wound to his groin. His protracted and painful convalescence is exacerbated by what Tristram calls "the almost insurmountable difficulties he found in telling his story intelligibly" (64). Only after examining a map of Namur does Toby find any relief:

> He was one morning lying upon his back in his bed, the anguish and nature of the wound upon his groin suffering him to lye in no other position, when a thought came into his head, that if he could purchase such a thing, and have it pasted down upon a board, as a large map of the fortifications of the town and citadel of *Namur*, with its environs, it might be a means of giving him ease.—I take notice of his desire to have the environs along with the town and citadel, for this reason,—because my uncle *Toby*'s wound was got in one of the traverses, about thirty toises from the returning angle of the trench, opposite to the salient angle of the demi-bastion of *St. Roch*;——so that he was pretty confident he could stick a pin upon the identical spot of ground where he was standing in when the stone struck him.
>
> All this succeeded to his wishes, and not only freed him from a world of sad explanations, but, in the end, it prov'd the happy means . . . of procuring my uncle *Toby* his HOBBY-HORSE. (65)

Far from an uncertain impression, Toby's wound imprints itself so violently that he cannot find the words to describe, to make sense of, the effraction. It continues to fester, erasing the distinction between body and mind, disarticulating his personal narrative as it waits for the signifier that would bind it to the understanding. A pin on Toby's map provides a mute spatial localization, a plug for the hole in the symbolic to which his trauma corresponds. It is a partial solution that saves Toby from the "insurmountable difficulties" of "telling his story intelligibly" by permitting him to avoid speaking about the wound at all. The pin procures for Toby his hobby-horse because this partial and imaginary evasion of narrative intelligibility does not contain the trauma, but only anchors it to a point from which the symptom—the train of his singularity—will proceed.

His obsessive interest in military history thus treats the trauma through its imperfect repetition in the proliferating representations of what cannot be named. In all these inadequate representations, Toby returns to the trauma, again and again leaping at every inopportune opportunity to interject his symptom into an otherwise successive train of ideas, bringing the rest of the conversation with him. So, years after the siege of Namur but years earlier than Walter's failed disposition on the nature of time, during her extended siege on Toby's affections, widow Wadman finds that she can only infiltrate his defenses by incorporating herself into his symptom, engaging him as an enemy would in battle, with strategies of "Love-militancy" (446) and "stroke[s] of generalship" (448); and when she repeatedly inquires after the location of his injury, attempting surreptitiously to determine his sexual viability, Toby tenderly takes her hand and draws her finger to . . . the pin on his map of Namur. The sexual relation is foreclosed before it can begin, made impossible by the castration that sets the symptom on its way. Where the sexual relation ought to be, there is instead Toby's libidinal fixation upon military adventurism and military history.

This, then, is a form of duration that is both inconsistent and consistent with Locke's rational temporality. Inconsistent, because the hobby-horse operates according to another temporality, the timeless time of the zone of catastrophe we encountered already on Crusoe's island, where the subject cannot take hold of language so that time itself, the differential articulation of past and future, ceases to have any meaning. Consistent, because the stubbornness of the catastrophe is what affords the subject's consistency, its durability and duration, its synchrony within an otherwise diachronic universe. The symptom does not budge, and here it is what Locke calls "the Existence, or the Continuation of the Existence of our selves." As Toby makes clear, there is nothing rational about it; it is indifferent to the movements of the clock or the succession of ideas, and certainly to his brother's rationalist pontifications, or even to widow Wadman's contrapuntal love-militancy. But nor is it without its reasons, unspeakable though they may be. Outside of rational time, the cause of his fixation is there in the symptom, not beyond or before but immanent within Toby's untimely interruptions.

Built out of these two faulty mechanisms—the self-defeating preposterousness of digressive enhancement, and the disruptive meanderings of the hobby-horse around and around an open wound—Tristram's textual body and his being are the site of a multiple inheritance: a patchwork of overlapping but incongruous symptoms, singular and thus incommunicable fixations, whose stitching and weaving together is the narrator's symptom, his hobby-horse. As allobiography, the traumatic origins of this symptom are the originary traumas from which unfold the singular symptoms characterizing the other characters comprising his singular reality. And because even these origins can be traced only as the lack around which every hobby-horse meanders or dances, Tristram is only the inheritance of this lack, which he therefore does not own but nevertheless must live in his own way.

The novel thus figures and is motored by two modes of *jouissance*. The first, as with Sade, is oriented toward the horizon of an impossible fulfillment, onanistically enjoying each of its failures because every frustration is an occasion to try again, to keep stroking the pen. The second is indifferent to success or failure—indifferent, then, to the Sadean schema we traced in the previous chapter—and only wants to wander, unpredictably, therefore irreverently, and to proliferate ever more errant avenues of signification. There is no "outside" of the phallic function, no being beyond castration; there is no subject or object without the cut which instantiates them both within the logic of fantasy, and across this cut there is no possible union between them. There is no sexual relation, the sexual relation is impossible. But one may explore rather than lament that impossibility, one may enjoy the gap between desire and its fulfillment, and make something monstrous and beautiful, beautifully monstrous, out of what doesn't stop not being written.

Between Men: The Primal Scene in Shandy Hall

To this point we have established how Sterne subverts the empiricist doctrine of natural purposiveness, and its ally, the emergent paradigm of practical aesthetics, at the site of the concept of time on which they depend. Within and against this concept he opposes not timelessness but the untimely. Duration is not an effect of the subject's rational reflection (nor, recalling Hume, is it an effect of imagination, which can only secure the illusion of the self's durability, or what psychoanalysis calls the ego); rather, *the subject's duration is in the symptom*. The subject is there where time is out of joint, where the signifier representing it returns to the unwritten scene of originary trauma, the zone of catastrophe which is both the end and the beginning of the world. The subject is the fiction generated by the friction between the signifier's wanting to say and its failure to say, between what it desires and what it can have, between the impossible and the linguistically, socially, even perceptually determined confines of possibility.

In a clinical mode, this is a fine definition of the subject of the unconscious, whose address to the analyst is in those acts that disturb the pretended coherence of the ego narrative, those frictions between what one says and what one does, which disclose a logic of desire other than that which is imposed or admitted by the social link and therefore for which there are no words. In the work of literature, the subject of literature similarly acts through, upon, and against the language of which it is comprised, to the extent that those acts are addressed to the desire of the critic. Like the subject of the unconscious, which is immanent but inarticulable within the discourses surrounding it, this subject is there in the written yet is irreducible to it. This is the subject for which Sterne's "laying bare the device" provides a narrative, novelistic formalization, should we be called by the desire to read it.

From the beginning, I have explored the space between these two structures of address according to an analogy between the ethics of criticism and the ethics of psychoanalysis, articulated through the Freudian concept and clinical technique of construction. This is where the literary essence of psychoanalysis is most compelling and where the invitation to think literature with psychoanalysis is most apparent. For it is in construction that the collaboration between interpreting and interpreted, between the action and the object of interpretation, requires an intervention that dissolves or disregards the distinction between the critical and the creative. In this dissolution we also recognize the concept of literature and its origins in the literary absolute. In the clinical or the critical, the composition of the impossible at stake in the fantasy is definitionally a matter and consequence of speculation. Now, *Tristram Shandy* affords us an opportunity to test this analogy by constructing the fantasy at stake in this most typical novel.

Freud's case histories, textual records of the action of unconscious fantasy, provide a practical pattern for such a test. The case of Sergei Pankejeff, the so-called "Wolf Man," is the most extensive and the most useful one for our purposes. In that text's construction of the primal scene, Pankejeff is posed as an infant watching from the foot of the bed as his parents copulate, three times, *a tergo*, studying their contorted faces and strange gruntings, while he is also inside his mother's womb where he usurps her enjoyment of the exquisite torture his father brings upon her. This is impossible. As with any fantasy, that is the point. The scene appears interstitially in the case history, after the interpretation of the wolf dream from which its subject gets his nickname and on the way to the analysis of additional inexplicable behaviors, screen memories, somatic symptoms. . . . The construction situates the dream, these fragments and symptoms, and their interpretations, all in relation to one another, making sense of an otherwise senseless matrix of desire. This making sense systematizes desire, and is therefore an aftereffect of the primal scene's effects, an *après-coup*, a historical truth which can only be articulated after the facts— "divined," as Freud often writes, from the history it motors. The structure of the unconscious fantasy is a product of, not a precedent to, its structuration. It is not discovered, rather it is made through the work of analysis.

The value of any construction is in its function, which is to narrativize an otherwise obscure logic for which there are no words. On the trail of the subject of literature, our aim is to arrange the interplay of textual symptoms and their interpretations in relation to one another according to the impossible desire around and around which they circulate. To strain the fantasy through the sieve of the symbolic in this way, we can follow Freud and Pankejeff by organizing it into a tableau inscribing the other's untimely irruptions and impotent digressions across and throughout the story of the self, posing these variances of *jouissance* in impossible relation to one another, systematizing the apparently senseless peregrinations of the signifier—and positioning the subject just where the Wolf Man's primal scene and Tristram's broken sex machine guide us: suspended between sex and death.

So, let us find the words.

Yorick watches as Walter copulates with Toby, his impotent phallus rubbing back and forth against Toby's open wound without penetrating it, out of which friction and wound Tristram is born.

Now, Freud often begged the conviction, the good faith, of his audience in the face of images and conclusions such as this, since they could not but seem incredible to anyone who had not themselves experienced psychoanalysis. Here, as well, the novel's primal scene may seem absurd and ridiculous. So it is. Again, however, that is the point. Or rather, the point is that the scene is impossible—the impossibility of the possible. What matters is only the effectiveness with which it composes, in the form of the fragment, a total system of desire and its effects.

The first evidence of our construction's effectiveness is in its configuration of the uncertainty surrounding Tristram's parentage. Critics and adroit readers have long speculated on who might be Tristram's real father, since by all indications it cannot be Walter.[28] Such speculation confines us within the realm of the plausible, as if Tristram and his characters are actual people, as if Sterne left a trail of clues to some soap-operatic surprise. But the true basis of the ambiguity surrounding Tristram's origin is that he has not one but *three* fathers. First, there is Toby, whose wound is the site of the trauma from which the formal components of Tristram's hobby-horse (the writing of his allobiography) are inherited. The wound is open because it is a generative gap in the order of the signifier which manifests and endures in the untimely interruption of the symptom. All those seemingly random outbursts where the narrator's attention swings from the plot's action to the fickle mechanics of its composition or a belated dedication or yet another sexual innuendo, where the materiality of the text is made into the very stuff of the novel (blank pages, black pages, marbled pages, archaic fonts, lacunae, serpentine lines, the flourish of the fiddlestick)—whenever Tristram's life and opinions are overrun by his mal/functioning writing machine, these are the marks of Toby's inheritance, which is not a substance but a structure. Alongside and upon Toby and his wound, there is Walter, whose efforts to wield the phallus are sustained and vitalized by his impotence and failure ever to arrive at the climax of his various disquisitions, as well as his ceaselessly returning with joy but no pleasure to the site of his failures. This is the sociability, the conversation without communication, exemplified in the two characters' discourse on duration. In Tristram, it is the inheritance of an untreatable feminine dissatisfaction, manifested in the digressive enhancements, the back-and-forth of the compensatory masculine histrionics, it provokes. Finally, there is Yorick. We will find that he is crucial to the construction because it is his gaze, like that of the child in the Wolf Man's construction, that frames and engenders the scene as, precisely, a scene.

Framing the origin of the novel as an impossible, hallucinatory sexual relation between men takes us further beyond the plausible, the realistic, the rational—in short, the imaginary—by decoupling sex from reproduction and locating it instead within the circuit of the drive, that broken machine that renders sex unnatural, monstrous, and ridiculous, where its aim is not reproduction but repetition. The construction makes conspicuous the fact that

Tristram's mother Elizabeth has *nothing at all* to do with him. His textual body is a composite and inheritance of his other characters' hobby-horses, an overlapping series of castrations and their consequences for the subject's duration in the symptom. The mother is an occasional outburst of labor pain, an impertinent question in the middle of her husband's sexual exertions, or a body without a voice, silent and silenced by all the men's talk, talk, talk. In this text as in the prescripts of eighteenth-century marriage law, as Elizabeth herself discovers early in the plot, Tristram is not his mother's heir; by the patriarchal rights of inheritance, she belongs to him. The child is the father of the woman.

Within the realm of the plausible, it is notable that Tristram will have been raised more by his mother and nursemaid while Walter was busy writing his *Tristrapoedia* and Toby and Trim fiddled with their kitchen-garden sieges. Yet the narrator insists on the mother's insignificance, the absence of any inheritance from her, asserting, "all the SHANDY FAMILY were of an original character throughout;——I mean the males,—the females had no character at all" (49).[29] Only the men are "original," originating, origins. Only they have hobby-horses, since only their traumas are indexed and inscribed, only their wounds set the writing machine in motion. This is further confirmed by Sterne's habit of never differentiating any man's speech from the narrative voice while every woman's speech is set apart within quotation marks (notice this detail, for example, in the above-quoted conflict between Tristram's great-grandparents on the woman's jointure as compensation for the man's too-small nose).[30] While the women are made marginal by even the text's typography and punctuation, the men's voices are woven inseparably together. Tristram's body is made by men, in the friction between them and the enjoyment it enjoins.[31]

This closed homosociality is one reason why Sterne has been accused of perpetuating women's social and literary disenfranchisement, or simply of misogyny. What is worse, he and other fixtures of sentimental fiction made their fame by appropriating literary strategies that had been innovated by women, thus not only marginalizing them in the pages of their fictions but robbing real women authors of the recognition and reward they and their writing deserved.[32]

Locating literature, literary experimentation, and the literary marketplace at the center of the history of hegemonic masculinity, these indictments make clear that the ideological configuration which dismisses, disallows, or robs women's voices, and thereby deprives women and their experiences of social and historical significance, is an effect of signification. Such critiques therefore ask, if implicitly, what "woman" and "man" signify, as well as what material consequences these significations have—or could have, were they signified otherwise.

So does psychoanalysis. Here we should recall that because sexual difference pertains to two modalities of *jouissance*—two different experiences of the effect of the signifier upon the living being, two forms of relation to the phallic function—it does not rely upon a predetermined, natural, immutable, or inevitable definition of men and women. Nor, for the same reason, does it permit us to presume some essential relation between men and the masculine or women and the feminine. Nor does it suppose any natural complementarity between them; if the masculine and the feminine are related, it is always in the form of a non-relation: without conjunction, compatibility, or symmetry. If Man and Woman, masculine and feminine, male and female, are not categories of being but *signifiers*, they do not designate subjects. They mark, in culturally and historically specific ways, the absence of the subject upon whom they are imposed. Psychoanalysis is concerned with and constituted by the address of that absent subject, but it also knows that such an address only issues from the discrepancies between the subject and the signifiers that want and fail to represent it, including the signifiers of gender and sexuality.

There is no metalanguage, no outside of culture and history and their interests and effects, no beyond of ideology. Psychoanalysis therefore operates within the same discourse from which the subject is exiled. It retains the terms "masculine" and "feminine" in order to invest them with an ontological value that does not reduce sex, gender, or indeed desire to some immutable essence, but radically subverts their habitual connotations. Every person is both masculine and feminine. Everyone is riven and driven by this irreconcilable difference because it is the intrinsic incompatibility of the self with itself. To be subject to the phallic function, as we all are, does not mean to be determined by it; it means to be rendered indeterminate and indeterminable. The task of analysis is never to reconcile the subject with ideology and its prescriptions concerning sex, gender, and power, but to assist the subject in signifying otherwise.

To bring this to bear on the most typical novel in world literature means neither to rescue *Tristram Shandy* from feminist critique nor to surrender the text fully to its cultural and historical context. It means to affirm that it is an artifact and agent of that context and, *because* of this complicity, to explore the ways in which the work of literature also signifies sex and sexual difference otherwise. How, we must ask, does the novel frustrate the sexual?

Like the modes of enjoyment personified by Walter and Toby, and their impossible coupling in the novel's primal scene, the masculine and the feminine are two mutually constitutive, incompatible, asymmetrical halves of the novel's discourse. No congress between them will produce a unity. With all its generativity, with its forever forestalled potential for a final meaning, the sexual relation cannot but be a non-relation. The creativity at stake in the sexual relation is not reproduction, since it is borne of the conjunction and disconnect between the two halves of this ontological asymmetry. And so its creativity is always novel. With *Tristram Shandy* it is *the* novel.

The Nonsense of an Ending

This leaves us with Yorick's curious and essential place within the narrative's fantasmatic structure. Like his Shakespearean namesake, Yorick enjoys the protagonist's affection—immortalized in the only way Tristram knows, by an immense quantity of ink, spilled *in memoriam* over those two solid black pages—at a distance from the family romance that sustains the drama's development.[33] His death overflows the order of the signifier, drowns or eclipses it, like a curtain drawn across the stage. Yorick thus is no disinterested observer. His gaze is not passive but generative. Here and in his other writings, Yorick is the figure through whom Sterne collapses the distinction between author and character, the avatar of Sterne's presence within, not beyond or above, his text. Elsewhere, "Yorick" is the pseudonym under which Sterne signed much of his personal correspondence and two published volumes of his sermons, as well as the name of his semi-autobiographical first-person narrator in his later novel, *A Sentimental Journey*. We therefore locate him at the spectatorial position in the novel's primal scene because, watching from the margins, Yorick disappropriates the family drama of its intimacy, shifting the otherwise unintelligible obscenity of the primal scene to the social scene. He is the vector through which the novel's unspeakable, because purely fantasmatic, origin is made legible, made to be read, sublimated: given over to the work of literature.

Unlike *Robinson Crusoe*, whose author narrates his character's adventures from a transcendental, omniscient, essentially psychotic position relative to the history he animates, and who thereby is made into a correlate and representative of the divine Providence which Defoe arrogates to himself as omnipotent author of his text, Sterne/Yorick reveals that the author is not beyond the time of writing. He is not the subject of knowledge acting upon the subject of experience and molding it in his own image. Against Defoe's pretensions to totality and infinity, Sterne insists upon and celebrates the fact that, here or elsewhere, in Tristram's tiny world at the outskirts of York or on Crusoe's limitless little island, the author operates in security from neither the violence nor the promiscuity of the signifier. Yorick disallows the metalinguistic position of an exceptional, because omniscient and omnipotent, author-ity who would not be subject to the phallic function.

Thus, as a character in his own novel, Sterne more than watches his characters from behind the veil covering the fantasmatic scene. Through a strange—or, with Shklovsky, enstranging—redoubling of the narrative gaze back upon itself, Sterne *watches himself watching and being watched*, enjoying being enjoyed by a gaze that both is and is not his own. His text expresses a simultaneously narcissistic and self-effacing spectatorial self-regard. The author, like his character Yorick, watches not because he is exempt from the inarticulable enjoyment that circulates throughout the text, but because his scopophilia is the text's condition of possibility; the text is oriented and motivated by *the desire to be seen and to see himself being seen*. And like his characters' symptoms—those hobby-horses that constitute, define, and sustain them—Sterne's symptom, his text, is generative of his own position with respect to the order of the signifier in which he is happily captured: subjecting himself to the gaze of the other, he is made a subject by it.

This is further corroborated by the well-known fact that Sterne's commercial success was far from serendipitous. He wrote to please, and strived to guarantee his celebrity by exploiting emergent cultural and economic conditions for the profitable cultivation of a readership increasingly sensitive to modalities of *jouissance*—that is, ways of relating and being subject to the signifier—which traditionally masculine social, intellectual, and aesthetic hierarchies could no longer repress. To these ends, he fashioned himself into Yorick, the likeably ribald and appropriately sentimental man of both reason and feeling whose sole ambition is to be enjoyed, *to enjoy being enjoyed*, by the characters populating his small but far from insignificant world. And should that world grow to encompass the vast, anonymous reading public, so much the better for a symptom whose appetite for fame was also a desire to be consumed.[34]

Watching the other watching oneself, and inscribing this double gaze through the eyes and from the position of the other, enjoying being enjoyed—this is the bedrock and organizing principle of allobiography. It means making oneself into a subject, inscribing one's being, composing oneself, telling one's story, by quilting a patchwork of stories that at once comprise and incomplete one's reality, interminably. It means writing oneself being written.

Confounding the differences between subject and object, completion and incompletion, or finally self and other is the narrative correlate of Lacan's formalization of the logic of fantasy. The novel doesn't stop being written because what it desires to write is what doesn't stop not being written. It is an emphatically masculine text not only because it is a tale of intimacy and affection between men, a story of a COCK and a BULL, in which women are at best the representatives of an interminable dissatisfaction, but also because in its urgency to escape its own conditions of possibility, in its desperation to fill the lack in being without which it would not exist, to heal its opening wounds, it is a failure. And it enjoys that failure, or else it would not be. It is a fundamentally feminine text, too, because it enjoys its incompleteness, evades or subverts or parrots or mocks or simply ignores the masculine, torments it with its incapacity to satisfy the signifier's urge to wander. It is an impossible text and yet the most typical novel in world literature because its stage is the impossibility of the relation between the two modalities of *jouissance* that, however covertly or inadvertently, attend every signification of a subject.

So, even when the novel does arrive at its conclusion, it will not stop being written and unwritten. It will keep on with its mal/functioning motion because the signifier continues to misfire in the reader to whom the novel is addressed and who, through the work of literature, reanimates the body of the text, disappropriating the subject from the writing machine in order to return it to the work—if in another language, then still on its own terms. "Tristram" is Sterne's name for the subject of literature, a signifier that represents a subject. His readers, you and I—our stories, and the indefinitely extensive web of others' stories-all-the-way-down that comprise us—we are these other signifiers to whom that representative is addressed. This is why the subject is not outside the text, why the subject is only the text, but is both more and less than the web of signification comprising it. Reading, too, is allobiography.

Laying bare the device in this way, *Tristram Shandy* reveals why the subject of literature is necessarily a sexed subject. It completes itself only by incompleting itself. Its being is inseparable from the materiality of its body, the scribbles on the page within which it is inscribed and without which it does not exist. But it is irreducible to that materiality, because the materiality of the sign is also the medium through which the text is animated and reanimated by an experience and ethics of reading that discover within it an infinity of novel possibilities. Our construction of *Tristram Shandy*'s primal scene is one such possibility, an artifact of this critic's hobby-horse, a symptom of my engagement with the text. It is not, however, a one-sided imposition. It is the consequence of a relation between reader and text which, like the sexual relation, is as impossible as it is real. In the end, after the writing is done, that relation too will remain unwritten.

Epilogue

✦

Between Ideology and the Unconscious

Fantasy and ideology are co-implicated and irreducible, inseparable yet non-identical. Everything in the preceding pages illustrates and emphasizes this because the difference between fantasy and ideology is axiomatic for the ethics of psychoanalysis, and therefore also for any theory or practice of reading it would inform. Throughout this book, I have aligned this ethics with the ethics of literary criticism and have brought this to bear upon a few of the most established, influential, and enduring examples of the eighteenth-century novel and novelistic discourse for two interwoven reasons.

First, these texts are inseparable from the larger project of philosophical and social reform, the event in the history of mediation, that bestowed upon itself the mantle and arrogated to itself the mythical power of Enlightenment. It is the Enlightenment that furnishes the particularly modern strategies of representation by which the systems of thought and phenomena that constitute our contemporary realities are made to seem inevitable and irresistible. It accomplishes this effacement of social and historical contingency by introducing systematicity as a paradigm and an imperative, orienting the validity of any system—political, philosophical, scientific, technological—around a new, and newly valorized, concept of *nature* because of the supposition of necessity it provides. If the systematic organization of ideas and their signification takes place upon the ground of natural necessity, then the resulting knowledge and, more importantly, mundane practices of everyday life are made to seem as though they could not be otherwise. The Enlightenment thereby becomes the master signifier of modernity: that which moves history but is unmoved by it; in the name of which other key signs of ideology, such as progress or liberty or the pursuit of happiness, are reified and reproduced. In short, the modern history of ideology—and this is perhaps all we can mean by "modern history" as such—is the history of the Enlightenment. This is why its mythical status and function do not undermine but instead enforce its action upon the reality it continues to orient.

The eighteenth-century novel was instrumental to the constitution of this myth not only as an emissary through which specialized discourses (scientific, philosophical, and political) were made available and persuasive to a general public, but also as the experimental field in which was forged the relation between experience, identity, and representation comprising the modern individual. This most powerful of the Enlightenment's ideological innovations, the paradigm of the autonomous, sovereign, self-interested, self-contained "I," the total subject at the center of its own story, operator of its own narrative, was a novel invention.

The second reason I have asserted the relation and difference between ideology and fantasy by way of the eighteenth-century novel is to make clear, at this vital point in the ideological history of the present where the novel and the Enlightenment's paradigmatic individualism are all but indistinguishable, why the work of literature and the work of analysis both enjoin a radical resistance against ideological totalization. Criticism and psychoanalysis resist, without imagining a liberation from, every well-intended or nefarious, intentional or accidental, attempt to reduce the subject—of the unconscious; of literature—to an artifact, effect, or tool made to serve some extrinsic (economic, political, aesthetic, theoretical) interest or agenda. They do so for the subject but only insofar as their work is undertaken with the subject, in a joint enterprise. In this way, for and with the subject, criticism and psychoanalysis are more than variations on or servants to ideology critique, they are constituted out of a concern for its cause and condition: that bit of the human, that unwritten desire, that logic of fantasy, which is forever undoing, and therefore always provoking, ideological inscription and determination. For it is the subject at stake in unconscious fantasy that remains interminably unpersuaded by appeals to nature, unsatisfied by the apparent and the given, and unconcerned with the logic and limits of necessity. Following the action of this subject within and upon (but never without) its history, analysis or criticism, too, are animated by another logic, another sort of reason, one that can act upon and perhaps change the world.

In these remaining pages, I want to insist that this is neither romance nor hyperbole. I will do so by further delimiting fantasy from ideology without, however, eclipsing their inseparability—rather by drawing the limit between them as a line of convergence and divergence, a line that both conjoins and differentiates. To assert this difference, I argue, is a vital, even urgent corrective to the recent record of their confusion, and can reorient or revitalize the relation between psychoanalysis, ideology critique, and finally literary criticism on more ethically considered ground.

The Politics of Fantasy

To suggest that fantasy can change the world is first of all to deploy this signifier, "world," as the name for an ideological configuration of "reality," which means above all a configuration of representations and our relation to and place within them.[1] After exploring *Robinson Crusoe*'s literary psychosis and what it reveals about the delusional qualities of the Enlightenment, we know that reality is not inert, given, and inevitable. Reality is a matter and effect of interpretation. "The point," as Lacan puts it not only apropos of psychosis but with respect to reality as such, is that "the signifier in fact enters the signified—namely, in a form which, since it is not immaterial, raises the question of its place in reality."[2] Reality, in other words, is the materiality or materialization of the signifier, which is neither disinterested nor eternal, neither neutral nor inevitable; reality is the way in which the codes of recognition and intelligibility (the symbolic order) we impose upon our perceptive experience (the imaginary) constitute that experience and make it meaningful or available to meaning-making. Reality does not grow from the ground or fall from the sky. It is constructed, contingent, and always in flux. This formative relation of the signifier to the reality it invents and organizes is precisely what ideology wants to elide.

All this is quite basic for ideology critique, at least since Barthes's *Mythologies*, if not Marx's critique of political economy.[3] Reality is a social, historical, and therefore linguistic construct. What our Lacanian terminology stresses, however, and this was also stressed by Althusser, is that *ideology is imaginary.*[4] It is the imaginary distortion and the distortion in the imaginary of the subject's social predicament, the (mis)representation of that predicament as an existential necessity, enforced through the strictures and expectations of the social link.

Fantasy, on the other hand, is the point at which the subject touches upon and finds, or seeks and fails to find, its own purchase in reality. The logic of fantasy formalizes, which is to say universalizes, this peculiar mode of being that is the human, and thereby describes the way in which every singular instance of the human, called the subject of the unconscious, carves its own path along its way toward the impossible object and cause of its desire. This quest for the impossible which inscribes the subject there in what doesn't stop not being written, this sexual non-relation, is what pushes the subject beyond the pleasure principle, beyond the limits of the social link and what is useful there, beyond the given and the general, beyond good and evil. It is why desire will not be appeased—which is to say, nullified—by any actually existing thing, nor by any representation or idea. Fantasy is what compels the subject, against the lure of every bauble and prize and trifle, against anything that promises to put an end to this tortuous quest and the torturous *jouissance* it exacts, to cry in protest or disappointment, *No! This is not it!* and to keep on questing after whatever *it* is, interminably. In this way, fantasy both urges the subject to fill the lack which constitutes it as a subject—thus annihilating the subject's own conditions of possibility, whence Lacan's famous insistence that there is but one drive and it is the death drive—and yet ensures that every possible object cannot but prove inadequate to that task, thereby ensuring that the subject will go on desiring, which is to say, being.

The stakes of fantasy therefore are nothing short of ontological. This is why no appeal to reality can dispel or dissipate it. Unlike reality, fantasy is real.

Of course, it is also fantasy just the same. If we stress its ontological stakes, this is not because it is ontically uninteresting or irrelevant to ideology. Nor should we resuscitate the dichotomy between the subject and the world, the inside and the outside, *res cogitans* and *res extensa* that the Freudian discovery ought thoroughly to have debunked, especially after its Lacanian iteration. The point is that fantasy, like any frame, any enlightenment, both reveals and conceals; it is this duality more than any stale dualism that concerns psychoanalysis, because this simultaneous revealing and concealing is what confounds the subject, what ensures that it is not transparent to itself.

So, fantasy is not reality but it is real for the subject. It is the real of the subject's existential exile from a symbolically constructed world, the logic by which that exile is lived. Unlike the ego, however, which is the power broker in this world of representations, the fantasmatically oriented subject of the unconscious has no regard for what Freud termed the *reality principle*, which acts on behalf of the ego as the pleasure principle's custodial attendant.[5] Whereas the reality principle constrains the ego's actions according to external (moral or practical) constraints, the fantasy is not interested in what a given configuration of the social link makes possible or permissible.[6] Or, if the subject is captured according to these historically conditioned parameters, if the fantasy alights upon some partial object or substitute satisfaction, the capture is temporary, and this or that (partial or substitute) object soon proves insufficient to quell the desire that sustains the subject in its quest beyond the pleasure principle. Yes, fantasy does compel the subject to embrace these partial satisfactions, but this is only its secondary movement; its primary, determining logic concerns a desire that will only be satisfied at the vanishing horizon of the impossible.

This is why ideology wants to collapse the distinction between fantasy and itself. Ideology has but one interest in the subject, which is to render it efficient: to maximize its use as a tool for the reproduction of the means and relations of production that organize the social order, thus also to minimize, ideally to annihilate, the friction between the subject's desire and what is useful to that order. To minimize tension, as we emphasized with Rousseau, is also the aim of the pleasure principle. What is "good" for the social link is what is useful to it, including those forms of pleasure and expectations for the taking of pleasure imposed upon the subject, no matter how seemingly transgressive these pleasures may be. To close the interval of desire, to fill the gap in which the vacillations of unconscious fantasy are ever unsettling the social link's hold on the subject, to smother it with pleasure, would ensure the frictionless reproduction of the order of things. Ideology operates (according to) the pleasure principle.

Social reproduction without friction or remainder, without the tension between desire and its impossible satisfaction, without the grating and grinding of *jouissance* beyond pleasure, would accomplish ideology's core ambition: to present reality not as the unstable reification of a set of historical conditions and a hegemonic struggle, but as if the situation could not be other-wise. ("What could not be otherwise" has been a common refrain throughout this book, and is a variation on the "what-goes-without-saying" that you recall from the first chapter is Barthes's succinct definition of ideology.) Such frictionless reproduction would convert the historically delimited and con-tingent processes of subject formation into a matter of course as natural, and as irresistible, as the whirlings of the cosmos. If ideology could triumph, if what the subject desires and what reality has to offer could be fixed in perfect consonance, then we would arrive at what William Blake, that great eighteenth-century ambassador of fantasy, once contemptuously labeled "the ratio of all things," and we would be "unable to do other than repeat the same dull round over again."[7] Under these hypothetical conditions—and fan-tasy teaches that they are only hypothetical—the human would be entirely calculable, controllable, a mere work/pleasure machine from which certain outputs could be extracted following the right set of inputs. Thus would resistance be not only futile but absurd. "History" would entail duration without difference or change, the eternal recurrence of the same, the purely fictional stasis of Thomas More's *Utopia* or its modern iteration, the perfect tyranny of pleasure in Aldous Huxley's *Brave New World*.

But we do not live in a brave new world. History is not a closed loop. No place is utopia. Despite the ever more sophisticated and always proliferating means by which we are entrapped or entrap ourselves within a maze of plea-sures, despite the infinite creativity with which pleasure is made into the aim of a universal moral (super-egoic) imperative or the ways in which unplea-sure can be converted into its own moral end, the human still surprises. The subject resists. History moves. Again, this is not a romantic sentiment but a matter of fact. Such resistance and its movement take shape not only as the sort of critical consciousness to which Paulo Freire or Edward Said—or before them, Rousseau—call us. The subject's resistance can be detected casually and pervasively in the panoply of everyday disappointments, frus-trations, irritations, and anxieties that accumulate and metastasize into plain old unhappiness, or in popular outrages, outbursts, or insurrections express-ing some unbearable discontent with the state of our civilization, in acts of destruction or creation—including our primary concern, acts of literature, whose at-once creative and destructive potential is nowhere more explosively demonstrated than in the works of Rousseau's most notorious acolyte, the Marquis de Sade. These spectacular or mundane resistances, even in their very banality, in yet another dreaded day at the office, or as cartoonishly and monstrously rendered in the tediousness of Sade's tableaux, testify to reality's insufficiency to satisfy and the preposterousness of its pretensions to do so.

Psychoanalysis calls this resistance *the symptom* because it entails the dis-placed expression of some frustrated or forbidden desire, the return of the repressed, which is to say that the symptom is not the effect of some under-lying cause but the cause itself. It is the unconscious in action, in search of an addressee. And the unconscious does not exist except as this action—this recalcitrance, subversion, evasion, revolt—for which the ego cannot account, since it (the ego) is built and fortified by the exclusion of the subject the symptom expresses. The ego is this exclusion. Its trouble is that the symptom slips from every effort of containment, including especially those ideological containments that prohibit or redistribute the desire of the subject in ways that reinforce the order of things. The symptom is that slippage, the slippage of the real of the subject from beneath the thumb of reality.

Psychoanalysis is on the side of the symptom. It is the position of the analyst, the locus of the desire of the analyst (the grammar of the double-genitive indicates both the analyst's desire for the unconscious and the subject's desire for the analyst), where the symptom finds its addressee. To be on the side of the symptom does not imply some valuative or moralistic endorsement of the specific contents of this or that symptom, this or that mode or strategy of resistance. The work of analysis reroutes the truth of the symptom through the position of the analyst and back to the subject as if that truth had come from outside; without the ethical guardrails such work affords, the symptom can be ballasted by love or hate, kindness or cruelty, and can tend toward beatific or horrific ends. But it is a symptom all the same, and this is what concerns us. Any judgments as to the morality of the symptom belong on the side of the social link. But psychoanalysis is for the subject, and the symptom is the subject's means of making a way for itself—for better or often for worse—in an indifferent or hostile world.

This is not to suggest that, being on the side of the subject, psychoanalysis is simply opposed to the social link. Since the ethics of psychoanalysis involves making a way for the subject against the totalizing ambitions of the ego and its ideological supports, against the censorship and repression that want to quiet the subject's protest resounding from beyond the pleasure principle, this ethics is not merely that of the inward-facing imperative to know thyself. Nor is it an ethics of pure refusal or negation. Lacanians rightly tend to emphasize the subject as *lack*, but it must also be remembered that this lack is not a deficit so much as it is a provocation. The ethics of psychoanalysis therefore is also oriented outwardly, toward the social link and its hostility to the subject. It orients the subject's efforts to rupture or transform the terms and conditions of its ideological entrapment in order to open and defend a space in which may be realized the transformative potential of the unconscious fantasy and the dissatisfaction it motors. It must undertake to change the social link and the language which structures it, not to escape reality like some shipwrecked sailor at the end of the world. To undertake the ethics of psychoanalysis is to constitute a transformational solidarity with the unconscious that works to change reality, in ever more novel ways.

The difference between fantasy and ideology reveals, then, an inherent politics of the unconscious. For the ethics of psychoanalysis, this is not a politics in which one can decline to participate.

Literature, Ideology, and the Unconscious

By the same measure, there is also a politics of literary criticism, to the extent that the critic is the position to which the subject of literature is addressed and through which that subject's truth is returned to itself in another, differently illuminated form. Any critical exercise that only concerns a literary text's complicity with its historical and ideological situation, but declines to attend to the text's resistances against or its potential to rupture that situation, thereby declines the address of the subject and the work of literature. It is ideology critique.

This is all well and good. It will always be necessary for criticism to clear the ideological distortions that constitute and sustain the dehumanizing structures and relations comprising our world. And this sort of criticism occupies not a small part of *The Unwritten Enlightenment*, and even inaugurates it. The histories of reading that have assimilated the texts in question here to the interests of imperialism and antiblackness (Defoe), liberalism and neoliberalism (Rousseau), moral monstrosity (Sade), or phallic authority (Sterne), to which my own readings are indebted and from which they depart, demonstrate the obvious: that literature can be put *to work*, that it is no more immune to ideology than any other field of human endeavor and can be a powerful weapon in ideology's arsenal.

But this weaponization happens without regard for or aggressively opposes what literature is, essentially and originally, as a category and a concept: the incalculable creative potential of a critical encounter between a reader and a text. This encounter never takes place beyond language or history, but nor is it entirely circumscribed by, and condemned merely to reproduce, them. The interminable realization of its potential is the work of literature; the cause of this realization, its reason for being, is the subject of literature. As critics invested in and ethically committed to the work of literature, we are constitutively on the side of this subject. And as with the ethics of psychoanalysis, this alliance looks both toward the text and outward toward the reality in which it, and we, find or fail to find ourselves.

If we believe that literature can change the world—and this is no mere conviction; it is a fact of broad historical record—we therefore operate the work of literature in ways that rigorously and emphatically distinguish ideology from fantasy, writing from and for the unwritten, for both ethical and tactical reasons.

Perhaps such militance itself seems symptomatic. Maybe it is my own hobby-horse. Even if so, however, it is not news. The distinction between ideology and fantasy, and the relation between ideology critique and psychoanalysis this distinction permits, were fundamental to Lacan and Althusser. The latter's theorization of immanent causality, fashioned after Lacan's reclamation of psychoanalysis from depth psychology but oriented toward an object of inquiry other than the unconscious, is the basis of Fredric Jameson's (in)famous and enduring imperative to "Always historicize!" which means also to historicize the position of the literary critic and the ideological stakes of any given instance or school or ethics of criticism.[8] Without the difference between fantasy and ideology there can be no possible relation, thus no alliance, between psychoanalysis and ideology critique, in the space of literature or anywhere else.

And yet, the last decades of psychoanalytic cultural and literary criticism have seen this distinction erode and at times collapse. Fantasy increasingly has been conflated with ideology in ways that mitigate the clinical and conceptual specificity of psychoanalysis and what it can offer to any theory or practice of resistance against ideology's total hold on the subject. It is as though "fantasy" has become another, perhaps more specialized name for ideology.

This trend is already evident in moments of Jameson's *The Political Unconscious*,[9] but can be traced more directly to Slavoj Žižek's *The Sublime Object of Ideology*, which theorizes precisely the relation between ideology and fantasy, and in ways that support what we are charting here. In fact, much of Žižek's psychoanalytic cultural criticism (if we may distinguish this from his more strictly philosophical investigations) in and after *The Sublime Object* exposes the ruses of ideology by demonstrating how they elide or attempt to appropriate an underlying fantasmatic structure. Often with Žižek, it is fantasy's discrepancies with respect to a given ideological maneuver that reveal how such a maneuver constructs, manipulates, and distorts the subject's position within what is called reality.[10] Or inversely, Žižek at times shows ideology to be the materialization of a fantasy of which the subject or social milieu is unaware, because it is unconscious; in other words, Žižek locates ideology as a consequence of fantasy and a means to its repression, and finds in fantasy a recalcitrant residue of desire that ideology cannot digest. Suffice it to say that *The Unwritten Enlightenment* carries on in this vein and is thoroughly indebted to Žižek's interweaving of ideology critique with psychoanalysis.

The trouble thus is not with the whole of *The Sublime Object* or its ambition to explore the interplay of fantasy (the real) and reality (the imaginary). The trouble rather is with Žižek's insistence there and throughout his works, especially via his notorious, copious references to popular culture, on the ways in which fantasy and ideology can overlap. This seems to have induced, or at least to exemplify, the tendency of many critics (of culture, film, literature, art, and so on) to neglect, overlook, disregard, or otherwise fail to consider the question prior to such a relation: namely, that of the difference between fantasy and ideology. Given how pervasive this tendency has become, it is impossible to enumerate its every instance, and it makes little sense to single out those after Žižek who repeat it. I only want to raise the red flag in hopes that anyone operating at the intersections of psychoanalysis and ideology critique, whether in the field of literature or elsewhere, will interrogate their methods and theoretical assumptions, squaring them with the ethics of psychoanalysis before putting its concepts to use. To this end, I will confine my complaint only to one example from Žižek, the pattern for which can be found throughout many of his later works.[11]

The first chapter of *The Sublime Object* includes a section titled "Ideological Fantasy," which already confounds these two concepts. Still, Žižek helpfully defines ideology here in terms consistent with our own: the ideological illusion, he argues, is "not on the side of knowledge," it does not operate in the disconnect between what the people are doing and what they think they are doing; rather, the illusion "is an error, a distortion which is already at work in the social reality itself. . . . What they do not know," he continues, "what they misrecognize, is not the reality but the illusion which is structuring their reality, their real social activity." Ideology is social reality spontaneously experienced as if it were not the effect of a history of representation and the reification of an ideologically invested illusion. We may know this; we may be perfectly aware of the contingency and even the absurdity of our world, yet we carry on despite this knowledge. This is ideology. So far, so good.

But Žižek goes further: "The illusion is therefore double: it consists in overlooking the illusion which is structuring our real, effective relationship to reality. And this overlooked, unconscious illusion is what may be called the *ideological fantasy*." Hold on. What is double about the illusion? On reading this formulation again, it seems rather that ideological fantasy is not a double of ideology but only Žižek's new name for it. There is a circularity here: ideology is fantasy because fantasy is ideology: thus, ideological fantasy. And what justifies this naming? All too easily, "unconscious" is invoked as an adjective, reviving the sort of use and abuse of the unconscious Lacan has enjoined us to refuse. It is not that we owe Lacan a dogmatic allegiance, but if we are going to depart from his definition of the unconscious, and especially if we do so in the name and under the sign of Lacan, then we ought at least to contend with that definition and offer a compelling alternative. But here Žižek defines "unconscious," at best, implicitly, as an adjectival modifier of ideological illusion, which thereby retains its primacy in the formulation. Žižek then repeats this move in even more striking terms that mean to invert the hierarchy but have the opposite effect: "The fundamental level of ideology," he writes, "is not that of an illusion masking the real state of things but that of an (unconscious) fantasy structuring our social reality itself."[12] Thus is fantasy absorbed, subsumed—literally made into the bedrock of ideology.

It is certainly true that ideology and fantasy often seem consonant. Instances of this abound throughout Žižek's work. Indeed, we have already noted that this is ideology's core aim, its own (impossible) fantasy: to encircle the coordinates of the unconscious so as to entrap and inscribe the subject alongside the other units of account in ideology's ledger. But too often their consonance drowns out the dissonance. As *The Sublime Object* also makes clear, an ideological formation will never fit its fantasmatic motivation perfectly and without remainder, but only ever partially and therefore insufficiently. What *The Unwritten Enlightenment* emphasizes is that it is there in the disharmony between reality (ideology) and fantasy, whether in the work of analysis or the work of literature, where the ethical regard for the subject is concerned.[13] Our task when confronting their consonance is not to dampen but to amplify the dissonance.

Žižek knows this, even if occasionally he seems to forget it, and it bears repeating that *The Unwritten Enlightenment* descends from the same theoretical tradition *The Sublime Object* represents. But what I have foregrounded throughout—particularly in my various embellishments upon the figure of the broken writing machine—is that this fantasy framework is *ill-fitted* to the reality it frames.

Difference is the condition for the possibility of any relation; the specific differences at stake here specify the conditions and the logic of *this* relation. But by developing pointedly Lacanian interventions that often ease into complementary but distinct Hegelian/Marxian analyses without accounting for their distinctions—indeed, by positioning Marx as the first true Lacanian, which has the added effect of transforming Lacan into a Marxist—Žižek has inspired or is at the forefront of a panoply of critics who overlook the difference altogether. Psychoanalytic concepts are applied without regard for their clinical origins and stakes or for their value as anything other than variations on the conceptual tools already provided by ideology critique. The unconscious becomes just another way to explain. And so psychoanalysis is swallowed up by the alliance. The cause for which it stands—the subject, the human—is reduced to a pure contingency, a pliable object molded by the forces of social reproduction, captured entirely within the field of manipulative representations comprising its ideological situation. Fantasy is interpolated as merely the spring of libidinal energy driving this or that ideological maneuver, and not as the crucial excess of energy that overflows and cannot be captured by ideology and converted to its own ends. What moves the subject—the drive as such, the death drive—is therein conceived, if it is considered at all, only as an accomplice to ideology, as a sort of subjective hinge upon which it turns, and is widely misread as an explanation or excuse for the economic and ecological depredations motoring the war machine or the collapse of Civilization As We Know It.

Such are the incalculable, unforeseeable consequences of psychoanalysis. It does not always live up to its commitments. Sometimes—or as Lacan and Freud both insisted, much of the time, even or especially with the best of intentions—psychoanalysis is its own worst enemy.

Reducing psychoanalysis in this way to an instrument of cultural critique often results in theoretical confusion and political imprecision that could be resolved by a reliance on ideology critique alone. Worse, it misrepresents psychoanalysis as an apparatus of thought to be wielded or applied rather than what it truly is: a structure of address, instantiated through the ethics of an experience and a practice that pries a modicum of separation from the social link. It is out of this separation—again, not a liberation, but a momentary suspension, an interstice—that the truth of the subject has a chance to be expressed in terms other than those of the symptom, and with this expression, within this interval, to turn upon and transform the social link. This is where the subject's radical potential, and the inherent radicalism of psychoanalysis, lies. If fantasy were merely a subspecies of ideology, if it were only an individualized vector of ideological transmission or the fountain from which ideology springs, then there would be no unconscious. The unconscious would only be false consciousness by another name. But psychoanalysis already has another name for false consciousness: *consciousness*.[14]

Psychoanalysis confirms this again (and again) by way of experience, from which psychoanalytic theory, abstraction, formalization, or application all follow as endeavors not to master but to orient the history and direction of that experience. Although arrived at by empiricist means, through a rigorous investigation of the experience of the unconscious, even under the banner of the Enlightenment, psychoanalytic knowledge is not on the order of empirical fact. It is rather know-how, *savoir faire*; it is knowledge that must be as nimble, unsettled, dynamic, as its object and cause.

This holds true, as well, when our attention shifts analogously from the subject of the unconscious to the subject of literature. It is ethically incumbent upon any critic operating on the side, for the cause, of the subject to hold the line between ideology and fantasy. This line is analogous to the limit at which the work of literature takes place: between the written and the unwritten, between the text and what it desires but fails to say, between what it is made (commanded) to say and what it refuses to surrender to the order of the signifier, between what of it is useful and what is excessive or useless or disconsonant. This infinitesimal but therefore infinite "between" marks the text's difference from itself. This is the opening and condition for the structure of address through which the subject of literature returns to itself by way of the critic's creative and reflective mediation. Otherwise, what is called "literature" is merely an artifact or consequence of its conditions: a reflection of its history and its ideologically saturated situation, as if it could not be otherwise: a representation of ideology, which is to say, just another instance of it.

If we critics do not hold the line between fantasy and ideology; if we do not follow the unwritten truth around which the text circulates and for which it continues to be read; if we do not undertake the work of literature with and against the text, constructing this work along the seams of its internal falterings and hesitations, in its slippages and displacements, in all those momentary incoherencies or more-than-paradoxical contradictions signifying a breakdown of signification—if, in short, we do not read for the subject of literature, we risk surrendering the question of literature, and the special and powerful ways in which it asks the question of the human, to the same inhuman and dehumanizing ideological maneuvers we want to challenge. We abdicate our cause precisely in our efforts to defend it.

This is the provocation to which this book has been dedicated. I have attempted to peel fantasy apart from ideology in a categorical, openly polemical fashion, not to deny but rather to insist that they are intertwined—co-implicated and irreducible, inseparable yet non-identical. As the composition of a knot cannot be grasped so long as its threads remain clustered and compressed into one another, our task has been to separate the threads of psychoanalysis and ideology critique in order to better understand how they are interwoven and why they should not be confounded into a single object. By disentangling and situating these essential critical allies with respect to the subject and experience of literature, I hope to have buttressed the ethical supports upon which the work of analysis and the work of literature, and with them, the need for incessant ideology critique, all must stand.

NOTES

Introduction

1. Roland Barthes, *Mythologies*, trans. Richard Howard and Annette Lavers (New York: Hill and Wang, 2012), esp. 226–27 and 234–36.

2. Jacques Lacan, "Position of the Unconscious," in *Écrits: The First Complete Edition in English*, trans. Bruce Fink (New York: Norton, 2006), 708.

3. Lacan intimated as much on the back cover of the first edition of his *Écrits*: "One must read this collection cover to cover to realise that a single debate is engaged in here, always the same. Should it seem dated, it proves nevertheless to be that of the Enlightenment [*le débat des lumières*]" (*Écrits* [Paris: Seuil, 1966]; translated by Danny Nobus in "Lacan's *Écrits* Revisited: On Writing as Object of Desire," *Psychoanalytische Perspectieven* 36, no. 4 [2018]: 347–48, fn. 4; translation slightly modified).

4. This is a variation on the Freudian theme of desire and loss: "The finding of an object is in fact a refinding of it" (Sigmund Freud, *Three Essays on the Theory of Sexuality*, in *The Standard Edition of the Complete Psychological Works of Sigmund Freud* [hereafter *S.E.*], vol. 7, ed. and trans. James Strachey et al. [London: Hogarth, 1953–74], 221).

5. See, for instance, Colette Soler, "Literature as Symptom," in *Lacan and the Subject of Language*, ed. Ellie Ragland-Sullivan and Mark Bracher (New York: Routledge, 1991), 213–19; and Jacques Lacan, "Préface," in *Lacan*, by Robert Georgin (Paris: Cistre, 1984), 9–17. The best and most extensive survey of this debate is still Jean-Michel Rabaté, *Jacques Lacan: Psychoanalysis and the Subject of Literature* (New York: Palgrave, 2001).

6. Francesco Orlando, *Toward a Freudian Theory of Literature with an Analysis of Racine's "Phèdre,"* trans. Charmaine Lee (Baltimore, MD: Johns Hopkins University Press, 1978); Marthe Robert, *Origins of the Novel*, trans. Sacha Rabinovitch (Bloomington: Indiana University Press, 1980); Peter Brooks, *Reading for the Plot: Design and Intention in Narrative* (Cambridge, MA: Harvard University Press, 1984); Leo Bersani, *The Freudian Body: Psychoanalysis and Art* (New York: Columbia University Press, 1986). On the difficulties of establishing a formalist psychoanalytic literary criticism, see Peter Brooks, *Psychoanalysis and Storytelling* (Oxford: Blackwell, 1994), esp. 20–45.

7. Joan Copjec, *Read My Desire: Lacan Against the Historicists* (Cambridge, MA: MIT Press, 1994), 13–14.

8. Barthes, *Mythologies*, xi; italics in original.

9. Shoshana Felman, "To Open the Question," in *Literature and Psychoanalysis: The Question of Reading: Otherwise*, ed. Felman (Baltimore, MD: Johns Hopkins University Press, 1982), 10. Felman continues: "literature *in* psychoanalysis functions precisely as its 'unthought': as the condition of possibility

and the self-subversive blind spot of psychoanalytical *thought*" (10, emphasis in original).

10. Lacan, "Position of the Unconscious," esp. 703–5.

11. For a more exhaustive account of what the co-constitutivity of critic and literature means for the theory of the novel, see my "What Is the Novel? The Fundamental Concepts of a Literary Phenomenon," *Continental Thought and Theory* 2, no. 3 (January 2019): 134–66.

12. See Nancy Armstrong, *How Novels Think: The Limits of Individualism from 1719–1900* (New York: Columbia University Press, 2005), esp. 1–52.

13. Philippe Lacoue-Labarthe and Jean-Luc Nancy, *The Literary Absolute: The Theory of Literature in German Romanticism*, trans. Philip Barnard and Cheryl Lester (Albany: SUNY Press, 1998), 83.

14. Early Romanticism represents "the *theoretical* institutionalization of the *literary genre* (or, if you like, of literature *itself*, of *literature* as absolute)" (Lacoue-Labarthe and Nancy, *The Literary Absolute*, 3; emphasis in original).

15. Allen Tate, "Miss Emily and the Bibliographer," in *Praising It New: The Best of the New Criticism*, ed. Garrick Davis (Athens, OH: Swallow, 2008), 44; John Crowe Ransom, "Criticism, Inc.," in *Praising It New*, 58.

16. Ransom, "Criticism, Inc.," 61. Also see Cleanth Brooks, *The Well Wrought Urn: Studies in the Structure of Poetry* (Orlando, FL: Harcourt Books, 1947), esp. "Preface" and "Appendix One: Criticism, History, and Critical Relativism." According to Brooks, "the question of form, of rhetorical structure . . . is the primary problem of the critic. . . . If there is such a thing as poetry," which would be at issue in the question of form, "we [critics] are compelled to deal with it" (222).

17. The most notable example of a New Critical effort to think this relation is Ian Watt's *The Rise of the Novel: Studies in Defoe, Richardson and Fielding* (Berkeley: University of California Press, 1957), the strengths and deficiencies of which have been extensively rehearsed elsewhere.

18. Mikhail Bakhtin, *The Dialogic Imagination*, ed. Michael Holquist, trans. Caryl Emerson and Michael Holquist (Austin: University of Texas Press, 1981), 11, 22. Bakhtin's definition of the novel resonates at the foundation of modern literary criticism, in Friedrich Schlegel's famous fragment 116 from the *Athenaeum*: "Other kinds of poetry are finished and are now capable of being fully analyzed. The romantic kind of poetry"—which for Schlegel was epitomized by the novel—"is still in the state of becoming; that, in fact, is its real essence: that it should forever be becoming and never be perfected" (Schlegel, *Philosophical Fragments*, trans. Peter Firchow [Minneapolis: University of Minnesota Press, 1991], 32). Earlier, in the "Critical Fragments," Schlegel also castigated the ancient poetic genres for being "ridiculous in their rigid purity" (ibid., 8).

19. This is borne out by the history of the novel. Miguel de Cervantes's genius for irony helped establish that the novel resembles its world without merely reproducing it (*Don Quijote*, trans. Burton Raffel, ed. Diana de Armas Wilson [New York: Norton, 1999]). Whence the enduring legitimacy of Bakhtin's insight: the novel's resemblance to and difference from its "unfinished, still-evolving, contemporary reality" (*The Dialogic Imagination*, 7), a reality that informs but does not exhaust its literary potential. By a sort of deferred action, Cervantes's literary experiment would wait a century before finding its place at the

foundation of the eighteenth-century novel, thus also at the root of its contemporary manifestations. The novel as such is thus not coincident with its own history; through this hundred-year genealogical hiatus, its origin was an aftereffect of its repetition.

20. Roman Jakobson, "Closing Statement: Linguistics and Poetics," in *Semiotics: An Introductory Anthology*, ed. Robert E. Innis (Bloomington: Indiana University Press, 1985), 145–75.

21. See John Bender, "Novel Knowledge: Judgment, Experience, Experiment," in *Ends of Enlightenment* (Stanford, CA: Stanford University Press, 2012), 21–37.

22. Edgar Allan Poe, "Critical Notices," *Southern Literary Messenger* 2, no. 2 (January 1836): 127–28.

23. Jakobson, "Closing Statement," 167.

24. Schlegel, *Philosophical Fragments*, 51.

25. Walter Benjamin, "The Concept of Criticism in German Romanticism," in *Selected Writings: Volume 1, 1913–1926*, ed. Marcus Bullock and Michael W. Jennings (Cambridge, MA: Harvard University Press, 1996), 148.

26. Benjamin, "The Concept of Criticism," 155.

27. For instance, see Jacques Lacan, *The Seminar of Jacques Lacan, Book III: The Psychoses, 1955–1956*, trans. Russell Grigg, ed. Jacques-Alain Miller (New York: Norton, 1993), 166–68; and *The Seminar of Jacques Lacan, Book VII: The Ethics of Psychoanalysis, 1959–1960*, ed. Jacques-Alain Miller, trans. Dennis Porter (New York: Norton, 1992), 12.

28. Sigmund Freud, *The Interpretation of Dreams*, in *S.E.* 5: 525; and 4: 111 n. 1. Also see J. Laplanche and J.-B. Pontalis, *The Language of Psycho-Analysis*, trans. Donald Nicholson-Smith (New York: Norton, 1973), 293–94; and David Sigler, "The Navel of the Dream: Freud, Derrida and Lacan on the Gap where 'Something Happens,'" *SubStance* 39, no. 2 (2010): 17–38.

29. Jacques Derrida variously theorizes the generativity of this lack under the heading of supplementarity; see esp. "Structure, Sign, and Play in the Discourse of the Human Sciences," in *Writing and Difference*, trans. Alan Bass (Chicago: University of Chicago Press, 1978), 289.

30. Sigmund Freud, "Constructions in Analysis," in *S.E.* 23: 257–69.

31. Freud drew this analogy as early as his first major case history, that of "Dora," where he also offers a similar qualification: "like a conscientious archaeologist I have not omitted to mention in each case where the authentic parts end and my constructions begin" (Freud, "Fragment of an Analysis of a Case of Hysteria," in *S.E.* 7: 12).

32. Numerous other examples pervade Freud's work, most notoriously the murder of the primal father first in *Totem and Taboo* (*S.E.* 13, esp. 125–61) and again in his last book, *Moses and Monotheism* (*S.E.* 23, esp. 41–53 and 80–102). In these writings, Freud poses the historical truth of civilization in terms of a *necessary fiction* that explains the logic of the present by projecting it backward to the break with prehistory. The construction of the primal horde thus resembles the Enlightenment convention of the "state of Nature" and its interruption by the covenant or social contract, which similarly imagines, thereby produces a model for, contemporary society according to the fiction of its foundation. Freud himself employs the term "state of nature" in "The Future of an Illusion" (*S.E.* 15: 15–20).

33. Jacques Lacan, *1966–1967: La Logique du fantasme* (unpublished seminar; my translation), November 16, 1966; retrieved from https://nosubject.com/Seminar_XIV. Remaining within the context of the Enlightenment, Willy Apollon invokes Kant's concept of the *noumenon* to articulate this notion of the subject as a site of "pure representations . . . that do not correspond to anything that can be contained within the limits of reality and of the pleasure principle" (Apollon, "The Untreatable," trans. Steven Miller, *Umbr(a): A Journal of the Unconscious*, no. 1: "The Incurable" [2006]: 28).

34. In this regard but with extended attention to the form of Freud's writing, see Michel de Certeau, "The Freudian Novel: History and Literature," in *Heterologies: Discourse on the Other*, trans. Brian Massumi (Minneapolis: University of Minnesota Press, 1986), esp. 19–21.

35. An extended consideration of this point can be found in Rabaté, *Jacques Lacan*, throughout but esp. 1–28 and 183–85.

36. This sense of "unworking" borrows from Jean-Luc Nancy's term *désoeuvrement*, "that which, before or beyond the work, withdraws from the work, and which, no longer having to do either with production or with completion, encounters interruption, fragmentation, suspension" (Nancy, *The Inoperative Community*, ed. Peter Connor [Minneapolis: University of Minnesota Press, 1991], 31).

37. Charles W. Mills, "The Illumination of Blackness," in *Antiblackness*, ed. Moon-Kie Jung and João H. Costa Vargas (Durham, NC: Duke University Press, 2021), 18–19. Antiblackness will be addressed again in chapter 1, on *Robinson Crusoe*.

38. Clifford Siskin and William Warner, "*This Is Enlightenment*: An Invitation in the Form of an Argument," in *This Is Enlightenment*, ed. Siskin and Warner (Chicago: University of Chicago Press, 2010), 1–33, esp. 1–12.

39. See Clifford Siskin, "Mediated Enlightenment: The System of the World," in *This Is Enlightenment*, ed. Siskin and Warner, 164–172.

40. Michel Foucault similarly diagnoses this epistemic shift, by way of the origin of the modern novel (for him, this is *Don Quixote*), as a move from the paradigm of interpretation to that of classification, that is, from the discovery of a system of meaning already intrinsic to observable phenomena to the construction of such systems and their overlay upon the phenomenal. See *The Order of Things: An Archaeology of the Human Sciences* (New York: Vintage, 1994), 125–65.

41. For a full elaboration of the philosophical history of the subject, see Étienne Balibar, "Subjection and Subjectivation," in *Supposing the Subject*, ed. Joan Copjec (New York: Verso, 1994), 1–15.

42. According to Foucault, "it is when the legitimate use of reason has been clearly defined in its principles that its autonomy can be assured. The [Kantian] critique is . . . the handbook of reason that has grown up in Enlightenment; and, conversely, the Enlightenment is the age of the critique" (Foucault, "What Is Enlightenment?" trans. Catherine Porter, in *The Foucault Reader*, ed. Paul Rabinow [New York: Pantheon Books, 1984], 38).

43. "Oldest Programme for a System of German Idealism," trans. Stefan Bird-Pollan, in *Classical and Romantic German Aesthetics*, ed. J. M. Bernstein (Cambridge: Cambridge University Press, 2003), 185–87. This does not oppose poetry to philosophy, but collapses the distinction between them. If philosophy

is to reach the hearts and minds of the people, "The philosopher must possess as much aesthetic power as the poet" (185–87). According to Bernstein, the "Oldest Programme" "crystallizes the rogue moment in idealist thought when philosophical rationality in its role as mimic and defender of scientific reason is displaced by the claims of aesthetics. Aesthetic reason is a reason aestheticized, drawn out of its logical shell where the rules of deductive reason are constitutive to become, in its reformed disposition, imbued with spirit, feeling, sensuousness, life" (Bernstein, "Introduction," in *Classical and Romantic German Aesthetics*, ix).

44. Rodolphe Gasché, "Forward: Ideality in Fragmentation," in Friedrich Schlegel, *Philosophical Fragments*, xxvii, xxx.

45. Jacques Lacan, *The Seminar of Jacques Lacan, Book VI: Desire and Its Interpretation*, ed. Jacques-Alain Miller, trans. Bruce Fink (Medford, MA: Polity, 2019), 326.

46. Willy Apollon, "Four Seasons in Femininity or *Four Men in a Woman's Life*," *Topoi* 12 (1993): 114. Lacan offers another variation on this fenestrating metaphor: "It is thus as representation's representative in fantasy—that is, as the originally repressed subject—that $, the barred S of desire, props up the field of reality here; and this field is sustained only by the abstraction of object *a*, which nevertheless gives it its frame" (Lacan, "On a Question Prior to Any Possible Treatment of Psychosis," in *Écrits*, 487, fn. 14). The best extended meditation on the incurable tension between the imaginary other and the *objet a* (though this does not exhaust the book's range) is Roland Barthes's *A Lover's Discourse: Fragments*, trans. Richard Howard (New York: Hill and Wang, 2010).

47. Jacques Lacan, *Encore: The Seminar of Jacques Lacan, Book XX: On Feminine Sexuality, the Limits of Love and Knowledge, 1972–1973*, ed. Jacques-Alain Miller, trans. Bruce Fink (New York: Norton, 1998), 93–94 and 144–45.

48. Lacan, *Encore*, 93.

49. On the undecidable conjunction and difference between literature and philosophy, see Philippe Lacoue-Labarthe, *The Subject of Philosophy*, ed. Thomas Tresize (Minneapolis: University of Minnesota Press, 1993).

50. Diagnosis and the supposition of neutrality are two primary means of resistance, on the part of the critic or the analyst, against the work of literature or analysis. See Jean-Max Gaudillière and Françoise Davoine, *Madness and the Social Link: The Jean-Max Gaudillière Seminars 1985–2000*, trans. Agnès Jacob (New York: Routledge, 2021), 9–10.

51. Lacan, *Encore*, 121.

Chapter 1

1. Daniel Defoe, *Robinson Crusoe*, ed. Michael Shinagel (New York: Norton, 1994), 4. Subsequent references appear parenthetically and refer to this edition of the text; unless otherwise noted, all typological peculiarities, italics, and abbreviations are in the original.

2. Freud's short essay on "Family Romances" famously begins with the simultaneous banality and radicalism of this rebellion: "The liberation of an individual, as he grows up, from the authority of his parents is one of the most necessary though one of the most painful results brought about by the course of his development. . . . Indeed, the whole progress of society rests upon the opposition between successive generations" (Freud, "Family Romances," in *S.E.* 9: 235–42).

3. See Carol Kay, *Political Constructions: Defoe, Richardson, and Sterne in Relation to Hobbes, Hume, and Burke* (Ithaca, NY: Cornell University Press, 1988), esp. 66–92; and Maximillian Novak, *Defoe and the Nature of Man* (Oxford: Oxford University Press, 1963).

4. The most extensive study along these lines is Roxann Wheeler, "'My Savage,' 'My Man': Racial Multiplicity in *Robinson Crusoe*," *ELH* 62, no. 4 (Winter 1995): 821–61. Also see Derek Walcott, "The Figure of Crusoe," in *Critical Perspectives on Derek Walcott*, ed. Robert D. Hamner (Boulder, CO: Lynne Rienner, 1997), 33–41; and David Marriott, "The Figure of Crusoe," in *Modernism and Masculinity*, ed. Natalya Lusty and Julian Murphet (Cambridge: Cambridge University Press, 2014), 159–78. A key literary figuration of the relation between race, racism, and representation in Defoe's novel is J. M. Coetzee, *Foe* (New York: Penguin, 1986); also see Derek Attridge, *J. M. Coetzee and the Ethics of Reading* (Chicago: University of Chicago Press, 2004), 65–90.

5. See J. Paul Hunter, *The Reluctant Pilgrim: Defoe's Emblematic Method and Quest for Form in Robinson Crusoe* (Baltimore, MD: Johns Hopkins University Press, 1966); and G. A. Starr, *Defoe and Spiritual Autobiography* (Princeton, NJ: Princeton University Press, 1965).

6. I am grateful to Professor Laird Easton for this evocative formulation.

7. See Sigmund Freud, "Psychoanalytic Notes upon an Autobiographical Account of a Case of Paranoia (*Dementia Paranoides*) (1911)," in *S.E.* 12: 71.

8. Rosemary Dinnage suspects that Schreber's book "must be the most written-about document in all psychiatric literature" ("Introduction," in Daniel Paul Schreber, *Memoirs of My Nervous Illness*, trans. Ida Macalpine and Richard A. Hunter [New York: New York Review Books, 2000], xi). Lacan is conspicuously absent from Dinnage's introduction, but it is a useful compendium of many major works on Schreber since Freud's 1911 case history.

9. Jacques Lacan, "On a Question Prior to Any Possible Treatment of Psychosis," in *Écrits*, 454.

10. Lacan, *The Psychoses*, 101.

11. Lacan, *The Psychoses*, 209. Also see 167. Jeffrey Rodman has shown that Defoe's novel and Lacan's theory of the psychoses both investigate how individuals can become dislocated from shared structures of relation (Rodman, "Defoe and the Psychotic Subject," in *Ethics and the Subject*, ed. Karl Simms [Amsterdam: Rodopi, 1997], 245–51). Rodman's comparison is preliminary and does not extrapolate the historical import and lasting effects of the novel's psychotic dimension. It also does not consider Schreber's *Memoirs* and takes no account of actual psychotic experience or the clinical specificity of Lacan's teaching. It is, however, the only prior consideration of *Robinson Crusoe* and psychosis, other than Lacan's, of which I am aware.

12. Lacan, "On a Question Prior," 481.

13. Psychosis thus names "the subjective position in which what responds to the appeal to the Name-of-the-Father is not the absence of the real father, for this absence is more than compatible with the presence of the signifier, but the lack of the signifier itself. . . . At the point at which the Name-of-the-Father is summoned . . . a pure and simple hole may thus answer in the Other" (Lacan, "On a Question Prior," 465; on the paternal metaphor, see 481).

14. Lacan, "On a Question Prior," 463–64. The metaphor's prohibiting function is represented by the bar which crosses the subject of the unconscious in the formula for the logic of fantasy ($\bar{S} \lozenge a$) and is also one of Lacan's figurations for symbolic castration: what compels the subject to sacrifice its attachment to a primordial (retroactively conceived, fantasmatic) satisfaction. At the same time, as Lacan indicates in the inverted formula for this same logic ($S \lozenge \bar{A}$), in which the "A" of the big Other is barred and the S of the subject is not, it also marks the Other as incomplete, desiring and therefore lacking the subject; the prohibition thus is the condition of the subject's possibility in the sense that it constitutes a lack in the Other to which the subject's (non-)being in the fantasy corresponds. Symbolic castration is the mark of the lack in both the subject and the Other.

15. Danielle Bergeron, "The Work of the Dream and Jouissance in the Treatment of the Psychotic," in Willy Apollon, Danielle Bergeron, and Lucie Cantin, *After Lacan: Clinical Practice and the Subject of the Unconscious*, ed. Robert Hughes and Kareen Ror Malone (Albany: SUNY Press, 2002), 72.

16. Lacan finds here the crux of Schreber's conviction, from which the whole of his ensuing delusion unfolds, that the world's salvation hinges upon his transformation into a woman: "Divination by the unconscious no doubt warned the subject very early on that, unable to be the phallus the mother is missing, there remained the solution of being the woman that men are missing" ("On a Question Prior," 472).

17. Schreber, *Memoirs*, 58. For another startling example of the difficulty Schreber faces in translating this sense of an inner experience imposed from without, see 120–21, fn. 61.

18. Schreber, *Memoirs*, 26. 139, 250, 258.

19. So Freud also says of Schreber: "It [is] incorrect to say that the perception which was suppressed internally is projected outwards; the truth is rather . . . that what was abolished internally [*innerlich Aufgehobene*] returns from without" (Freud, "Psychoanalytic Notes," 71).

20. Schreber, *Memoirs*, 131; emphasis in original. The translators of Freud's *Standard Edition* render *Luder* as "Scoundrel!" (Freud, "Psychoanalytic Notes," 23, fn. 4). Lacan suggests that the peculiarities of what Schreber calls the "basic language" permit us to translate *Luder* via its etymological relation to the English "lure"—"which is certainly the best *ad hominem* address to be expected coming from the symbolic: the Other with a capital O can be awfully impertinent" (Lacan, "On a Question Prior," 477–78).

21. Lacan, "On a Question Prior," 481.

22. *The Freud/Jung Letters*, ed. William McGuire, trans. Ralph Manheim and R. F. C. Hull (Princeton, NJ: Princeton University Press, 1974), 220.

23. "The question is what this testimony by the subject is worth. Well then, he is giving us his experience, which imposes itself as the very structure of reality for him" (Lacan, *The Psychoses*, 210).

24. For an extensive theorization of this undecidable limit between fiction and testimony, see Maurice Blanchot and Jacques Derrida, *The Instant of My Death / Demeure: Fiction and Testimony*, trans. Elizabeth Rottenberg (Stanford, CA: Stanford University Press, 2000), esp. 32–43.

25. Without referencing *Robinson Crusoe*, Mikhail Bakhtin demonstrates that this split between temporal action and atemporal narration is a characteristic of

the novel form that indicates its generic specificity; see "Epic and Novel," in *The Dialogic Imagination*, ed. Michael Holquist, trans. Caryl Emerson and Michael Holquist (Austin: University of Texas Press, 1981), 27.

26. Gaudillière, *Madness and the Social Link*, 6, 31.

27. For a survey of the political philosophies that intersect with *Robinson Crusoe* and the two sequels Defoe authored, see Novak, *Defoe and the Nature of Man*, 22–64. Also see Kay, *Political Constructions*, 66–68.

28. According to Locke: "nothing will be in the mind as a present good, able to counter-balance the removal of any *uneasiness*, which we are under, till it raises our desire, and the *uneasiness* of that has the prevalency in determining the *will*" (*An Essay Concerning Human Understanding*, ed. Peter H. Nidditch [Oxford: Oxford University Press, 1979], 254–55; italics in original).

29. This discontinuity is not accidental. As Michael McKeon explains, "Defoe was aware of the problem," which was less a problem than a deliberate narrative device by which Defoe strengthened the text's prefatory claim to historicity, in order "to sensitize us to the personalized veracity of Robinson's experience, which is all the more authentic for having this subjective volatility" (McKeon, *The Origins of the English Novel, 1600–1740* [Baltimore, MD: Johns Hopkins University Press, 1987], 316–17).

30. According to John Bender, Defoe "showed how, in confinement, the internal forces of psychological motivation fuse dynamically with the physical details of perceptual experience" (*Imagining the Penitentiary: Fiction and the Architecture of Mind in Eighteenth-Century England* [Chicago: University of Chicago Press, 1987], 43). This is the core of Bender's larger argument that Defoe's novels interweave representation, empirical observation, and psychological dynamism to present a systematic model of consciousness and subjectivity that enabled the rise of the penitentiary at the end of the eighteenth century.

31. For Burke, astonishment names "that state of the soul, in which all its motions are suspended" such that "the mind is so entirely filled with its object, that it cannot entertain any other, nor by consequence reason on that object which employs it" (Edmund Burke, *A Philosophical Enquiry into the Origin of Our Ideas of the Sublime and Beautiful and Other Pre-Revolutionary Writings*, ed. David Womersley [New York: Penguin, 1998], 101). Contrary to its later, Romantic reformulation as the domain of the absolute, aesthetics in the eighteenth century was an extension of Locke's epistemology; see Michael McKeon, "Mediation as Primal Word: The Arts, the Sciences, and the Origins of the Aesthetic," in *This Is Enlightenment*, ed. Clifford Siskin and William Warner (Chicago: University of Chicago Press, 2010), 385.

32. Thus Crusoe reflects, "I had been fed even by Miracle, even as great as that of feeding *Elijah* by Ravens; nay, by a long Series of Miracles" (96). Yet another instance of prophetic significance is the warning Crusoe receives from the man of fire who visits him in the dream just prior to his awakening of conscience—"*Seeing all these Things have not brought thee to Repentance, now thou shalt die*" (65). While the language is not identical, this clearly resonates with the litany of threats the prophet Ezekiel is commanded to deliver to the House of Israel; see esp. Ezekiel 18.

33. See Luke 16:19–31.

34. Without referencing *Robinson Crusoe*, Anthony Paul Farley finds in the logic of such a scene the perfection of slavery: "Slavery is perfect when the slaves themselves willingly become things. The perfect slave makes itself a slave by bowing down before the rule of law, and this it can do only after its so-called emancipation. Perfecting slavery is what the slave does when it bows down before the law and prays for relief" (Farley, "Toward a General Theory of Antiblackness," in *Antiblackness*, ed. Moon-Kie Jung and João H. Costa Vargas [Durham, NC: Duke University Press, 2021], 87).

35. In fact, after the awakening of Conscience the term "wretch" is applied not only to Friday but numerously to the other cannibals (121, 123, 126, 133, 143, 150, 167, 169, 170), and to Friday's father (176), confirming that the paternal appellation marks the spiritual destitution that precedes both temporal and spiritual deliverance. This narrative function will be revived when Crusoe delivers the English captain from his mutinous crew.

36. As McKeon observes, Crusoe's "increasingly confident internalization of God's society . . . entails a reciprocal expansion of his own identity as one not only delivered by God but able to deliver others as well" (*Origins of the English Novel*, 330).

37. This and the narrative teleology we have uncovered here place us squarely at odds with Carol Kay's claim that "Crusoe refuses to pretend to any special status as the arm of Providence" (*Political Constructions*, 91).

38. John Richetti calls Crusoe "the perfect mediator" who in Hegelian fashion progressively resolves his own internal contradictions and ultimately those that proliferate throughout his island world while retaining, and even extending and enriching, the onto-theological, metaphysical foundations of his Christian cultural context (Richetti, *Defoe's Narratives: Situations and Structures* [Oxford: Clarendon, 1975], 47).

39. Elias Canetti and Eric L. Santner have separately situated Schreber and the structure of psychosis in general with respect to the paranoia of rule, particularly regarding fascism and Nazism. For Canetti, see *Crowds and Power*, trans. Carol Stewart (New York: Farrar, Straus and Giroux, 1962 [1984]), esp. 434–63; and for a secondary commentary on Canetti's position, see Davide Tarizzo, *Political Grammars: The Unconscious Foundations of Modern Democracy* (Stanford, CA: Stanford University Press, 2021), esp. 149–53. From Santner, see *My Own Private Germany: Daniel Paul Schreber's Secret History of Modernity* (Princeton, NJ: Princeton University Press, 1996). Through such comparative analyses, Schreber is made to reveal Nazism's delusional structure. Winding back the question of delusion to *Robinson Crusoe* and the Enlightenment suggests that these political terrors were not aberrations or deviations into the realms of the irrational. Nazism is not the exception but the result of this history of the psychosis of reason—not its only or inevitable result, but one of its outcomes. Apropos of the question of antiblackness (see n. 34 above), this is consistent with Aimé Césaire's well-known critique of Enlightenment humanism in the context of colonialism: "through the mouths of the Sarrauts and the Bardes, the Mullers and the Renans, through the mouths of all those who considered—and consider—it lawful to apply to non-European peoples 'a kind of expropriation for public purposes' for the benefit of nations that were stronger and better equipped, it was already

Hitler speaking!" (Césaire, *Discourse on Colonialism*, trans. Joan Pinkham [New York: Monthly Review Press, 1972], 39).

40. Sigmund Freud, "Creative Writers and Day-Dreaming," in *S.E.* 9: 149–50.

41. See, for instance, Sigmund Freud, *Civilization and Its Discontents*, in *S.E.* 21: 74; and Freud, *The Future of an Illusion*, in *S.E.* 32: 15–20.

42. Claude Lévi-Strauss, *Tristes Tropiques*, trans. John Weightman and Doreen Weightman (New York: Penguin, 2012), esp. 321–415. Also see my "Psychoanalysis at the End of the World," in *Lacan and the Environment*, ed. Clint Burnham and Paul Kingsbury (New York: Palgrave, 2021), 221–37.

Chapter 2

1. Sigmund Freud, "Analysis Terminable and Interminable," in *S.E.* 23: 248.

2. Freud, "Analysis Terminable and Interminable," 220, 235, 223, 249.

3. Freud, "Analysis Terminable and Interminable," 248–49.

4. Sigmund Freud, "From the History of an Infantile Neurosis," in *S.E.* 17: 10.

5. Jacques Lacan, *My Teaching*, trans. David Macey (New York: Verso, 2008), 43.

6. Said's version of critical consciousness includes a rebuke against any literary criticism that does not engage the historicity of its texts; see his "Introduction: Secular Criticism," in *The World, the Text, and the Critic* (Cambridge, MA: Harvard University Press, 1983), 1–30. Also see Erich Auerbach, "Philology and 'Weltliteratur,'" trans. Marie and Edward Said, *Centennial Review* 13, no. 1 (Winter 1969): 1–17; and Paulo Freire, *Pedagogy of the Oppressed*, trans. Myra Bergman Ramos (New York: Continuum, 2005), esp. 71–86.

7. As Althusser notes, "the ideological State apparatus which has been installed in the *dominant* position in mature capitalist social formations . . . is the *educational ideological apparatus*" (Louis Althusser, *On Ideology* [New York: Verso, 2008], 26; emphases in original).

8. The term "neoliberalism" has become something of an empty signifier in contemporary discourse about the limits and imperatives of self-governance within and beyond democracy. Here, I refer to the broad institutional reconfiguration that since the 1940s has situated the role of the state primarily in service to the market, in order to maximize individual interests by binding price, as much as possible, to individual consumer choice, regardless of other interests, especially those concerning the public good. The best account of this shift, even according to neoliberal economists themselves, is Michel Foucault, *The Birth of Biopolitics: Lectures at the Collège de France, 1978–79*, trans. Graham Burchell, ed. Michel Senellart (New York: Palgrave Macmillan, 2008).

9. Henry Giroux, *Education and the Crisis of Public Values: Challenging the Assault on Teachers, Students, & Public Education* (New York: Peter Lang, 2012), 119–20. Another representative set of arguments regarding the neoliberal onslaught on progressive education is Kenneth J. Saltman and David A. Gabbard, eds., *Education as Enforcement: The Militarization and Corporatization of Schools* (London: Routledge, 2003).

10. To cite just two prominent examples of Enlightenment education discourse: John Locke situates education as a moral problem, and thus a matter of collective welfare: "of all the Men we meet with Nine Parts of Ten are what they are, Good or Evil, useful or not, by their Education. 'Tis that which makes the great

Difference in Mankind" (*The Educational Writings of John Locke*, ed. James L. Axtell [Cambridge: Cambridge University Press, 1968], 114); and Montesquieu's *The Spirit of the Laws* holds that in a republic "love of the laws and the homeland" requires "a continuous preference of the public interest over one's own," and therefore demands a mode of education according to which the concept of private interest is founded upon the public good (*Spirit of the Laws*, ed. Ann M. Cohler, Basia C. Miller, and Harold S. Stone [Cambridge: Cambridge University Press, 1989], 35–36).

11. Jean-Jacques Rousseau, *The Social Contract and Other Late Political Writings*, ed. and trans. Victor Gourevitch (Cambridge: Cambridge University Press, 1997), 41. For a broader history including Rousseau, Diderot, and the other philosophes, see Peter Gay, *The Enlightenment: An Interpretation: The Science of Freedom* (New York: Norton, 1969), 497–552.

12. This is consistent with the later revolutionaries' self-understanding according to which they were not overturning but restoring the order of the world according to a movement of natural necessity; see Hannah Arendt, *On Revolution* (New York: Penguin, 2006), 32–45.

13. Romain Rolland, "Jean-Jacques Rousseau," in *French Thought in the Eighteenth Century* (London: Morrison and Gibb, 1953), 16. Rolland is the friend from whom Freud borrowed the term "oceanic feeling" in the opening pages of *Civilization and Its Discontents* (*S.E.* 21: 64–66).

14. For a detailed history of *Émile*'s complicated and shifting reception in the eighteenth century, see Jean Bloch, *Rousseauism and education in eighteenth-century France* (Oxford: Voltaire Foundation, 1995).

15. John Dewey, *Education Today*, ed. Joseph Ratner (New York: Greenwood, 1940), 174; on Rousseau's absolutism, see John Dewey, *Democracy and Education: An Introduction to the Philosophy of Education* (New York: Macmillan, 1928), 130–37.

16. Gerald L. Gutek, "Introduction," in *Emile*, by Jean-Jacques Rousseau (New York: Barnes & Noble, 2005), vii.

17. In response to an acerbic review of his *Les Crimes de l'amour*, for example, Sade situates himself within a literary tradition that includes Rousseau, Richardson, Fielding, Voltaire, and Marmontel while disputing the accusation that his book glorifies misconduct: "what are the two principal mainsprings of dramatic art? Have all the authors worthy of the name not declared that they are *terror* and *pity*? Now, what can provoke *terror* if not the portrayal of crime triumphant, and what can cause *pity* better than the depiction of virtue a prey to misfortune?" (Marquis de Sade, "The Author of *Les Crimes de l'Amour* to Villeterque, Hack Writer," in *The 120 Days of Sodom & Other Writings*, trans. Austryn Wainhouse and Richard Seaver [New York: Grove, 1966], 124).

18. Jacques Lacan, "Kant with Sade," trans. James B. Swenson, Jr., *October* 51 (Winter 1989): 55.

19. For a more exhaustive list and a selection of other references, see Yvon Belaval, "Préface," in *La Philosophie dans le boudoir*, by Marquis de Sade (Paris: Gallimard, 1976), esp. 26–27; and Pierre Klossowski, *Sade My Neighbor*, trans. Alphonso Lingis (Evanston, IL: Northwestern University Press, 1991), 67–98.

20. Marquis de Sade, "Reflections on the Novel," in *The 120 Days*, 106.

21. Sade, "Reflections on the Novel," 105–6.

22. Marquis de Sade, *Letters from Prison*, trans. Richard Seaver (New York: Arcade, 1999), 314.

23. This definition of "discourse" is adapted from its etymology in the *Oxford English Dictionary*, 3rd ed.

24. Paulo Freire also emphasizes the narrative dimension of education as such: "A careful analysis of the teacher-student relationship at any level, inside or outside the school, reveals its fundamentally *narrative* character"; for Freire, the basis of oppression is that education today "is suffering from narration sickness" (*Pedagogy of the Oppressed*, 71).

25. Jean-Jacques Rousseau, *Emile or On Education*, trans. Allan Bloom (New York: Basic Books, 1979), 187–88; all subsequent references are to this edition and appear parenthetically.

26. The dialectical progression and teleological structure of Rousseau's text all seem quite Hegelian. The resonance is not coincidental. Hegel, that most systematic of thinkers from whose totalizing dialectic nothing escapes, found in *Émile* substantial inspiration for his *Phenomenology of Spirit*, particularly the subject's teleological movement toward self-consciousness. According to Jean Hyppolite:

> Hegel had read Rousseau's *Emile* at Tübingen and had found in it a preliminary history of natural consciousness rising to liberty through particularly educative experiences which were specific to it. The preface to the *Phenomenology* emphasizes the pedagogical nature of Hegel's book, as well as the relation between the evolution of the individual and that of the species, a relation also considered in Rousseau's book. (Hyppolite, *Genesis and Structure of Hegel's "Phenomenology of Spirit,"* trans. Samuel Cherniak and John Heckman [Evanston, IL: Northwestern University Press, 1979], 11)

H. S. Harris also notes that at Tübingen Hegel was "known among his friends as a constant student of Rousseau and Lessing" (Harris, *Hegel: Phenomenology and System* [Indianapolis, IN: Hackett, 1995], 7). Also consistent with *Émile*, both the *Philosophy of Right* and the *Encyclopedia Logic* describe education as the externalization of the inherently inward presence of human Reason, which travels back to its inwardness in its total assimilation of all difference and, in the end, becomes the closed, self-motivated movement of the Concept. Hegel provides what could be a fine summary of Rousseau's philosophy of education in the first part of his *Encyclopedia of Philosophical Sciences*:

> A child, for instance, [considered] as human in a general sense, is of course a rational essence; but the child's reason as such is present at first only as something inward, i.e., as a disposition or vocation, and this, which is merely internal, has for it equally the form of what is merely external, namely, the will of its parents, the learning of its teachers, and in general the rational world that surrounds it. The education and formation of the child consists therefore in the process by which it becomes *for-itself* also what it is initially only *in-itself* and hence for others (adults). Reason, which is at first present in the child only as an inner possibility, is made actual by education, and conversely, the child becomes in like manner conscious that the ethics, religion, and science which it regarded initially as

external authority are things that belong to its own inner nature. (Hegel, *The Encyclopaedia Logic: Part I of the Encyclopaedia of Philosophical Sciences with the Zusätze*, trans. T. F. Geraets, W. A. Suchting, and H. S. Harris [Indianapolis, IN: Hackett, 1991], 211)

No doubt, Hegel is more Rousseauian than Rousseau is Hegelian. The point, though, is that Hegel found order among the chaos of *Émile*, that the chaos or apparent paradoxicality are ordered by a teleology according to which the ending is already there in its origin, and the origin there again in the ending.

27. "Since we absolutely must have books, there exists one which, to my taste, provides the most felicitous treatise on natural education. This book will be the first that my Emile will read. For a long time it will alone compose his whole library, and it will always hold a distinguished place there. It will be the text for which all our discussions on the natural sciences will serve only as a commentary. It will serve as a test of the condition of our judgment during our progress; and so long as our taste is not spoiled its reading will always please us. What, then, is this marvelous book? Is it Aristotle? Is it Pliny? Is it Buffon? No. It is *Robinson Crusoe*" (Rousseau, *Émile*, 184).

28. For an analysis of the complicated status of gender and sexuality in Rousseau, see Mira Morgenstern, "Strangeness, Violence, and the Establishment of Nationhood in Rousseau," *Eighteenth-Century Studies* 41, no. 3 (Spring 2008): 359–81. Also see Penny Weiss, *Gendered Community: Rousseau, Sex, and Politics* (New York: NYU Press, 1993).

29. See Jean-Jacques Rousseau, *The Discourses and Other Early Political Writings*, ed. and trans. Victor Gourevitch (Cambridge: Cambridge University Press, 1997).

30. Jean-Jacques Rousseau, "Essay on the Origin of Languages," in *The Discourses*, 248.

31. Rousseau, "Essay on the Origin of Languages," 253.

32. Rousseau, "Essay on the Origin of Languages," 253.

33. For a detailed discussion of late eighteenth- and early nineteenth-century attempts to read Rousseau's state of Nature as an anthropologically verifiable fact, see Nancy Yousef, "Savage or Solitary? The Wild Child and Rousseau's Man of Nature," *Journal of the History of Ideas* 62, no. 2 (April 2001): 245–63. Bizarrely, this tendency to literalize Rousseau persists, if more obliquely, among anthropologists and economic and political theorists today. For a summary of recent works along these lines, see David Graeber and David Wengrow, *The Dawn of Everything: A New History of Humanity* (New York: Farrar, Straus and Giroux, 2021), 9–12.

34. Jacques Derrida notes how this innovation led Lévi-Strauss to privilege Rousseau as the "fondateur des sciences de l'homme" (*Of Grammatology*, trans. Gayatri Chakravorty Spivak [Baltimore, MD: Johns Hopkins University Press, 1976], 107). Here and throughout his other early writings, Derrida commits significant attention to the undecidable limit between Nature and Culture, similarly examining how both sides of the dichotomy are constituted by the cut that divides them.

35. Rousseau, "Essay on the Origin of Languages," 272–73.

36. Rousseau, "Essay on the Origin of Languages," 273.

37. Sigmund Freud, "Beyond the Pleasure Principle," in *S.E.* 18: 38; italics in original.

38. This is a pedagogical variation on Lacan's insistence that *"transference is the enactment of the reality of the unconscious"* (*The Seminar of Jacques Lacan, Book XI: The Four Fundamental Concepts of Psychoanalysis*, ed. Jacques-Alain Miller, trans. Alan Sheridan [New York: Norton, 1981], 149; italics in original).

39. Marquis de Sade, *Philosophy in the Bedroom*, in *Justine, Philosophy in the Bedroom, & Other Writings*, ed. and trans. Richard Seaver and Austryn Wainhouse (New York: Grove, 1965), 230–31; all subsequent references in the text are to this edition and appear parenthetically.

40. See, for instance, Georges Bataille, *The Accursed Share, Volume 1: Consumption*, trans. Robert Hurley (New York: Zone Books, 1991), esp. 9–41 and 63–77.

41. See, for instance, Voltaire, *Candide, or Optimism*, trans. Theo Cuffe (New York: Penguin, 2005), 10–12.

42. Roland Barthes notes that there is nevertheless a pleasure at stake in the text itself: "Neither culture nor its destruction is erotic; it is the seam between them, the fault, the flaw, which becomes so. The pleasure of the text is like that untenable, impossible, purely *novelistic* instant so relished by Sade's libertine when he manages to be hanged and then to cut the rope at the very moment of his orgasm, his *jouissance* (Barthes, *The Pleasure of the Text*, trans. Richard Miller [New York: Hill and Wang, 1975], 6–7; emphasis in original; translation modified).

43. Marquis de Sade, "Last Will and Testament of Donatien-Alphonse-François Sade, Man of Letters," in *Justine*, 157.

44. As Alenka Zupančič explains, "life as life is not yet a declination from death or the opposite of death; rather, it is its continuation by other means" (*What Is Sex?* [Cambridge, MA: MIT Press, 2017], 91). Zupančič further contests the assumption that the death drive is an unconscious will to destruction: "there is only the death drive. Yet it cannot be described in terms of destructive tendencies that want (us) to return to the inanimate, but precisely as constituting *alternative paths to death* (from those immanent in the organism itself)" (ibid., 106; emphasis in original). Elsewhere, Zupančič explains apropos of Sade, "Pleasure—that is, the limit of suffering that a body can still endure—is thus an obstacle to enjoyment [*jouissance*]. Sade's answer to the impossibility of surpassing this limit is fantasy, the fantasy of infinite suffering" (Zupančič, *Ethics of the Real: Kant, Lacan* [New York: Verso, 2000], 81).

45. Steven Miller, *War after Death: On Violence and Its Limits* (New York: Fordham University Press, 2014), 7.

46. It is this *jouissance* which Sade hopes to excite for his audience, the anonymous addressees in whom his revolutionary vision would be realized. This is apparent as early as *The 120 Days of Sodom*: "Many of the extravagances you are about to see illustrated," he writes in this inaugural apology to the reader, "will doubtless displease you . . . but there are among them a few which will warm you to the point of costing you some fuck, and that, reader, is all we ask of you" (Sade, *The 120 Days*, 254). His introductory epistle in *Philosophy in the Bedroom* is a variation on the same theme: "Voluptuaries of all ages, of every sex, it is to you only that I offer this work; nourish yourselves upon its principles: they

favor your passions, and these passions, whereof coldly insipid moralists put you in fear, are naught but the means Nature employs to bring man to the ends she prescribes to him" (185).

47. Orgasm, moreover, represents a purely physical expulsion of the tension Dolmancé cultivates through the intermixture of his philosophy and his sexual acts; "[Sade] knows that orgasm is but a tribute paid to the norms of the species and is thus a counterfeit of the ecstasy of thought" (Klossowski, *Sade My Neighbor*, 32).

48. Apropos of both Freud and Kant, Joan Copjec writes: "the freedom of the ethical subject . . . [is] the freedom to resist the lure of the pleasure principle and to submit oneself to the law of the death drive" (*Read My Desire*, 96).

49. Writing in a different idiom, Bataille reaches a similar conclusion: "Interminable and monotonous enumeration alone managed to present him [Sade] with the void, the desert, for which he yearned, and which his books still present to the reader" (Bataille, *Literature and Evil*, trans. Alastair Hamilton [London: Marion Boyars, 1973], 116).

50. "Libertinage, standing up to power, is still a passion of power" (Marcel Hénaff, *Sade: The Invention of the Libertine Body*, trans. Xavier Callahan [Minneapolis: University of Minnesota Press, 1999], 10).

51. Maurice Blanchot, "Sade's Reason," in *Lautréamont and Sade*, trans. Stuart Kendall and Michelle Kendall (Stanford, CA: Stanford University Press, 2004), 10; my italics.

52. On this failure, see Lacan, *Encore: The Seminar of Jacques Lacan, Book XX*, 59.

53. Lacan, "Kant with Sade," 58; translation modified.

54. Lacan, "Kant avec Sade," in *Écrits 2: Nouvelle Édition* (Paris: Éditions du Seuil, 1966), 247.

55. Fink's translation:

> "I have the right to enjoy your body," anyone can say to me, "and I will exercise this right without any limit to the capriciousness of the exactions I may wish to satiate with your body" (Lacan, *Écrits*, 648).

Along with the added quotation marks, Fink adds "with your body" to the end of the maxim, which also is not in the French original but seems (?) to be based on the adverbial pronoun, "y," in "le goût d'y assouvir."

56. Rousseau exemplifies a broader truth of the bourgeois revolutions, poetically articulated by Hannah Arendt in her book on the subject: "The trouble has always been the same: those who went into the school of revolution learned and knew beforehand . . . that a revolution must devour its own children" (Arendt, *On Revolution*, 47–48).

57. To reduce Sade to an exemplar of perversion is to commit what Hénaff calls the "strange and remarkably naïve error" of conflating the author with his heroes (*Sade*, 7). Sade himself warned against such naiveté, in no uncertain terms, in his response to Villeterque's review of his *Les Crimes de l'amour*: "Loathsome ignoramus: have you not yet learned that every character in every dramatic work must employ a language in keeping with his character, and that, when he does, 'tis the fictional personage who is speaking and not the author?" (Sade, "The Author of *Les Crimes de l'Amour*," 127–28; compare. n. 17 above). Freud famously

located the logic of the pervert in the disavowal of the reality of castration, which manifests as a fixation on some partial object that substitutes for the lack in the Other (see "Fetishism," in *S.E.* 21: 147–58); Hénaff makes clear that this, too, is inapposite: "for Sade, nothing could be further from libertine desire. The selective dividing up carried out by the eye on the desired body is marked not at all by a fetishistic emphasis, but rather by the precision of taxonomic reason" (*Sade*, 29).

58. Eliyahu Rosenow, for example, notices that Rousseau's ideal tutor (Rousseau himself) "is the one who regulates the child's natural curiosity, who shapes his judgment, ambitions and hopes; he decides what head he will have on his shoulders; he determines his desires and controls his most hidden impulses and inclinations" (Rosenow, "Rousseau's 'Emile,' an Anti-Utopia," *British Journal of Educational Studies* 28, no. 3 [October 1980]: 217). Following this analysis, Scott Walter has criticized the free school movement's reliance upon Rousseau's text; he isolates and emphasizes the tutor's "pervasive manipulation" of Émile's surroundings, and concludes: "An education devoted to social control and a parent-child relationship built on the worst kind of authoritarianism are the hidden legacies of *Emile*" (Walter, "'The 'Flawed Parent': A Reconsideration of Rousseau's 'Emile' and Its Significance for Radical Education in the United States," *British Journal of Educational Studies* 44, no. 3 [September 1996]: 268, 272).

59. This a matter of historical fact. The American and French revolutions were motivated and bankrolled by an emergent propertied class that was disaffected with royal prerogatives surrounding trade and commerce. Royalty and aristocracy interfered with this new colonial class's unchecked wealth accumulation. See, for instance, C. L. R. James, *The Black Jacobins: Toussaint L'Ouverture and the San Domingo Revolution* (New York: Vintage, 1989), esp. 47–61.

60. Lacan, *Ethics of Psychoanalysis*, 302.

61. Lacan, *Ethics of Psychoanalysis*, 303.

Chapter 3

1. Laurence Sterne, *The Life and Opinions of Tristram Shandy, Gentleman* (New York: Modern Library Classics, 2004), 226; all further references are to this edition and appear parenthetically. Unless otherwise noted, all italics, aposiopeses, and typographic anomalies are in the original.

2. T. S. Eliot, "The Love Song of J. Alfred Prufrock," in *Collected Poems 1909–1962* (New York: Harcourt Brace, 1963), 6.

3. The sexual non-relation is not simply the absence of a relation but the condition for the possibility of relationality as such. As Alenka Zupančič notes, it "gives, dictates the conditions of, what ties us, which is to say that it is not a simple, indifferent absence, but an absence that curves and determines the structure with which it appears" (*What Is Sex?*, 24).

4. Viktor Shklovsky, *Theory of Prose*, trans. Benjamin Sher (Normal, IL: Dalkey Archive, 1990), 170.

5. Shklovsky, *Theory of Prose*, 4–6; emphasis in original.

6. Shklovsky, *Theory of Prose*, 153.

7. E. M. Forster, *Aspects of the Novel* (New York: Harcourt, 1927), 164.

8. A. Alvarez, "The Delinquent Aesthetic," *Hudson Review* 19, no. 4 (Winter 1966–67): 590–91.

9. See, for example, Ronald Paulson, *Don Quixote in England: The Aesthetics of Laughter* (Baltimore, MD: Johns Hopkins University Press, 1998), 150–58; and Robert Folkenflik's introduction to the Modern Library edition of *Tristram Shandy*, viii.

10. Although the two never met, it is well known that Sterne was taken by Hogarth's "discovery" of the universal principal of beautiful composition. He also cultivated an alliance with Hogarth, England's most renowned mid-century artist, in order to foster his novel's mass appeal and artistic legitimacy. (See Ian Campbell Ross, *Laurence Sterne: A Life* [Oxford: Oxford University Press, 2001], 5–6.) At Sterne's request, Hogarth provided the illustrations accompanying several volumes of *Tristram Shandy*, including volume 2, in which Tristram explicitly references the *Analysis* (other references are apparent, though more oblique) as an especially informative basis for his method of writing. For an extended discussion of Sterne's interest in and adherence to Hogarth's aesthetic, see William Blake Gerard, *Laurence Sterne and the Visual Imagination* (Surrey, UK: Ashgate, 2006).

11. William Hogarth, *The Analysis of Beauty: Written with a View to Fixing the Fluctuating Ideas of Taste* (London: J. Reeves, 1753), 40. The most popular aesthetic treatises with which Hogarth was in debate were Francis Hutcheson's *An Inquiry into the Original of Our Ideas of Beauty and Virtue, in Two Treatises* (London: J. and J. Knapton et al., 1729); and its predecessor, Lord (Anthony Ashley Cooper) Shaftesbury's 1711 collection *Characteristicks of Men, Manners, Opinions, Times* (Indianapolis, IN: Liberty Fund, 2011).

12. Hogarth, *Analysis of Beauty*, 38–39.

13. Hogarth, *Analysis of Beauty*, 25; emphasis in original.

14. See McKeon, "Mediation as Primal Word," 384–412.

15. Hogarth, *Analysis of Beauty*, 70. Hogarth continues: "—But in nature's machines, how wonderfully do we see beauty and use go hand in hand!" (71).

16. For an excellent survey of the emergent discourses of automation in eighteenth-century culture and sentimental fiction, including Sterne's two novels, see Alex Wetmore, "Sympathy Machines: Men of Feeling and the Automaton," *Eighteenth-Century Studies* 43, no. 1 (Fall 2009): 37–54. Also see William C. Mottolese, "Tristram Cyborg and Toby Toolmaker: Body, Tools, and Hobbyhorse in *Tristram Shandy*," *SEL: Studies in English Literature* 47, no. 3 (Summer 2007): 679–701.

17. Translated in the Modern Library edition of *Tristram Shandy* (n. 628).

18. Lila V. Graves examines the Lockean dimension of the relation between death and writing in *Tristram Shandy*, arguing that Tristram's authorial consciousness is given its full range of play only when it is secured from physical destruction (Graves, "Locke's *Essay* and Sterne's 'Work Itself,'" *Journal of Narrative Technique* 12, no. 1 [Winter 1982]: 36–47). This insightful reading does not quite consider how death is also the *condition* for Tristram's symbolic elaboration.

19. This characterization is consistent with Alenka Zupančič's characterization of sublimation from *What Is Sex?* but less so with Tim Dean's interpretation that "sublimation represents the transformation of erotic into cultural aims" (*Beyond Sexuality* [Chicago: University of Chicago Press, 2000], 275). My account of the relation between sex and death is, however, thoroughly indebted to Dean's

explanation of the logic of fantasy (ibid., esp. 57–60) and its implications for the theory of sublimation, or theory as sublimation (274–76).

20. Melvyn New, "Sterne and the Narrative of Determinateness," *Eighteenth-Century Fiction* 4, no. 4 (July 1992): 323.

21. These and other references, to the extent that they can be accepted as citations of actual works, are provided in Nicolas Baker, "The Library Catalogue of Laurence Sterne," *The Shandean* 1 (1989): 9–24. And no, I am not oblivious to the irony of referencing a reference to a list of references in a parody of the phallic preposterousness of paratextual authority; taking Sterne seriously often has the effect of making one seem ridiculous.

22. An indispensable explanation of how the Lacanian conception of sexual difference can be based in Saussure's structural linguistics and (apropos of the Enlightenment) Kant's critical philosophy, as well as its radical implications for the politics of gender and sexual identity, is Joan Copjec's formative "Sex and the Euthanasia of Reason," in *Read My Desire*, 201–36. On the universal dimension and political consequences of the unsettledness of sex from a Lacanian point of view, see Patricia Gherovici, *Transgender Psychoanalysis: A Lacanian Perspective on Sexual Difference* (New York: Routledge, 2017), esp. 87–93.

23. Locke, *Essay Concerning Human Understanding*, 182; italics in original.

24. Locke, *Essay Concerning Human Understanding*, 182; italics in original.

25. See, for instance, David Hume, *A Treatise on Human Nature*, ed. David Fate Norton and Mary J. Norton (Oxford: Oxford University Press, 2000), especially 2.1.11, 206–11, and 2.2.5, 231–36. Hume also accounts for the relation between the experience of duration (time) and the persistence of identity, but holds (contrary to Locke) that the faculty of imagination, not reason or the understanding, is the mental agency of this persistence, and thus the basis of the self; see the *Treatise*, 1.4.2, 125–44. On Hume's possible influence on Sterne and his novel, see Arnold E. Davidson, "Locke, Hume, and Hobby-Horses in *Tristram Shandy*," *International Fiction Review* 8, no. 1 (1981): 17–21. For a compelling account of the confluences and divergences between *Tristram Shandy* and Hume's *Treatise*, as well as some ways in which Sterne subverts Locke by staying true to him, see Christina Lupton, "*Tristram Shandy*, David Hume, and Epistemological Fiction," *Philosophy and Literature* 27, no. 1 (April 2003): 98–115. An intriguing investigation into the ways Hume and Sterne were entangled, precisely, in the discourse of entanglement, is Andrew Warren, "'Incomprehensible Contexture[s]': Laurence Sterne and David Hume on Entanglement," *SEL: Studies in English Literature* 59, no. 3 (Summer 2019): 581–603.

26. This is especially true given that the world of which Tristram writes is nothing more than "a small circle described upon the circle of the great world, of four *English* miles diameter" (Sterne, *Tristram Shandy*, 7).

27. In Ronald Paulson's words, "All of the Shandy hobby-horses can be summed up as showing 'where you were wounded'" (*Don Quixote in England*, 154).

28. Paulson, for instance, estimates that Tristram's father is Yorick, "whom Tristram resembles both physically and spiritually more closely than Walter," inferring from innuendo—always a hazardous enterprise with Sterne—that Yorick has usurped Walter's position without his knowledge (*Don Quixote in England*, 157). J. Paul Hunter argues that Walter is probably not the narrator's

real father, but concludes that no other character is a more likely candidate for the position, and thus perhaps—why not?—that he has no father at all (Hunter, "Clocks, Calendars, and Names: The Troubles of Tristram and the Aesthetics of Uncertainty," in *Rhetorics of Order / Ordering Rhetorics in English Neoclassical Literature*, ed. J. Douglas Canfield and J. Paul Hunter [Cranbury, NJ: Associated University Presses, 1989], 173–98). These two positions exemplify but do not exhaust the debate.

29. This alludes to one of Sterne's favorite predecessors, Alexander Pope, whose "An Epistle to a Lady" begins: "Nothing so true as what you once let fall, / 'Most women have no characters at all'" (*The Major Works*, ed. Pat Rogers [New York: Oxford University Press, 1993], 350).

30. Eve Kosofsky Sedgwick was the first to emphasize that the lack of punctuation distinguishing Sterne's conversationalists from one another enables the narrator to assimilate others' speech into and as his own consciousness. She further demonstrates that the conspicuous absence of women's personalities in Sterne's work is a central motif within an aesthetics of male homosocial desire that emerged in the mid-eighteenth century in response to the sudden, market-driven erosion of patriarchal authority (Sedgwick, *Between Men: English Literature and Male Homosocial Desire* [New York: Columbia University Press, 1985], esp. 67–82). Although Sedgwick's investigation is limited to Sterne's second novel, *A Sentimental Journey*, her conclusions are just as applicable to *Tristram Shandy*.

31. For a Lacanian reading of the architecture of sexual difference in the novel, the ways in which it literally separates men from women in terms consistent with Lacan's conception of sexual difference, see Daniel Thomičres, "When Tristram Meets Nannette: An Inquiry into Sexual Anxiety in Laurence Sterne's *Tristram Shandy*," *PSYART: A Hyperlink Journal for the Psychoanalytic Study of the Arts* (November 2012), https://psyartjournal.com/article/show/thomires-when _tristram_meets_nannette_an_inquiry_.

32. Claudia L. Johnson exemplifies this charge, arguing that Sterne and his contemporaries appropriated the discourse of sentiment in order to "validate . . . male authority figures by representing them as men of feeling," and that this "bars the women whose distress occasions their affective displays from enjoying any comparable moral authority by representing their affectivity as inferior, unconscious, unruly, even criminal" (Johnson, *Equivocal Beings: Politics, Gender, and Sentimentality in the 1790s: Wollstonecraft, Radcliffe, Burney, Austen* [Chicago: University of Chicago Press, 1995], 14).

33. Hunter's assessment that Yorick is an unlikely candidate for the position of Tristram's father shares this supposition: "Tristram, for all his fondness for Yorick, never lets him get physically close to the central action, and Yorick is curiously distant, too, from the novel's sexual ambiguities, an odd exclusion. He is almost too removed" (Hunter, "Clocks, Calendars, and Names," 189).

34. As Ian Campbell Ross has argued, "Sterne owed his literary fame not to . . . personal patronage from any . . . of the noblemen, politicians or royalty at whose tables he found so ready a welcome. The secret of Sterne's success lay instead in the skill with which—in collaboration with his booksellers—he reached out to patrons of a different kind: those prosperous middle-class readers who increasingly made up the great bulk of the reading public" (Ross, *Laurence Sterne*, 11).

Epilogue

1. As Louis Althusser has it, "it is not their real conditions of existence, their real world, that 'men' 'represent to themselves' in ideology, but above all it is their relation to those conditions of existence which is represented to them there" (Althusser, *On Ideology*, 38).

2. Jacques Lacan, "The Instance of the Letter in the Unconscious, or Reason since Freud," in *Écrits*, 417.

3. Barthes's *Mythologies* emphasizes that ideology's primary function is to naturalize the historical; his is the first and still the most extensive semiotics of this function and its consequences. As early as the *Economic and Philosophic Manuscripts of 1844*, Marx criticized political economy for basing its account of the contemporary organization of labor upon "a fictitious primordial condition," a (Hobbesian) fiction and philosophical hypothesis, that naturalizes the economic principle of competition (*The Marx-Engels Reader, Second Edition*, ed. Robert C. Tucker [New York: Norton, 1978], 71). With his later investigation of the commodity form, Marx revealed, well in advance of the invention of semiotics, how the signifier enters into the signified, in his theorization of exchange-value's usurpation of use-value. For an excellent extended consideration of this, see A. Kiarina Kordela, *Epistemontology in Spinoza-Marx-Freud-Lacan: The (Bio) Power of Structure* (New York: Routledge, 2018).

4. Althusser, *On Ideology*, 38–39. Also see Copjec, *Read My Desire*, 21.

5. Sigmund Freud, "Beyond the Pleasure Principle," in *S.E.* 18: 10.

6. This is one practical consequence of the more profound fact that "in analysis we never discover a 'no' in the unconscious" (Sigmund Freud, "Negation," in *S.E.* 19: 239).

7. William Blake, "THERE is NO Natural Religion" [b], in *The Complete Poetry & Prose of William Blake*, rev. ed., ed. David V. Erdman (New York: Anchor Books, 1982), 2.

8. Fredric Jameson, *The Political Unconscious: Narrative as a Socially Symbolic Act* (Ithaca, NY: Cornell University Press, 1981), 9.

9. Jameson rightly insists that every formation or instance of unconscious fantasy will be subjected to ideological conscription (*The Political Unconscious*, 142). But throughout *The Political Unconscious*, even in the book's title, he conflates ideology with the unconscious as if both name the operations of objective historical processes of which the political subject is generally unaware.

10. "Lacan's basic thesis," according to Žižek, does not amount to the subject's "radical alienation" in the exteriority of the alienating symbolic order, but also includes "a possibility for the subject to obtain . . . some kind of positive consistency, also outside the big Other, the alienating symbolic network. The other possibility is that offered by fantasy: equating the subject to an object of fantasy." And so, "the only way to break the power of our ideological dream is to confront the Real of our desire which announces itself in this dream" (Slavoj Žižek, *The Sublime Object of Ideology* [New York: Verso, 1989], 46–48). Or later, "the Unconscious is the *inaccessible phenomenon*, not the objective mechanism which regulates my phenomenal experience" (Slavoj Žižek, *The Plague of Fantasies* [New York: Verso, 1997], 158; emphasis in original). Also see Slavoj Žižek, "The Spectre of Ideology," in *Mapping Ideology*, ed. Žižek (New York: Verso, 2012), 1–33.

11. From among the dozens of additional examples of how Žižek's work both disentangles and conflates ideology and fantasy, the best and most extensive is *The Plague of Fantasies*. One can see these same operations throughout his more specialized studies of specific subjects or texts and their misuse or ideological abuse, such as his efforts to reclaim Christianity from, well, Christianity in *The Puppet and the Dwarf: The Perverse Core of Christianity* (Cambridge, MA: MIT Press, 2003) and *The Fragile Absolute; or, Why Is the Christian Legacy Worth Fighting for?* (New York: Verso, 2000); and to reclaim Lenin from his consignment to an archaic past (*Repeating Lenin* [Zagreb: Arkzin, 2002]). *The Parallax View* (Cambridge, MA: MIT Press, 2006) is perhaps Žižek's most theoretically explicit elaboration of the difference between reality and fantasy and what it means for thought and politics.

12. Žižek, *The Sublime Object*, 27–30; emphasis in original.

13. See, for instance, Mladen Dolar, "'I Shall Be with You on Your Wedding-Night': Lacan and the Uncanny," *October*, vol. 58, "Rendering the Real" (Autumn 1991): 5–23, esp. 19–21. For a related critique of the ways in which Žižek has inspired more than committed the theoretical missteps I am elaborating here, particularly with regard to aesthetic artifacts (i.e., literature), see Tim Dean, "Art as Symptom: Žižek and the Ethics of Psychoanalytic Criticism," *Diacritics* 32, no. 2 (Summer 2002): 21–41.

14. "The only homogenous function of consciousness," Lacan reminds us, "is found in the ego's imaginary capture by its specular reflection, and in the function of misrecognition that remains tied to it" (Lacan, "Position of the Unconscious," in *Écrits*, 705).

BIBLIOGRAPHY

Althusser, Louis. *On Ideology*. New York: Verso, 2008.

Alvarez, A. "The Delinquent Aesthetic." *Hudson Review* 19, no. 4 (Winter 1966–67): 590–600.

Apollon, Willy. "Four Seasons in Femininity or *Four Men in a Woman's Life*." *Topoi* 12 (1993): 101–15.

———. "The Untreatable." Translated by Steven Miller. *Umbr(a): A Journal of the Unconscious*, no. 1: "The Incurable" (2006): 23–39.

Arendt, Hannah. *On Revolution*. New York: Penguin, 2006.

Armstrong, Nancy. *How Novels Think: The Limits of Individualism from 1719–1900*. New York: Columbia University Press, 2005.

Attridge, Derek. *J. M. Coetzee and the Ethics of Reading*. Chicago: University of Chicago Press, 2004.

Auerbach, Erich. "Philology and 'Weltliteratur.'" *Centennial Review* 13, no. 1 (Winter 1969): 1–17.

Baker, Nicolas. "The Library Catalogue of Laurence Sterne." *The Shandean* 1 (1989): 9–24.

Bakhtin, Mikhail. *The Dialogic Imagination*. Edited by Michael Holquist, translated by Caryl Emerson and Michael Holquist. Austin: University of Texas Press, 1981.

Balibar, Étienne. "Subjection and Subjectivation." In *Supposing the Subject*, edited by Joan Copjec, 1–15. New York: Verso, 1994.

Barthes, Roland. *A Lover's Discourse: Fragments*. Translated by Richard Howard. New York: Hill and Wang, 2010.

———. *Mythologies*. Translated by Richard Howard and Annette Lavers. New York: Hill and Wang, 2012.

———. *The Pleasure of the Text*. Translated by Richard Miller. New York: Hill and Wang, 1975.

Bataille, Georges. *The Accursed Share, Volume 1: Consumption*. Translated by Robert Hurley. New York: Zone Books, 1991.

———. *Literature and Evil*. Translated by Alastair Hamilton. London: Marion Boyars, 1973.

Belaval, Yvon. "Préface." In Marquis de Sade, *La Philosophie dans le boudoir*, 7–34.

Bender, John. *Ends of Enlightenment*. Stanford, CA: Stanford University Press, 2012.

———. *Imagining the Penitentiary: Fiction and the Architecture of Mind in Eighteenth Century England*. Chicago: University of Chicago Press, 1987.

Benjamin, Walter. "The Concept of Criticism in German Romanticism." In *Selected Writings: Volume 1, 1913–1926*, edited by Marcus Bullock and Michael W. Jennings, 116–200. Cambridge, MA: Harvard University Press, 1996.

Bergeron, Danielle. "The Work of the Dream and Jouissance in the Treatment of the Psychotic." In Willy Apollon, Danielle Bergeron, and Lucie Cantin, *After Lacan: Clinical Practice and the Subject of the Unconscious*, edited by Robert Hughes and Kareen Ror Malone, 71–85. Albany: SUNY Press, 2002.

Bernstein, J. M., ed. *Classic and Romantic German Aesthetics*. Cambridge: Cambridge University Press, 2003.

Bersani, Leo. *The Freudian Body: Psychoanalysis and Art*. New York: Columbia University Press, 1986.

Blake, William. *The Complete Poetry & Prose of William Blake*, revised edition. Edited by David V. Erdman. New York: Anchor Books, 1982.

Blanchot, Maurice. *Lautréamont and Sade*. Translated by Stuart Kendall and Michelle Kendall. Stanford, CA: Stanford University Press, 2004.

Blanchot, Maurice, and Jacques Derrida. *The Instant of My Death / Demeure: Fiction and Testimony*. Translated by Elizabeth Rottenberg. Stanford, CA: Stanford University Press, 2000.

Bloch, Jean. *Rousseauism and Education in Eighteenth-Century France*. Oxford: Voltaire Foundation, 1995.

Borges, Jorge Luis. *Collected Fictions*. New York: Penguin, 1999.

Brooks, Cleanth. *The Well Wrought Urn: Studies in the Structure of Poetry*. Orlando, FL: Harcourt Books, 1947.

Brooks, Peter. *Psychoanalysis and Storytelling*. Oxford: Blackwell, 1994.

———. *Reading for the Plot: Design and Intention in Narrative*. Cambridge, MA: Harvard University Press, 1984.

Burke, Edmund. *A Philosophical Enquiry into the Origin of Our Ideas of the Sublime and Beautiful and Other Pre-Revolutionary Writings*. Edited by David Womersley. New York: Penguin, 1998.

Canetti, Elias. *Crowds and Power*. Translated by Carol Stewart. New York: Farrar, Straus and Giroux, 1962 [1984].

Certeau, Michel de. *Heterologies: Discourse on the Other*. Translated by Brian Massumi. Minneapolis: University of Minnesota Press, 1986.

Cervantes, Miguel de. *Don Quijote*. Edited by Diana de Armas Wilson, translated by Burton Raffel. New York: Norton, 1999.

Césaire, Aimé. *Discourse on Colonialism*. Translated by Joan Pinkham. New York: Monthly Review Press, 1972.

Coetzee, J. M. *Foe*. New York: Penguin, 1986.

Cooper, Anthony Ashley, Third Earl of Shaftesbury. *Characteristicks of Men, Manners, Opinions, Times*. Indianapolis, IN: Liberty Fund, 2011.

Copjec, Joan. *Read My Desire: Lacan Against the Historicists*. Cambridge, MA: MIT Press, 1994.

Davidson, Arnold E. "Locke, Hume, and Hobby-Horses in *Tristram Shandy*." *International Fiction Review* 8, no. 1 (1981): 17–21.

Davis, Garrick, ed. *Praising It New: The Best of the New Criticism*. Athens, OH: Swallow, 2008.

Dean, Tim. "Art as Symptom: Žižek and the Ethics of Psychoanalytic Criticism." *Diacritics* 32, no. 2 (Summer 2002): 21–41.

————. *Beyond Sexuality*. Chicago: University of Chicago Press, 2000.

Defoe, Daniel. *Robinson Crusoe*. Edited by Michael Shinagel. New York: Norton, 1994.

Derrida, Jacques. *Of Grammatology*. Translated by Gayatri Chakravorty Spivak. Baltimore, MD: Johns Hopkins University Press, 1976.

————. *Writing and Difference*. Translated by Alan Bass. Chicago: University of Chicago Press, 1978.

Dewey, John. *Democracy and Education: An Introduction to the Philosophy of Education*. New York: Macmillan, 1928.

————. *Education Today*. Edited by Joseph Ratner. New York: Greenwood, 1940.

Dinnage, Rosemary. Introduction to Daniel Paul Schreber, *Memoirs of My Nervous Illness*, xi–xiiv.

Dolar, Mladen. "'I Shall Be with You on Your Wedding-Night': Lacan and the Uncanny." *October* 58 (Autumn 1991): 5–23.

Eliot, T. S. *Collected Poems 1909–1962*. New York: Harcourt Brace, 1963.

Farley, Anthony Paul. "Toward a General Theory of Antiblackness." In Moon-Kie Jung and João H. Costa Vargas, *Antiblackness*, 82–104.

Felman, Shoshana, ed. *Literature and Psychoanalysis: The Question of Reading: Otherwise*. Baltimore, MD: Johns Hopkins University Press, 1982.

Folkenflik, Robert. Introduction to Laurence Sterne, *The Life and Opinions of Tristram Shandy, Gentleman*, xi–xxx.

Forster, E. M. *Aspects of the Novel*. New York: Harcourt, 1927.

Foucault, Michel. *The Birth of Biopolitics: Lectures at the Collège de France, 1978–79*. Edited by Michel Senellart, translated by Graham Burchell. New York: Palgrave Macmillan, 2008.

————. *The Order of Things: An Archaeology of the Human Sciences*. New York: Vintage, 1994.

————. "What Is Enlightenment?" In *The Foucault Reader*, edited by Paul Rabinow, 32–50. New York: Pantheon Books, 1984.

Freire, Paulo. *Pedagogy of the Oppressed*. Translated by Myra Bergman Ramos. New York: Continuum, 2005.

Freud, Sigmund. "Analysis Terminable and Interminable." In Strachey, ed., *The Standard Edition*, 23: 209–54.

————. "Beyond the Pleasure Principle." In Strachey, *The Standard Edition*, 18: 1–64.

————. "Civilization and Its Discontents." In Strachey, *The Standard Edition*, 21: 57–146.

————. "Constructions in Analysis." In Strachey, *The Standard Edition*, 23: 257–69.

————. "Creative Writers and Day-Dreaming." In Strachey, *The Standard Edition*, 9: 141–54.

————. "Family Romances." In Strachey, *The Standard Edition*, 9: 235–41.

————. "Fetishism." In Strachey, *The Standard Edition*, 21: 147–58.

————. "Fragment of an Analysis of a Case of Hysteria." In Strachey, *The Standard Edition*, 7: 1–122.

————. "From the History of an Infantile Neurosis." In Strachey, *The Standard Edition*, 17: 1–124.

———. "The Future of an Illusion." In Strachey, *The Standard Edition*, 21: 1–56.

———. *The Interpretation of Dreams*. In Strachey, *The Standard Edition*, 4–5.

———. *Moses and Monotheism: Three Essays*. In Strachey, *The Standard Edition*, 23: 1–138.

———. "Negation." In Strachey, *The Standard Edition*, 19: 233–40.

———. "Psychoanalytic Notes upon an Autobiographical Account of a Case of Paranoia (*Dementia Paranoides*) (1911)." In Strachey, *The Standard Edition*, 12: 1–82.

———. *The Psychopathology of Everyday Life: Forgetting, Slips of the Tongue, Bungled Actions, Superstitions and Errors*. In Strachey, *The Standard Edition*, 6: vii–296.

———. *The Standard Edition of the Complete Psychological Works of Sigmund Freud*. Edited by James Strachey et al. London: Hogarth, 1974.

———. *Three Essays on the Theory of Sexuality*. In Strachey, *The Standard Edition*, 7: 123–246.

———. *Totem and Taboo*. In Strachey, *The Standard Edition* 13: vii–162.

Gasché, Rodolphe. "Forward: Ideality in Fragmentation." In Schlegel, *Philosophical Fragments*, vii–xxxii.

Gaudillière, Jean-Max. *Madness and the Social Link: The Jean-Max Gaudillière Seminars 1985–2000*. Transcribed by Françoise Davoine, translated by Agnès Jacob. London: Routledge, 2021.

Gay, Peter. *The Enlightenment: An Interpretation: The Science of Freedom*. New York: Norton, 1969.

Gerard, William Blake. *Laurence Sterne and the Visual Imagination*. Surrey, UK: Ashgate, 2006.

Gherovici, Patricia. *Transgender Psychoanalysis: A Lacanian Perspective on Sexual Difference*. New York: Routledge, 2017.

Giroux, Henry. *Education and the Crisis of Public Values: Challenging the Assault on Teachers, Students, & Public Education*. New York: Peter Lang, 2012.

Gorelick, Nathan. "Psychoanalysis at the End of the World." In *Lacan and the Environment*, edited by Clint Burnham and Paul Kingsbury, 221–37. New York: Palgrave, 2021.

———. "What Is the Novel? The Fundamental Concepts of a Literary Phenomenon." *Continental Thought and Theory* 2, no. 3 (January 2019): 134–66.

Graeber, David, and David Wengrow. *The Dawn of Everything: A New History of Humanity*. New York: Farrar, Straus and Giroux, 2021.

Graves, Lila V. "Locke's *Essay* and Sterne's 'Work Itself.'" *Journal of Narrative Technique* 12, no. 1 (Winter 1982): 36–47.

Gutek, Gerald L. Introduction to Jean-Jacques Rousseau, *Emile* (2005), vii–xv.

Harris, H. S. *Hegel: Phenomenology and System*. Indianapolis, IN: Hackett, 1995.

Hegel, G. W. F. *Elements of the Philosophy of Right*. Edited by Allen W. Wood, translated by H. B. Nisbet. Cambridge: Cambridge University Press, 1991.

———. *The Encyclopaedia Logic: Part I of the Encyclopaedia of Philosophical Sciences with the Zusätze*. Translated by T. F. Geraets, W. A. Suchting, and H. S. Harris. Indianapolis, IN: Hackett, 1991.

———. *Phenomenology of Spirit*. Translated by A. V. Miller. Oxford: Oxford University Press, 1977.

Hénaff, Marcel. *Sade: The Invention of the Libertine Body.* Translated by Xavier Callahan. Minneapolis: University of Minnesota Press, 1999.

Hogarth, William. *The Analysis of Beauty: Written with a View to Fixing the Fluctuating Ideas of Taste.* London: J. Reeves, 1753.

Hölderlin, Friedrich. "Oldest Programme for a System of German Idealism." Translated by Stefan Bird-Pollan. In Bernstein, *Classic and Romantic German Aesthetics*, 185–87.

Hume, David. *A Treatise on Human Nature.* Edited by David Fate Norton and Mary J. Norton. Oxford: Oxford University Press, 2000.

Hunter, J. Paul. "Clocks, Calendars, and Names: The Troubles of Tristram and the Aesthetics of Uncertainty." In *Rhetorics of Order / Ordering Rhetorics in English Neoclassical Literature*, edited by J. Douglas Canfield and J. Paul Hunter, 173–98. Cranbury, NJ: Associated University Presses, 1989.

———. *The Reluctant Pilgrim: Defoe's Emblematic Method and Quest for Form in Robinson Crusoe.* Baltimore, MD: Johns Hopkins University Press, 1966.

Hutcheson, Francis. *An Inquiry into the Original of Our Ideas of Beauty and Virtue, in Two Treatises.* London: J. and J. Knapton et al., 1729.

Huxley, Aldous. *Brave New World.* New York: Harper, 2006.

Hyppolite, Jean. *Genesis and Structure of Hegel's "Phenomenology of Spirit."* Translated by Samuel Cherniak and John Heckman. Evanston, IL: Northwestern University Press, 1979.

Jakobson, Roman. "Closing Statement: Linguistics and Poetics." In *Semiotics: An Introductory Anthology*, edited by Robert E. Innis, 145–75. Bloomington: Indiana University Press, 1985.

James, C. L. R. *The Black Jacobins: Toussaint L'Ouverture and the San Domingo Revolution.* New York: Vintage, 1989.

Jameson, Fredric. *The Political Unconscious: Narrative as a Socially Symbolic Act.* Ithaca, NY: Cornell University Press, 1981.

Johnson, Claudia L. *Equivocal Beings: Politics, Gender, and Sentimentality in the 1790s: Wollstonecraft, Radcliffe, Burney, Austen.* Chicago: University of Chicago Press, 1995.

Jung, Moon-Kie, and João H. Costa Vargas, eds. *Antiblackness.* Durham, NC: Duke University Press, 2021.

Kant, Immanuel. *Critique of Judgment.* Translated by Werner S. Pluhar. Indianapolis, IN: Hackett, 1987.

———. *Critique of Practical Reason.* Translated by Werner S. Pluhar. Indianapolis, IN: Hackett, 2002.

———. *Critique of Pure Reason.* Translated by Werner S. Pluhar. Indianapolis, IN: Hackett, 1996.

Kay, Carol. *Political Constructions: Defoe, Richardson, and Sterne in Relation to Hobbes, Hume, and Burke.* Ithaca, NY: Cornell University Press, 1988.

Klossowski, Pierre. *Sade My Neighbor.* Translated by Alphonso Lingis. Evanston, IL: Northwestern University Press, 1991.

Kordela, A. Kiarina. *Epistemontology in Spinoza-Marx-Freud-Lacan: The (Bio) Power of Structure.* New York: Routledge, 2018.

Lacan, Jacques. *Écrits: The First Complete Edition in English.* Translated by Bruce Fink. New York: Norton, 2006.

———. *Encore: The Seminar of Jacques Lacan, Book XX: On Feminine Sexuality, the Limits of Love and Knowledge, 1972–1973*. Edited by Jacques-Alain Miller, translated by Bruce Fink. New York: Norton, 1998.

———. "The Instance of the Letter in the Unconscious, or Reason since Freud." In *Écrits*, 412–41.

———. "Kant avec Sade." In *Écrits 2: Nouvelle Édition*, 243–69. Paris: Éditions du Seuil, 1999.

———. "Kant with Sade." In *Écrits*, 645–68.

———. "Kant with Sade." Translated by James B. Swenson, Jr. *October* 51 (Winter 1989): 55–103.

———. *La Logique du fantasme*. Unedited transcript. https://nosubject.com /Seminar_XIV.

———. *My Teaching*. Translated by David Macey. New York: Verso, 2008.

———. "On a Question Prior to Any Possible Treatment of Psychosis." In *Écrits*, 445–88.

———. "Position of the Unconscious." In *Écrits*, 703–21.

———. "Préface." In Robert Georgin, *Lacan*, 9–17. Paris: Cistre, 1984.

———. *The Seminar of Jacques Lacan, Book III: The Psychoses: 1955–1956*. Edited by Jacques-Alain Miller, translated by Russell Grigg. New York: Norton, 1993.

———. *The Seminar of Jacques Lacan, Book VI: Desire and Its Interpretation*. Edited by Jacques-Alain Miller, translated by Bruce Fink. Medford, MA: Polity, 2019.

———. *The Seminar of Jacques Lacan, Book VII: The Ethics of Psychoanalysis, 1959–1960*. Edited by Jacques-Alain Miller, translated by Dennis Porter. New York: Norton, 1992.

———. *The Seminar of Jacques Lacan, Book XI: The Four Fundamental Concepts of Psychoanalysis*. Edited by Jacques-Alain Miller, translated by Alan Sheridan. New York: Norton, 1981.

Lacoue-Labarthe, Philippe. *The Subject of Philosophy*. Edited by Thomas Tresize. Minneapolis: University of Minnesota Press, 1993.

Lacoue-Labarthe, Philippe, and Jean-Luc Nancy. *The Literary Absolute: The Theory of Literature in German Romanticism*. Translated by Philip Barnard and Cheryl Lester. Albany: SUNY Press, 1998.

Laplanche, J., and J.-B. Pontalis. *The Language of Psycho-Analysis*. Translated by Donald Nicholson-Smith. New York: Norton, 1973.

Lévi-Strauss, Claude. *Tristes Tropiques*. Translated by John Weightman and Doreen Weightman. New York: Penguin, 2012.

Locke, John. *The Educational Writings of John Locke*. Edited by James L. Axtell. Cambridge: Cambridge University Press, 1968.

———. *An Essay Concerning Human Understanding*. Edited by Peter H. Nidditch. Oxford: Oxford University Press, 1979.

———. *Two Treatises of Government*. Edited by Peter Laslett. Cambridge: Cambridge University Press, 1988.

Lupton, Christina. "*Tristram Shandy*, David Hume, and Epistemological Fiction." *Philosophy and Literature* 27, no. 1 (April 2003): 98–115.

Manheim, Ralph, and R. F. C. Hull, eds. *The Freud/Jung Letters*. Princeton, NJ: Princeton University Press, 1974.

Marriott, David. "The Figure of Crusoe." In *Modernism and Masculinity*, edited by Natalya Lusty and Julian Murphet, 159–78. Cambridge: Cambridge University Press, 2014.

McKeon, Michael. "Mediation as Primal Word: The Arts, the Sciences, and the Origins of the Aesthetic." In Siskin and Warner, *This Is Enlightenment*, 384–412.

———. *The Origins of the English Novel, 1600–1740*. Baltimore, MD: Johns Hopkins University Press, 1987.

Miller, Steven. *War after Death: On Violence and Its Limits*. New York: Fordham University Press, 2014.

Mills, Charles W. "The Illumination of Blackness." In Moon-Kie Jung and João H. Costa Vargas, *Antiblackness*, 17–36.

Montesquieu. *The Spirit of the Laws*. Edited and translated by Anne M. Cohler, Basia C. Miller, and Harold S. Stone. Cambridge: Cambridge University Press, 1989.

More, Thomas. *Utopia*. Edited by George M. Logan and Robert M. Adams. Cambridge: Cambridge University Press, 2002.

Morgenstern, Mira. "Strangeness, Violence, and the Establishment of Nationhood in Rousseau." *Eighteenth-Century Studies* 41, no. 3 (Spring 2008): 359–81.

Mottolese, William C. "Tristram Cyborg and Toby Toolmaker: Body, Tools, and Hobbyhorse in *Tristram Shandy*." *SEL: Studies in English Literature* 47, no. 3 (Summer 2007): 679–701.

Nancy, Jean-Luc. *The Inoperative Community*. Edited by Peter Connor. Minneapolis: University of Minnesota Press, 1991.

New, Melvyn. "Sterne and the Narrative of Determinateness." *Eighteenth-Century Fiction* 4, no. 4 (July 1992): 315–30.

Nobus, Danny. "Lacan's *Écrits* Revisited: On Writing as Object of Desire." *Psychoanalytische Perspectieven* 36, no. 4 (2018): 345–74.

Novak, Maximillian. *Defoe and the Nature of Man*. Oxford: Oxford University Press, 1963.

Orlando, Francesco. *Toward a Freudian Theory of Literature with an Analysis of Racine's "Phèdre."* Translated by Charmaine Lee. Baltimore, MD: Johns Hopkins University Press, 1978.

Paulson, Ronald. *Don Quixote in England: The Aesthetics of Laughter*. Baltimore, MD: Johns Hopkins University Press, 1998.

Poe, Edgar Allan. "Critical Notices." *Southern Literary Messenger* 2, no. 2 (January 1836): 127–28.

Pope, Alexander. *The Major Works*. Edited by Pat Rogers. New York: Oxford University Press, 1993.

Rabaté, Jean-Michel. *Jacques Lacan: Psychoanalysis and the Subject of Literature*. New York: Palgrave, 2001.

Ragland-Sullivan, Ellie, and Mark Bracher, eds. *Lacan and the Subject of Language*. New York: Routledge, 1991.

Ransom, John Crowe. "Criticism, Inc." In Davis, *Praising It New*, 49–61.

Richardson, Samuel. *Pamela*. Edited by Peter Sabor. New York: Penguin, 2003.

Richetti, John. *Defoe's Narratives: Situations and Structures*. Oxford: Clarendon, 1975.

Robert, Marthe. *Origins of the Novel*. Translated by Sacha Rabinovitch. Bloomington: Indiana University Press, 1980.

Rodman, Jeffrey. "Defoe and the Psychotic Subject." In *Ethics and the Subject*, edited by Karl Simms, 245–51. Amsterdam: Rodopi, 1997.

Rolland, Romain. *French Thought in the Eighteenth Century*. London: Morrison and Gibb, 1953.

Rosenow, Eliyahu. "Rousseau's 'Emile,' an Anti-Utopia." *British Journal of Educational Studies* 28, no. 3 (October 1980): 212–24.

Ross, Ian Campbell. *Laurence Sterne: A Life*. Oxford: Oxford University Press, 2001.

Rousseau, Jean-Jacques. *The "Discourses" and Other Early Political Writings*. Edited and translated by Victor Gourevitch. Cambridge: Cambridge University Press, 1997.

———. *Emile*. New York: Barnes & Noble, 2005.

———. *Emile or On Education*. Translated by Allan Bloom. New York: Basic Books, 1979.

———. *Émile ou de l'éducation*. Paris: Flammarion, 1966.

———. "Essay on the Origin of Languages." In *The "Discourses" and Other Early Political Writings*, 247–99.

———. *Julie, ou la nouvelle Héloïse*. Paris: Flammarion, 2007.

———. *The Social Contract and Other Late Political Writings*. Edited and translated by Victor Gourevitch. Cambridge: Cambridge University Press, 1997.

Sade, Marquis de. "The Author of *Les Crimes de l'Amour* to Villeterque, Hack Writer." In Wainhouse and Seaver, *The 120 Days of Sodom & Other Writings*, 121–29.

———. *Juliette*. Translated by Austryn Wainhouse. New York: Grove, 1968.

———. *Justine, Philosophy in the Bedroom, & Other Writings*. Compiled and translated by Richard Seaver and Austryn Wainhouse. New York: Grove, 1965.

———. "Last Will and Testament of Donatien-Alphonse-François Sade, Man of Letters." In Seaver and Wainhouse, *Justine, Philosophy in the Bedroom, & Other Writings*, 155–57.

———. *Le Philosophie dans le boudoir ou Les Instituteurs immoraux*. Paris: Gallimard, 1976.

———. *Les Crimes de l'amour*. Paris: Libraire Génerale Française, 1972.

———. *Letters from Prison*. Translated by Richard Seaver. New York: Arcade, 1999.

———. *The 120 Days of Sodom*. In Wainhouse and Seaver, *The 120 Days of Sodom & Other Writings*, 183–674.

———. *The 120 Days of Sodom & Other Writings*. Compiled and translated by Austryn Wainhouse and Richard Seaver. New York: Grove, 1966.

———. *Philosophy in the Bedroom*. In Seaver and Wainhouse, *Justine, Philosophy in the Bedroom, & Other Writings* 179–367.

———. "Reflections on the Novel." In Wainhouse and Seaver, *The 120 Days of Sodom & Other Writings*, 97–116.

Said, Edward. *The World, the Text, and the Critic*. Cambridge, MA: Harvard University Press, 1983.

Saltman, Kenneth J., and David A. Gabbard, eds. *Education as Enforcement: The Militarization and Corporatization of Schools*. London: Routledge, 2003.

Santner, Eric. *My Own Private Germany: Daniel Paul Schreber's Secret History of Modernity*. Princeton, NJ: Princeton University Press, 1996.

Saussure, Ferdinand de. *Course in General Linguistics*. Translated by Wade Baskin, edited by Perry Meisel and Haun Saussy. New York: Columbia University Press, 2011.

Schlegel, Friedrich. *Philosophical Fragments*. Translated by Peter Firchow. Minneapolis: University of Minnesota Press, 1991.

Schreber, Daniel Paul. *Memoirs of My Nervous Illness*. Translated by Ida Macalpine and Richard A. Hunter. New York: New York Review Books, 2000.

Sedgwick, Eve Kosofsky. *Between Men: English Literature and Male Homosocial Desire*. New York: Columbia University Press, 1985.

Shklovsky, Viktor. *Theory of Prose*. Translated by Benjamin Sher. Normal, IL: Dalkey Archive, 1990.

Sigler, David. "The Navel of the Dream: Freud, Derrida and Lacan on the Gap where 'Something Happens.'" *SubStance* 39, no. 2 (2010): 17–38.

Siskin, Clifford. "Mediated Enlightenment: The System of the World." In Siskin and Warner, *This Is Enlightenment*, 164–72.

Siskin, Clifford, and William Warner, eds. *This Is Enlightenment*. Chicago: University of Chicago Press, 2010.

Soler, Colette. "Literature as Symptom." In Ragland-Sullivan and Bracher, *Lacan and the Subject of Language*, 213–19.

Starr, G. A. *Defoe and Spiritual Autobiography*. Princeton, NJ: Princeton University Press, 1965.

Sterne, Laurence. *The Life and Opinions of Tristram Shandy, Gentleman*. New York: Modern Library Classics, 2004.

———. *A Sentimental Journey*. New York: Penguin, 2002.

Tarizzo, Davide. *Political Grammars: The Unconscious Foundations of Modern Democracy*. Stanford, CA: Stanford University Press, 2021.

Tate, Allen. "Miss Emily and the Bibliographer." In Davis, *Praising It New*, 39–48.

Thomičres, Daniel. "When Tristram Meets Nannette: An Inquiry into Sexual Anxiety in Laurence Sterne's *Tristram Shandy*." *PSYART: A Hyperlink Journal for the Psychoanalytic Study of the Arts* (November 2012), https://psyartjournal.com/article/show/thomires-when_tristram_meets_nannette_an_inquiry_.

Tucker, Robert C., ed. *The Marx-Engels Reader, Second Edition*. New York: Norton, 1978.

Voltaire. *Candide, or Optimism*. Translated by Theo Cuffe. New York: Penguin, 2005.

Walcott, Derek, "The Figure of Crusoe." In *Critical Perspectives on Derek Walcott*, edited by Robert D. Hamner, 33–41. Boulder, CO: Lynne Rienner, 1997.

Walter, Scott. "The 'Flawed Parent': A Reconsideration of Rousseau's 'Emile' and Its Significance for Radical Education in the United States." *British Journal of Educational Studies* 44, no. 3 (September 1996): 260–74.

Warren, Andrew. "'Incomprehensible Contexture[s]': Laurence Sterne and David Hume on Entanglement." *SEL: Studies in English Literature* 59, no. 3 (Summer 2019): 581–603.

Watt, Ian. *The Rise of the Novel: Studies in Defoe, Richardson and Fielding*. Berkeley: University of California Press, 1957.

Weiss, Penny. *Gendered Community: Rousseau, Sex, and Politics*. New York: NYU Press, 1993.

Wetmore, Alex. "Sympathy Machines: Men of Feeling and the Automaton." *Eighteenth-Century Studies* 43, no. 1 (Fall 2009): 37–54.

Wheeler, Roxann. "'My Savage,' 'My Man': Racial Multiplicity in *Robinson Crusoe*." *ELH* 62, no. 4 (Winter 1995): 821–61.

Yousef, Nancy. "Savage or Solitary? The Wild Child and Rousseau's Man of Nature." *Journal of the History of Ideas* 62, no. 2 (April 2001): 245–63.

Žižek, Slavoj. *The Fragile Absolute; or, Why Is the Christian Legacy Worth Fighting for?* New York: Verso, 2000.

———. *The Parallax View*. Cambridge, MA: MIT Press, 2006.

———. *The Plague of Fantasies*. New York: Verso, 1997.

———. *The Puppet and the Dwarf: The Perverse Core of Christianity*. Cambridge, MA: MIT Press, 2003.

———. *Repeating Lenin*. Zagreb: Arkzin, 2002.

———. "The Spectre of Ideology." In *Mapping Ideology*, ed. Slavoj Žižek, 1–33. New York: Verso, 2012.

———. *The Sublime Object of Ideology*. New York: Verso, 1989.

Zupančič, Alenka. *Ethics of the Real: Kant, Lacan*. New York: Verso, 2000.

———. *What Is Sex?* Cambridge, MA: MIT Press, 2017.

INDEX

address, 11, 50; *ad hominem*, 149n20; to the analyst, 13, 122; structure of, 12, 17–18, 23, 39, 62, 66, 122, 141; subject of, 89; of the subject, 126, 137

allobiography, 100, 105, 109, 114, 121, 124, 128–29

Althusser, Louis, 133, 137, 152n7, 162n1

Alvarez, A., 103–5

analysand, 18, 20, 22, 65–66, 81

analyst, the, 18, 20, 22, 67, 95; desire of, 11, 136; literature and, 7; resistance and, 147n50; in training, 65–66, 80; unconscious and, 11, 13, 28, 66, 122

antiblackness, 31, 57, 137, 151n39. *See also* whiteness

Apollon, Willy, 27, 146n33

Aristotle, 69, 155n27

Athenaeum, 13, 15, 144n18

autonomy, 76, 94, 146n42; aesthetic, 14; individual, 68; rational, 46; subjective, 62

Bakhtin, Mikhail, 14–15, 144nn18–19, 149n25

Barthes, Roland, 4, 10, 24, 135, 156n42; *A Lover's Discourse: Fragments*, 147n46; *Mythologies*, 133, 162n3

Bataille, Georges, 82, 157n49

beautiful, the, 106, 122, 159n10

beauty, 105, 107–8, 159n15

Benjamin, Walter, 16–18, 22, 41

Bergeron, Danielle, 43

Blanchot, Maurice, 87–91, 149n24

Brooks, Cleanth, 144n16

Brooks, Peter, 143n6; *Reading for the Plot*, 7

Buffon, Comte de, 70, 82, 155n27

Burke, Edmund, 38, 52, 108, 150n31

capitalism, 3, 38, 63, 152n7

castration, 122; pervert and, 158n57; symbolic, 43, 101, 105, 149n14; in *Tristram Shandy*, 112, 121, 125

catastrophe, 44, 60; delusion and, 38–39; modernity as, 40; rationalization and, 47, 59; in *Robinson Crusoe*, 35–36; zone of, 49–50, 56, 64, 121–22

Cervantes, Miguel de, 15, 144n19

Césaire, Aimé, 151n39

clinic, the, 12–13, 23, 66; fantasy and, 62; transference in, 67, 81

clinical, the, 11, 33, 123; experience, 23; practice, 9

colonialism, 3, 151n39

consciousness, 5, 9, 22, 45, 60, 150n30, 163n14; authorial, 159n18; critical, 31, 67, 70–71, 80, 95, 135, 152n6; Enlightenment, 61; false, 141; fantasy and, 20, 26–27; of the object, 16; self-consciousness, 154n26

construction, 19–23, 26–27, 29, 37, 42, 122–24, 145nn31–32; delusion as, 39; *Émile* (Rousseau) as, 70, 78; of fantasy, 33; Freudian, 34, 47; interminability of, 65; Oedipus complex as, 44; Sade and, 89; *Tristram Shandy* and, 102, 129

contingency, 5, 22, 28, 139–40; historical, 51, 131; of necessity, 29

Copjec, Joan, 9, 157n48; "Sex and the Euthanasia of Reason," 160n22

creation, 15–16, 22, 28, 36, 41, 135

creative, the, 13, 15, 123

critic, the, 23; desire of, 11, 122; literary, 41, 138; literature and, 16–17, 27, 39, 137, 144n11, 144n16, 147n50; subject and, 141; theory of reading and, 13. *See also* New Critics

criticism, 16–17, 22; Benjamin on Romantic, 18, 41; of the Enlightenment, 31, 61; ethics of, 17, 122, 138; ideology and, 4, 137; of the novel, 33; psychoanalysis and, 7–8, 12–13, 23, 132; Schlegel on, 15–16. *See also* literary criticism; New Criticism

cure, 5, 39–40